POPCORN DISABILITIES

POPCORN DISABILITIES

The Highs and Lows of Disabled Representation in the Movies

Kristen Lopez

BLOOMSBURY ACADEMIC
NEW YORK • LONDON • OXFORD • NEW DELHI • SYDNEY

BLOOMSBURY ACADEMIC

Bloomsbury Publishing Inc, 1359 Broadway, 12th Floor, New York, NY 10018, USA
Bloomsbury Publishing Plc, 50 Bedford Square, London, WC1B 3DP, UK
Bloomsbury Publishing Ireland, 29 Earlsfort Terrace, Dublin 2, D02 AY28, Ireland

BLOOMSBURY, BLOOMSBURY ACADEMIC and the Diana logo are trademarks of Bloomsbury Publishing Plc

First published in the United States of America 2026

Copyright © Kristen Lopez, 2026

Cover design: Sally Rinehart
Cover image © iStock.com/gojak

All rights reserved. No part of this publication may be: i) reproduced or transmitted in any form, electronic or mechanical, including photocopying, recording or by means of any information storage or retrieval system without prior permission in writing from the publishers; or ii) used or reproduced in any way for the training, development or operation of artificial intelligence (AI) technologies, including generative AI technologies. The rights holders expressly reserve this publication from the text and data mining exception as per Article 4(3) of the Digital Single Market Directive (EU) 2019/790.

Bloomsbury Publishing Inc does not have any control over, or responsibility for, any third-party websites referred to or in this book. All internet addresses given in this book were correct at the time of going to press. The author and publisher regret any inconvenience caused if addresses have changed or sites have ceased to exist, but can accept no responsibility for any such changes.

Library of Congress Cataloging-in-Publication Data

Names: Lopez, Kristen author
Title: Popcorn disabilities : the highs and lows of disabled representation in the movies / Kristen Lopez.
Description: New York, NY : Bloomsbury Academic, 2026.
Identifiers: LCCN 2025030795 (print) | LCCN 2025030796 (ebook) | ISBN 9781493086337 hardback | ISBN 9781493086344 epub | ISBN 9798765161272 pdf
Subjects: LCSH: Disabilities in motion pictures | LCGFT: Film criticism
Classification: LCC PN1995.9.H34 L67 2026 (print) | LCC PN1995.9.H34 (ebook)
LC record available at https://lccn.loc.gov/2025030795
LC ebook record available at https://lccn.loc.gov/2025030796

ISBN: HB: 978-1-4930-8633-7
ePDF: 979-8-7651-6127-2
eBook: 978-1-4930-8634-4

Typeset by Deanta Global Publishing Services, Chennai, India
Printed and bound in the United States of America

For product safety–related questions, contact productsafety@bloomsbury.com.

To find out more about our authors and books, visit www.bloomsbury.com and sign up for our newsletters.

To Mom. For every time you've had to explain to me the difference between *Lucas* and *Rudy*. I love you.

CONTENTS

Foreword viii
Acknowledgments x

Introduction: Surprise! Your Disability Is Now a Movie 1
1 Silent Saints and Tragic Monsters 11
2 "One of Us" 29
3 Disabled Actors: An All-Too-Brief History Lesson 39
4 War and the Rise of the Bitter Cripple 61
5 "You Never Go Full Retard" 77
6 Black and Disabled 95
7 Disabled Horror and the Horror of Disability 109
8 Pretty Disabilities 131
9 Caretaker Cinema 155
10 Cripping Up and the Oscar Myth 173

Epilogue: Are We There Yet? 195
Works Cited 209
Index 219

FOREWORD

I can't precisely recall which part of my life I was living when I met Kristen Lopez for the first time. It might have been in my capacity as a host at Turner Classic Movies. We hold a classic film festival every year in Hollywood, and Kristen is regularly working as a writer at the festival, sharing her profound love of the movies produced during Hollywood's Golden Age. It certainly might've been there. Or we may have met at a movie theater somewhere in Los Angeles, back when I also worked as a film critic, first for the old Siskel and Ebert show *At the Movies*, then later (after getting, you know, fired) for the online show *What the Flick?!*

I was a terrible film critic. I could fake it well at times, I suppose. Mostly, though, I felt like I was miming what a critic would say. What I learned in the process of reviewing films poorly was that I genuinely loved talking about movies. I just didn't want to be an official arbiter of whether they were any good. What I clearly remember about meeting Kristen was this immediate sense that I enjoyed talking movies with her. Kristen has this boundless passion for movies, their stories, and the people who make them. And it's her enthusiasm for film that makes her the right person to take on the content of *Popcorn Disabilities*.

In an era when we all recognize the cultural importance of seeing ourselves reflected on the screen, Kristen is not only the perfect writer but also the perfect film lover to examine the representation (and, critically, the lack of it) of those living with disabilities of varying kinds. As we strive to guarantee the future of movies to tell nuanced, layered, and complicated stories in front of audiences in theaters, we can't shy away from recognizing where the industry has fallen short. This isn't the time for resting on laurels and offering up vacuous platitudes about "how far we've come." Rather, we're in an era that calls for blunt honesty about where this industry we love—this art form we love—has fallen short.

For better than a hundred years, filmmakers have strived to represent the full breadth of the human condition on-screen. They've made beautiful pictures, moving pictures, funny pictures, heart-stopping pictures, and yes, change-making pictures. The representation of fully formed Black characters has arrived, as has—to a lesser extent—meaningful characterizations of other long caricatured "outsider" groups. Moreover, sometime in the past half century, writers started crafting female characters for actresses who had the chutzpah, the temerity, to turn forty-five years old and desire to keep working. But I think we can all recognize that those living with disabilities have yet to achieve the same standard of representation on the big screen. And as we move toward changing that imbalance, it's imperative for abled movie fans to examine our own perceptions and prejudices when we watch how people with disabilities are portrayed on-screen. In doing so, we need to remember that the responsibility to unpack our baggage lies with us: We can't demand that our disabled friends and family do the work for us.

However, *Popcorn Disabilities* will undoubtedly help expedite the process. It offers insight into Kristen's journey to see and secure her place inside an art form that has captivated her imagination since childhood. And as she takes us along for the ride, she'll get other movie lovers, both abled and disabled, to question why certain stereotypes endure while others are rightly tossed into the waste bin of history. If you care about the movies the way she does, the way I do, then you'll finish reading this book and immediately understand why Kristen Lopez is the right person to write *Popcorn Disabilities*.

Ben Mankiewicz

ACKNOWLEDGMENTS

It's hard to believe this book is done. A full year of my life has been dedicated to talking about disability 24/7, and that's saying something, considering I am actually disabled. That's to say I have to start by thanking the people who put up with me while I wrote this, starting with my mom. Mom, thank you for enduring my tears, my frustration, and the numerous times I thought about destroying this manuscript and throwing the covers over my head. You've always been my biggest supporter, and this book would never have seen the light of day without your support. At the same time, I'd like to thank my brothers, John and Steven . . . just so they can't say I didn't thank them at all.

A massive thank-you to my friend Emily Edwards. Thank you for reading this manuscript, giving me notes, and answering every single one of my texts asking if I should move a paragraph around. Your editing of this book made my themes stronger and more organized.

At the same time I need to thank my friends Antonio Romo, Sharareh Drury, and Dianna Berrian. You kept me sane with your friendship and encouragement.

I also want to show my immense gratitude to Mr. Ben Mankiewicz for graciously agreeing to write my foreword, even after I admitted to him he was my second choice. Thank you for putting this on your already stacked plate. I also have to shout out the Turner Classic Movies crew in general for keeping my spirits raised with your programming and letting me be part of the family.

Thanks to Mark Falkin, my literary agent, for helping get this book out in the world. Also thank you to the Bloomsbury team, specifically Chris Chappell, for understanding the type of book I wanted to write and letting me go for it.

Thank you for getting on Zoom and being open to my desire to write not just an academic text about disability but one that could be funny and a tad cheeky.

And, as always, a special thanks to the Hollywood Roosevelt Hotel. Not sure what you guys do, but when I hang out in your hotel, the words just flow. These last chapters would not have been done without ya.

INTRODUCTION
SURPRISE! YOUR DISABILITY IS NOW A MOVIE

The year 2025 marks the thirty-fifth anniversary of the passage of the Americans with Disabilities Act, commonly referred to as the ADA. It's a piece of legislation that, as a child, I couldn't have cared less about. I never felt limited in my life, despite being born with osteogenesis imperfecta, more commonly known as brittle bone disorder, and becoming a full-time wheelchair user at the age of five. But as I've gotten older, moved away from my hometown, and tried to live and work as a disabled adult in America I've seen the way the ADA's been undermined and limited. I realize now how important it's been to my life as a disabled person in the United States and that, as flawed as it is, it benefits countless people. It put numerous protections into place but, specifically, it required establishments that are open to the public to be accessible without the use of stairs. Without it, I'd probably never be able to access the spaces I love, from video stores to movie theaters to Disneyland. I might not have become the film lover that I am today.

Movies opened up new worlds for me. I was an outgoing child but understood that not being ambulatory meant I'd have to put some dreams aside—farewell, ballet and becoming an Olympic ribbon dancer—and place restrictions on where I could go: The cobblestones of Britain will probably never be my friend. I knew I'd never be a world traveler but I could come close through the power of cinema. In the movies, I could go anywhere or be anything—within reason.

I didn't have disabled role models in my everyday life. I had no disabled family members to give me a road map on how to navigate the world, nor were any of my friends disabled. My experience with disability began and ended with myself. And since Hollywood wasn't exactly tripping over itself to show wheelchair users on-screen, I had to take what I could get. The first time I saw a wheelchair that wasn't mine was on-screen; it belonged to Lieutenant Dan in

Forrest Gump. What young disabled girl doesn't automatically identify with a surly Vietnam vet? This experience seared itself into my brain. *This guy used a wheelchair!* Sure, it didn't look like mine and, in hindsight, was definitely not made for him, but it was a start. It was also the first time I noticed what disability stereotypes in the movies looked like.

Disability narratives in movies prioritize the stories of white men, whether in the Lon Chaney films of the 1920s or Al Pacino's Oscar-winning performance in *Scent of a Woman*. To watch disability in the movies is to see once-ambulatory male characters struck down by the presumed horrors of disability that force them to reevaluate their sense of masculinity and identity. Disability stories are stories of lack and loss. Able-bodied audiences internalize this, and disabled viewers have to work against it. Being a disabled teen girl, watching disability narratives on-screen that didn't prioritize women and did emphasize disability as something to mourn did a number on me mentally, as it has done for countless others. It caused me to struggle with self-loathing and self-esteem issues that I deal with to this day.

This isn't strictly a disability problem. The lack of representation on-screen plagues viewers of color as well as women in general. Ninety-one percent of Americans believe that the media has the power to shape society. As Geena Davis says in the documentary *CinemAbility*, movies act as codes of conduct to teach people how to deal with those who are different from us. They teach us how to interact with people and show us what is rude versus polite. "Disabled movies" prioritize disabled pain and suffering. They illustrate the worst parts of our disabled lives. For many watching disabled narratives, they teach them how to stand in the presence of someone with a disability and not embarrass themselves. If the representation is bad, the interactions they encourage will be bad. I've had my fair share of bad moments with people. I recall one with a neighbor I'd never met before who came out of her house one day when she saw me walking my dog. She praised me for "having the strength" to go outside. She saw my leaving my house as a personal struggle I apparently endured with pride. "When I see you outside, it makes me realize I can't complain about my life." I'm not sure whether movies inspired this woman to say what she did, but in watching films with disabled characters, it's easy to understand *why* she'd think this.

When you aren't represented on-screen, those codes of conduct leave you adrift, trying to figure out your place in the world. Rites of passage like prom, first dates, sex, and getting a job are not stories Hollywood tells from a disabled perspective. As a teenager I identified with the plight of Molly Ringwald's character, Samantha, in *Sixteen Candles* and Elle Woods's desire to be a lawyer in *Legally Blonde, but I still felt we were different*. Disabled viewers always have that sense of remove. Samantha and Elle were always going to succeed for me, not because they were the heroines of their stories but because they were able bodied. As much as I love the movies, they gave me little perspective on how to look at the ableist world around me, leaving everything to trial and error.

Because there wasn't a diversity of depictions to choose from (I was gravitating toward Lieutenant Dan, after all), I found characters who were coded as disabled: those who weren't explicitly disabled—no wheelchairs or walkers among them—but who were outcasts or physically or mentally repressed. These characters saw themselves as missing something, so I equated my real disability with their fictional challenges. Take the 1989 Disney animated feature *The Little Mermaid*. "*The Little Mermaid* isn't about disability," you might say. On the surface (pun intended), you're right. But look at the story: The titular little mermaid, Ariel, wants to be "where the people are," but she can't because she has a gigantic fish tail and an inability to breathe and walk on land. For a five-year-old who didn't walk, Ariel spoke to all the things I wanted to do and couldn't. I connected to Ariel through our shared isolation (and our mutual stubbornness and belief that no one understands us, but let's stick to the obvious for now).

Samuel L. Jackson is the wheelchair-using Mr. Glass in *Unbreakable* (2000). Archive Photos / Stringer / Moviepix

Want an example of how disability representation manifests in reality? In the fall of 2000, I was a naive middle-schooler who loved movies—and not necessarily the movies embraced by my tween peers. I saw anything and everything, even movies that my mom will tell you I shouldn't have seen. (Thanks, Mom!) When M. Night Shyamalan's *Unbreakable* debuted on November 22 of that year, it wasn't something I was interested in, despite my love of movies. No disrespect to Shyamalan—a director who deserves his flowers and gave us one of my favorite disabled characters: Ivy, from *The Village*—but after the amazing ride that was his 1999 horror feature *The Sixth Sense*, the action-oriented, superhero world he was creating just didn't appeal to me. *Unbreakable* was a stock superhero movie in a landscape where that genre just wasn't cool. (Yes, kids, before there were multiple Marvel movies dropping every year the stray comic-bookesque feature was a hokey rarity.) The film follows a man, played by Bruce Willis, who survives a train crash due to his superheroic powers of invincibility.

The movie was unavoidable for me though. Friends and teachers would run up to me and ask if I'd seen *Unbreakable*. "It's made for you!" they said. Why would this superhero movie starring two actors over thirty appeal to a precocious middle schooler, you ask? What was it that leapt off the screen that should have made me first in line to see this clearly life-altering film? It was because the film's villain, Elijah Price (Samuel L. Jackson), had the same disability as me and used a wheelchair. Price, like most OIers, deals with multiple bone fractures that are caused by doing simple things. As a child, I routinely broke bones doing things most kids did. But, at the time, I didn't realize until years later how revolutionary it was to get a movie with a wheelchair user who was also a Black man. At the time, I'll confess, I'd chalked it up to "I've already seen a wheelchair-using dude in a superhero film" that year—said dude being Patrick Stewart's Charles Xavier in the first *X-Men*, released just four months earlier. The aforementioned friends and teachers presumed the character had to have something in common with me and that I'd feel a sense of kinship seeing him. There was also the underlying feeling that I should feel honored that my able-bodied friends and teachers noticed this disabled character. Don't get me wrong, I appreciate their efforts now. Their intentions were good. But the belief that one character should represent and identify with every disabled person is a problem that still happens today because of the sheer lack of characters to begin with.

I wore my avoidance of *Unbreakable* as a badge of honor. I refused to watch it purely because everyone around me felt I *needed* to see it. That I'd *love* it.

That's a lot of pressure: not only to see a movie but to validate others' love for it. I didn't love myself (what adolescent does?) and didn't want to celebrate a disabled character for the sake of their disability alone. Why was I required to support any disabled character for the fact that a screenwriter decided to write them into existence? This was my wayward attempt at rebellion. It took seventeen years for me to watch *Unbreakable* and when I finally saw it in 2017 and wrote about my experience with it for the entertainment site Crooked Marquee, I was surprised that I *wasn't* offended by it. Actually, I didn't have any deep feelings toward it at all. It's a fine movie, nothing more. Jackson's character was good, but the villain is fairly straightforward and did not fall into any specific tropes that were particularly offensive or anger inducing. I was left with the fact that, after all these years, I didn't have anything to celebrate or be outraged by. It was a movie that just was. As I mentioned in the article, "This is by far the least offensive portrait of disability I've seen in mainstream cinema." That seems so trite today. I look at *Unbreakable* through a different lens now: that of cinema's power to unite people, for good and bad, regarding disability. And how disabled people are compelled to respond to movies about the subject. Friends and colleagues still refer to *Unbreakable* any time I bring up my disability. I once had a doctor call my diagnosis "the *Unbreakable* disease." I at least now can respond when they follow up with "Have you seen it?"

As far back as 1920, Hollywood has perceived disability as strange and unknowable. It seems the only way to illustrate it has been to remind audiences, "They were once like you!" Remember, it's always about what the disabled person has lost. Though one in four people in the United States have a disability, that's not reflected in entertainment. Films that focus on disability are mired in outdated stereotypes and beliefs to appeal to an able-bodied audience, a fact enhanced by nearly all of these movies being written, directed, and (usually) starring able-bodied people. This in spite of the fact that Hollywood has had disabled actors and directors for decades. During the studio era directors like Frank Capra (deafness), Harold Russell (limb difference), and Lionel Barrymore (wheelchair user due to arthritis) lived with disabilities. There are also disabled performers today, including Dame Judi Dench (blindness), Millie Bobby Brown (deafness), and Michael J. Fox (Parkinson's). But if one in four have a disability, that's three in four who don't. Majority rules, in this case. Disabled audiences, if they do connect with a disabled character or story, are considered a nice bonus. Because of this able-bodied majority, there is a presumption that able-bodied people won't understand the strange world of disability and will require either an able-bodied narrator or lead, or a focus on able-bodied people who have become disabled late in life. This is a technique you'll see and hear a lot that I've dubbed "the able-bodied buffer."

Presentations of disability shaped by the able bodied represent the specific time and place out of which they come while simultaneously shaping audiences' perception of disability in a way that lingers for decades after a film is first screened. "Representations of unusual bodies . . . reveal[s] more about an era's cultural norms and self-image than they do about disabled individuals, even as they inevitably shape the latter's experiences and perceptions," writes Angela M. Smith in the book *Hideous Progeny*. This doesn't just illustrate and cement enduring stereotypes but presents a stigma of disability as something fearful and shameful. Disability theorist Tobin Siebers says, "Most people do not want to consider that life's passages will lead them from ability to disability. The prospect is too frightening, the disabled body too disturbing." Thus, disabled narratives champion it as something to overcome and, if possible, cure. Because of this cure mentality, coupled with medical jargon or scenes of hospital stays, disability is couched in movies as a medical issue.

A 2023 study by USC Annenberg showed that, over an eight-year period, 2.4 percent of all speaking roles in mainstream movies had a disabled character, a 0.5 percent increase from the previous year. It's a small victory worth celebrating but not when you consider that, because of Hollywood's slow adoption of disabled representation, they're leaving a lot of money on the table: A 2018 study conducted by the American Institutes of Research said disabled consumers are a trillion (with a *t*) dollar industry. Today there is an awareness that disability should be in Hollywood films but it's difficult not to see it as limited in scope and performative. Films like Greta Gerwig's *Barbie*—which I love—insert disabled actors into the frame to acknowledge their existence but don't give them any lines or depth. These characters are memorable because they are the only disabled persons around. The audience watches them but never engages with them. Thankfully, movies like *CODA* and *A Different Man*, plus the documentary *Crip Camp*, are subverting audiences' expectations of disability, but it's not nearly enough.

I realize how often movies make me question who I am. As a disabled person. As a disabled woman. As a person in society. To have people routinely hear my medical diagnosis, or see my wheelchair, and immediately ask if I've seen a specific disabled character, or ask for my opinion about a specific movie with a disabled character, or share with me their alleged knowledge on my life and medical history because of a film they watched. It shows cinema's ability to educate audiences about situations they know nothing about and make those who already are marginalized compare themselves to what is or was on-screen.

I measured my career goals, my desirability, my life, in comparison to the able-bodied characters on-screen and to the few disabled characters Hollywood gave me. Movies taught me how disabled people lived and, by extension, how I should live. That is the problem. When your representation is problematic AF, you, as the viewer, internalize that. It's large-scale FOMO, the cinematic equivalent of looking at someone's "fabulous" life on Instagram. To paraphrase America Ferrera's character in *Barbie*, it's too hard to tie oneself into knots to try to live up to, or break through, the glass ceiling of the few disabled characters Hollywood prioritizes. I come to this topic from my own perspective, which has commonalities with other disabilities but also may diverge from someone who is blind, Deaf, or neurodivergent. In all instances, I have researched as best I could and, in cases where I know I do not have the ability to speak with credibility on the topic, like with specific depictions of neurodivergent issues like autism, I have only touched on those films and hope more nuanced writers can pick up on those topics and write about them.

When I started my career as a journalist, I never planned to talk about my disability or write content related to it. I didn't see myself as an expert—my major was English, not disability or anything related to medicine—nor was there anything compelling in my life story to warrant my talking about the subject. I didn't think I'd overcome anything, suffered enough, or endured anything too intriguing. I was the epitome of normal with the exception that I used a wheelchair and had a crap-ton of broken bones and surgeries as a kid. But since disabled narratives highlight stereotypes told by the able bodied, much of the preservation of these tropes is covered by able-bodied journalists who don't know what to look for. Because film is a global medium, with great power comes great responsibility. So I started writing from my perspective as a disabled person who happened to be a journalist. As my journalistic career took off, I was surprised by how many people, both disabled and non, reacted positively to my articles on disability in the movies. I've received numerous emails from people who, like me, are just trying to be seen. For them, reading a disabled journalist point something out does make them feel seen. Someone understands their experience in some way. I've heard from young people, too, who don't necessarily care about movies but want to enter journalism and are surprised to find there's a physically disabled entertainment journalist out there. Because of the lack of disabled writers looking at disabled narratives in movies, I've heard from my fair share of angry directors and screenwriters who presume their movies should connect with me or are irritated that I'm critiquing their characterization or pointing out when something is offensive. No, I won't name any names and, yes, I'm prepping for a few angry comments about this book. But when I see a wheelchair user army-crawl to get away from someone or see a blind person touch someone's face to "see" them better, it's impossible not to feel angry at the lack of understanding.

And that isn't me, the journalist, saying that. It angers me as a lover of movies. Movies like *The Wizard of Oz* and *Snow White and the Seven Dwarfs* left me hating the word "dwarf" or "munchkin" because people assumed that was part of my disability. (While I am small in stature, I don't identify as a member of the Little Person community.) But because most narratives about disability don't focus on nuance, the average film viewer lumps short people with unconventional body shapes into those categories. Because my bones are shaped differently, films like *Edward Scissorhands* and *Pet Sematary* terrified me because I presumed that's what being an older disabled person looked like. And the fact that most disabled people on-screen were men left me wondering if any disabled women other than myself existed at all.

Which brings me to the book you hold in your hands. This is the culmination of a lot of years of watching and writing about disability narratives. Here is where I champion the movies I believe got it right(ish) and question those that got it horribly wrong. I also wanted to showcase to able-bodied audiences how they can engage with disabled narratives better and avoid embarrassment in situations with disabled people by noticing specific stereotypes and questioning why directors and screenwriters choose to present disabled characters the way they do.

I want people to look at movies, past and present, a little more deeply and realize why ramps proliferated more in the 1990s than they did in the 1970s. Why Lon Chaney, though abled, made some very cool disabled features in the 1920s. Or why Hollywood really enjoys doing *The Hunchback of Notre Dame* every couple of decades. If you enjoy a problematic disabled narrative, that's okay. I love a few myself (hi there, *Forrest Gump*). The goal isn't to shame anyone for liking a movie that has a disabled character played by an able-bodied actor or for appreciating how a story is told. We'll look at numerous tropes commonly found in disabled stories and around disabled characters, starting with the silent era and Victorian concepts of disability—what I've been cheekily calling the "eugenics era"—and Hollywood's long history of tragic disabled characters. There's a brief pit stop at Tod Browning's 1932 film *Freaks*, celebrated as one of the most controversial—and beloved, in some circles—disabled movies. From there a brief exploration of disabled performers, leading into war movies and the reason why there are so many angry disabled hippies. We'll talk about disabled aesthetics and how they factor into movies. Just *how* disabled is too disabled? We'll also touch on disabled characters of color, disabled women, sexual desire on-screen, and the Oscar myth of "play disabled, win an award."

This book is by no means definitive though it is a start, focusing on physical and mental disabilities in film. You'll probably say, "What about this movie? Why not that disability?" The book focuses primarily on American cinema and physical disability as well as movies I've interacted with in my own journey as a disabled person. The hope is that this book is a launchpad for you to find more disabled narratives to watch, enjoy, and deconstruct. We're not all sad and lonely, I promise. I only speak for me and my experience as a disabled person and welcome those who disagree with my assessment of certain movies. We're not a monolith and what I might see as progressive, someone else can see as reductive. As far as language goes, unless I am quoting from a movie, my aim is to avoid as much ableist language as possible. I will also prioritize the fewest words possible and thus go with identity-first language ("disabled person") as opposed to person-first language ("person with disabilities"). In situations where a specific disability is named, I will say that.

1 SILENT SAINTS AND TRAGIC MONSTERS

Disabled characters have existed in art, theatrical plays, and operas. So it's not surprising that arrival of early film technology saw disability presented there as well. One of the earliest examples is an 1897 short by the Lumière brothers—the same duo behind the legendary 1902 short *A Trip to the Moon*—entitled *The False Cripple* (it was the 1900s). The story involves a police officer who grows suspicious of a disabled beggar. It turns out the beggar is faking his disability. This could possibly be the first time an able-bodied actor decided to "crip it up," albeit the film's plot makes it an intentional deception. Sadly, there was no prestige or Oscar in the offing. Upon movies entering the popular consciousness, disabled characters continued to be seen, with nearly every major studio of the silent era crafting disability narratives. Some that stand out, or just have the most unintentionally audacious names, include Gaumont's 1907 short *The Legless Runner* and *The Cripple's Marriage* (1909), as well as Biograph's *The Deaf Mute's Ball* (1907). It's comical how crass these titles were, considering they contained only a few seconds of disabled screen time.

Any good discussion on where disability representation in film is going begins with where it started. We have to go back to the good old days: the Victorian era. Specifically, the kid who ruined disability (and potentially Christmas) for all of us: Tiny Tim. The crutch-loving soft boy of Charles Dickens's 1843 novel *A Christmas Carol* has become shorthand for everything negative in disability discourse. As Julia Miele Rodas writes about the character, Tiny Tim presents those with disabilities as "childlike, dependent, and in need of charity and pity," and it's these traits that every filmic adaptation of *A Christmas Carol* exaggerates, though it starts with his physical traits: depicting him as a wide-eyed, waxy-pallored little boy whose exclamation of "God bless us, everyone" shows not just his inner purity and goodness but what society is capable of in honoring that goodness. Tim reminds abled readers what good people they can be! An 1844 review of the novel, written by fellow Victorian William Makepeace Thackeray, called the "little creature" (great choice of words, Bill) a "bond of union" between Dickens and the reader. Even the Muppets gave us a darling facsimile in their 1992 adaptation and you know when they do something it's definitely pop culture. Tiny Tim might be the first example of the able-bodied buffer, wherein Ebenezer Scrooge learns through his interactions with Tim how to be a better person. Tim doesn't need any personality or depth—his goodness is his only defining trait beyond his crutch—because Scrooge is the real protagonist.

Tiny Tim's disability reminded readers at the time about Britain's poor children. By situating disabled people as living saints whose truncated life expectancy makes them able to appreciate and champion humanity's inner goodness—kind of like a Spidey sense—it compelled Victorian readers to offer moral (and, more importantly, financial) support for them. Tiny Tim became a cause célèbre for Victorian England, this in spite of not being a real person. As Rodas lays out, "Dickens scholars almost uniformly identif[y] Tim as the object of Scrooge's most important 'lesson in empathy,' and as 'the emblem of an inexhaustible fund of sympathetic capital.'" The Queen of Norway annually sent presents that read "With Tiny Tim's Love" to disabled children in London homes and hospitals, while the character inspired a cottage industry of products such as "Tiny Tim cots" that were used in hospitals for disabled kids. This idea of the benevolent disabled was something early filmmakers and screenwriters ran with throughout the 1920s and 1930s, from the work of Lon Chaney Sr. to various characters in *Frankenstein*, *City Lights*, and *The Wizard of Oz*. For decades after the publication of Dickens's book, and as film took over as the dominant form of entertainment, disabled characters fell into three categories: saintly depictions of goodness, à la Tiny Tim; externally frightening creatures whose outer visage is a front for their good-hearted, tragic soul, like Frankenstein's monster or Quasimodo; or tortured monsters whose outward looks warp them into an inner madness and hatred against the world, like the Phantom of the Opera. All three groups end up in the same place: Death.

You can't discuss the Victorian era without looking at the science of eugenics, the now debunked theory of racial improvement and planned breeding that presumed that human beings could be corrected and social ills eliminated via genetics and heredity. Really, the history of disability in the movies in general is one where eugenics was a factor for several years. When movies suggest that disability is something to eliminate or cure that's derived specifically from the eugenics movement. As Angela M. Smith says in *Hideous Progeny*, "Disabled people are seen as monsters properly excluded from reproduction." So in movies of this time period nearly all of the characters are loners whose death at the end precludes even a hint of them bearing offspring. Because the Victorians connected outer appearance with a person's soul the eugenics movement emphasized that a person's outer deformities implied degeneracy, weakness, or inferiority. Those with disfigured faces had inner depravity, while wheelchair users were helpless or impassive. "Physical beauty and health were . . . exalted signs of worthy genetic material," according to Smith. This belief system declared that disabled people and their monstrous appearances needed to be removed from society and shouldn't continue to flourish.

The rise of freak shows, which tended to include both disabled people as well as colonized people from other countries, sold the idea that both groups should be feared and controlled. Freak shows were meant to "comfort . . . spectators because they are not the ones on display," says writer Cindy Lacom. This later manifested in movies where the goal of disabled characters was to show able-bodied people how much worse their own lives could be and leave them grateful to not be in the same situation. One may not be disabled right now, but those with disabilities served as living reminders that the audience could be in their position one day. The interrelationship of science and spectacle is why works by authors like Oscar Wilde, Robert Louis Stevenson, Mary Shelley, and Victor Hugo became ripe for film adaptations. Movies themselves were the ultimate union between technology and the extraordinary, so why not crib from the authors who told those stories best? It's not surprising that during the infancy of film disabled characters were relegated to horror pictures that show physical imperfection as the key motivator in turning a character mad, sad, or bad. It sold the idea of terror stemming from disability.

An actor with a profound effect on the portrayal of disability in movies during the 1920s and into the 1930s was able bodied. But no one exemplifies spectacle and disability, and one's ability to create a compelling character using disability, like silent film star Lon Chaney Sr., otherwise known as the "Man of a Thousand Faces." Chaney's legacy is a fraught one. Aside from being a magnetic acting talent, he also had a penchant for engaging in an early (and extreme) form of what we'd today call Method Acting. Much of his desire to play disabled characters stemmed from his own upbringing. Chaney was born Leonidas Frank Chaney in Colorado Springs, Colorado, as a CODA (child of Deaf adults). His parents, Frank H. Chaney and Emma Alice Kennedy, met as students at the former Colorado School for the Education of Mutes (now known as the Colorado School for the Deaf and Blind). Because of his parents' deafness, young Leonidas became highly skilled in American Sign Language (ASL). Chaney certainly sympathized with disabled characters and attempted to give them humanity in his portrayals. He's quoted as saying, "I wanted to remind people that the lowest types of humanity may have within them the capacity for supreme self-sacrifice. The dwarfed, misshapen beggar of the streets may have the noblest ideals. Most of my roles... have carried the theme of self-sacrifice or renunciation. These are the stories which I wish to do." But while Chaney's parents had a disability, it doesn't mean he knew every person with a disability or that he knew every disability. For all his good intentions, it's impossible to miss the ableism in his thinking of how to portray those types of characters, and how his performances launched their own tropes that are hard to eliminate today. When discussing how he secured the role in 1919's *The Miracle Man*, Chaney said, "I flopped down, rolled my eyes up in my head like a blind man, and started dragging my body along the ground." Sounds a bit extreme.

Chaney's performances as people with disabilities are feats of visual spectacle and, in some instances, extremely audacious and entertaining. A great example of his acting talent and deep commitment to the bit is found in director Wallace Worsley's ridiculously fun 1920 feature, *The Penalty*. Like all Chaney movies, it needs to be seen to be believed. Chaney plays Blizzard, San Francisco's "lord and master of the underworld." (Let's start by appreciating a movie that says disabled people can do anything, including becoming underground crime lords!) Blizzard is justified in his anger at the world. He's a dual amputee, having lost both legs after a case of severe medical malpractice. That's not an exaggeration either. In the opening scene, a young Blizzard is introduced to the audience as suffering from a fever and bump on the head. Fearing he might die, the doctor makes the decision to amputate the boy's legs at the knee—a *perfectly* rational diagnosis for a fever and head contusion. Of course, the operation is found to be unnecessary after the fact. Instead of embarking on a massive lawsuit, Blizzard becomes a criminal mastermind, eventually amassing a large San Francisco crime ring. Referred to by the chief of police as the "cripple from Hell," Blizzard plans to loot the city while simultaneously wooing the daughter of the doctor who "mangled" him.

It generally takes me fifteen seconds to point out something inaccurate in a disabled narrative, based on my own experience, or to be able to tell whether the actor playing the disabled character knows anything about disability. Chaney is an able-bodied actor and yet it is amazing to watch him move throughout *The Penalty*, interacting with the set and other performers. Without the aid of CGI, it looks like Chaney is an actual double amputee. The audience sees the cinematic equivalent of a great magic trick and wonders how the magician pulled it off. I still can't figure out how Chaney's legs are hidden in the film. Cinematographer Don Short has the camera track Blizzard as he moves through his apartment, taking note of where Blizzard places his hands and pushes off things with his weight. Next time you're watching a disabled narrative, notice how often the disabled person is actually in the frame alone, not with anyone else. The camera stays low, centering and prioritizing Blizzard within the frame. One scene sees Blizzard enter a room on his crutches, a ramp seamlessly integrated into the set design. It's doubtful anyone who isn't disabled will notice it, but it's wonderful to see. It's so minor that even a disabled viewer can miss it. Blizzard even has convenient climbing pegs inserted into a wall so he can scale it like a 1920s Spider-Man to peek out a window. Blizzard is also a skilled piano player, albeit one who utilizes his many molls to push the piano's pedals for him. This character trait serves a dual purpose. It doesn't just illustrate Blizzard's need for adaptations because of his disability. It also shows his misogyny by literally placing women in a subservient position beneath him.

Chaney's dedication to showing the struggles inherent in a disabled person's life by extreme acting techniques is similar to Daniel Day-Lewis's commitment in *My Left Foot* (1989), which we'll discuss further in chapter 10. As Smith points out, Chaney's extreme techniques were a means of connecting an audience to him through physical pain and trauma. They emphasized "the real pains and impairments endured by particular horror actors," which helped sell him as a great actor because of how much physical discomfort he endured. He wore painful leg harnesses playing Blizzard that, because of how long he wore them, cut off circulation to his legs and led to frequent collapses on set. This wasn't the last time Chaney underwent a brutal transformation either. He wore a fifty-pound rubber body suit for his role as Quasimodo in 1923's *Hunchback of Notre Dame* and used a "contoured wire appliance to flare back and pull his nose," causing pain and bleeding, while performing as the titled Phantom in 1925's *The Phantom of the Opera*. The physical toll was suffering for his art.

Looking at Chaney's silent roles in today's time, coupled with his personal family history, marks him as an early ally for disabled representation, flawed though he is. And it's important to remember that while disabled people shouldn't *exclusively* be villains, they are flawed people and can be racist, misogynist, and so forth, which Chaney showed audiences. It's the opposite of making them saintly Tiny Tims. He's downright charming in *The Penalty*. He's the perfect embodiment of the tortured bad boy we see in contemporary films ("I can change him!"). But the character isn't a romantic figure. At one point, after he's laughed at for confessing his love to Barbara (Claire

Adams), the doctor's daughter, the audience sympathizes with him. He tells her, "Forgive me for having dared lift my thoughts to you. Laughter burns a cripple like acid." The screenwriters must have had a ball crafting one-liners like that. Numerous callbacks to Blizzard's disability hit the audience with all the subtlety of a sledgehammer. My personal favorite? Blizzard snidely saying, "What an admirable pair of legs. I gave mine to science." It's a sick burn, all things considered. The eugenics element is also alive and well in *The Penalty*, with the chief of police giving an ominous warning to a woman that being forced to sleep with Blizzard is a fate worse than death. The implication here is not that Blizzard is a rapist but that his disability corrupts and destroys women. This is common in gendered depictions of disability. Disabled male characters are able to play different types of characters but are saddled with "spreading" their disability through sexual violence.

Chaney's most complex disabled portrayal comes in the 1927 feature *The Unknown*. Second only to 1932's *Freaks*, discussed in the next chapter, *The Unknown* is one of the most audacious pieces of disability cinema. Funnily enough, this and *Freaks* are directed by the same master of the macabre (and fellow questionable disabled ally) Tod Browning. Chaney portrays Alonzo the Armless, a circus performer who throws knives with his feet. The film tells the age-old story: Boy meets girl—the circus owner's daughter, Nanon, played by Joan Crawford—only to discover the girl is in love with the hot, brawny strongman Malabar (Norman Kerry). Sure, you've seen it before, but have you seen it when the boy decides to rip his rival's arms off? Similar to what Browning did with *Freaks*, *The Unknown* takes the time to show us Alonzo's day-to-day life, including lighting a cigarette with his feet, a scene mimicked in *Freaks*.

Chaney's Alonzo thinks he's perfectly situated to win Nanon and become her lover because he lacks arms. Nanon has an issue with men touching her; she clearly has some trauma responses. In a shocking reveal the audience learns Alonzo has actually been hiding his arms the entire time! Realizing that Nanon could one day discover his secret, Alonzo decides to truly cut his arms off. Let it never be said the plots of Chaney's movies weren't wildly unique. It's not a totally terrible plan. When he is alone, he uses his feet to do simple tasks. His assistant has to remind him, "You are forgetting you have arms."

This decision is subversive, as Alonzo believes that becoming disabled is advantageous for him. The idea that feigning disability has perks for the abled is a trope that pops up in other movies. Jordan Peele's 2017 film *Get Out*, discussed in chapter 6, treads similar territory as *The Unknown*, with a white photographer believing if he obtains the literal eyes of a Black photographer he'll find similar acclaim. The Farrelly brothers' 1998 comedy *There's Something About Mary* also does this, revealing that one of Mary's (Cameron Diaz) many paramours has been faking having cerebral palsy to garner her affection. Each film depicts an abled person with privilege, male and white, who presumes that disability yields superiority of some kind or an artistic or romantic advantage. It states a concept that there are perks disabled people are getting that abled people aren't, though the abled person ends up being proven wrong by the end.

Amputation and castration also go hand-in-hand in movies, though Alonzo's desire to remove his arms is a twisted take on a Disability 101 trope known as the "magic cure." As Johnson Cheu writes in Smith's *Hideous Progeny*, "[The] medical cure, the possibility of a 'normal' body, is a perspective that is assigned by the able-bodied viewer to the disabled body . . . it is the able-bodied viewer who assigns desire for normalcy, achievable through medical cure to the disabled body." A non-disabled body is not meant to be perceived as "normal" by the abled viewer and the best way to transcend that is via a medical cure. What screenwriters Browning, Waldemar Young, and Joseph Farnum do to counteract that is turn the cure on its head. Alonzo gets what he wants—to really most sincerely be disabled—but the disability doesn't yield him the happy ending he sought. Nanon decides she's gotten over her touch issues and wants Malabar, regardless of his big, hulking arms. Alonzo is now disabled and single. Disabled narratives often leave disabled people alone, but for the purposes of this story it's meant as a damn harsh lesson. In *The Penalty*, Blizzard's end goal is to have new legs grafted onto his body so he can "walk as men walk" (because masculinity and disability don't mix, either in the movie or society). But Alonzo doesn't want to be a normal man.

Chaney's characters are empathetic takes on disability but those characters live in accordance with the Victorian principles on display at the time. Thus, Chaney's characters are tragic and their deaths serve as a personal redemption, whether they've committed bad acts or not. In *The Unknown*, Alonzo's grief over losing Nanon manifests in his attempt to rip Malabar's arms off during a circus gimmick involving horses, though—honestly—Malabar should have seen that as a safety issue earlier on. Chaney's death becomes a sacrifice for love, with Alonzo placing himself in front of a kicking horse to save Nanon. He gets trampled . . . for love! He didn't die in vain. In the adaptation of Victor Hugo's *Hunchback*, Chaney's Quasimodo is stabbed in the process of saving the beautiful Esmeralda (Patsy Ruth Miller). *The Phantom of the Opera* sees Chaney's Phantom killed by an angry mob and thrown into the Seine but not before he realizes his love for opera singer Christine Daaé (Mary Philbin) isn't reciprocated. In each, the character's love for an abled woman, who will never truly accept him, is a death sentence for him, but he still gets a heavenly redemption in saving the pure, white, able-bodied heroine.

The Penalty has the harshest twist of the proverbial knife with its ending. Blizzard asks for a leg graft from the doctor who took his legs as a child. Why he'd want a terrible doctor to do another surgery on him, coupled with all the horrible things Blizzard's done to the doctor since—things that might make someone unwilling to let Blizzard live—is a question you won't get an answer to. While Blizzard is under anesthesia, the doctor realizes Blizzard's bad behavior and villainous personality stem from the head contusion he suffered as a child. Technically, Blizzard is not responsible for his actions! The doctor corrects the head injury and, while Blizzard is still disabled, he now accepts who he is. He becomes a good person and an upstanding member of society. He even gets married! Unfortunately, happiness isn't long for him, as he ends up shot by a former criminal associate who refuses to believe Blizzard's entire personality is changed by fixing a bump on the head. Fair. Blizzard isn't bad, he's mad, and medical science cures his mindset if not his physical disability. But Blizzard is still a tragic, disabled Chaney character, and thus his death leaves the audience mourning what could have been.

These characters don't become heroes but rather have their goodness validated through their desire to save someone presented as superior to them: the abled. Quasimodo's death in *Hunchback* redeems him at the end, but because his character is part of a larger ensemble, his demise is boiled down to his love for Esmeralda more than to anything good he does for the city of Paris. As for the Phantom, though equally bitter at the disrespect to his opera house, the original novel shows him in an even more negative light. The Phantom outright states he sees redemption through securing Christine's love, that her desire for him will give him the self-worth society has denied him as a man. If she can overlook his physical appearance, then what is everyone else's problem?

The establishment of decency laws in the 1930s saw the closure of freak shows across the United States. Despite the issues with these traveling shows, they were often the main source of income for disabled people. This went hand in hand with the rise of "medicalizing" disability, as Rodas writes, that saw an increase in private hospitals. So the mentally and physically disabled became "medical marvels," taken out of the circus and off the streets and placed in hospitals and museums where they could be cared for by medical staff. Gone was the belief that the disabled were "social parasites"; instead, they were pitiable orphans in need of care.

Chaney played several self-sacrificing, tragic characters, and they aren't too far off from another monstrous character of Gothic literature adapted in the 1930s: Frankenstein's monster, most famously embodied by Boris Karloff in James Whale's 1931 feature. Coded as a disabled character, Whale's Frankenstein—using the familiar name for him even though he isn't, technically, Frankenstein—falls into the childlike, pitiable, charity case stereotype evoked by Tiny Tim. As the 1930s developed and eugenics started becoming the foundational principles of dictatorial regimes in Europe, the United States started moving away from overt displays of eugenics in their features. Physically disabled characters like Frankenstein transitioned into kindhearted, childlike, tragic figures. Think less Chaney and more Dickens, wherein they are poor waifs thrown under the proverbial wheel of life. Where Chaney's villainy gave him agency, Frankenstein's monster is not wholly responsible for his actions because he is so infantile. When he throws a little girl into a lake and causes her to drown, the monster is genuinely shocked and upset, not realizing the consequences of his actions.

Interestingly, in Mary Shelley's original writing of Frankenstein, the monster is described as more human than how Karloff is made up to be in the movie. Shelley describes him as having "watery eyes . . . [a] shrivelled complexion and straight black teeth." She describes the character as downtrodden and sickly, not unlike the numerous people suffering from tuberculosis, typhoid, typhus, and malnutrition that ran rampant at the time the novel was written. The written monster is not the non-human-looking creature with the boxy, square head and bolts coming out of his neck, like Karloff's makeup design. Karloff, similar to Chaney, also underwent an intense physical transformation to play Frankenstein's monster, removing his partial bridgework to give the monster the right sunken-cheeked appearance and wearing thirteen-pound shoes to give him a shuffling gait.

Frankenstein's 1935 sequel, *Bride of Frankenstein*, makes a stronger argument for being a disabled narrative due to an extended sequence originally written in Shelley's book. The monster meets a blind man and learns about things like tobacco, alcohol, and, most important, friendship. The blind man is equally pitiful, lonely, and isolated, seeking solace and companionship just as much as the creature is. The man's blindness sets up a stereotype commonly seen in romantic dramas: the "love is blind" trope. When two hunters find out the monster is living with the blind man they immediately react with violence, destroying what the creature presumes is his only chance at finding a friend. Though the movie is titled "the bride of Frankenstein," the movie ends by refusing to let the creature have a romantic relationship—the undesirables can't procreate while being alive and well—albeit it is Frank who decides "we belong dead," destroying himself and his new bride, wonderfully played by Elsa Lanchester, in the process ... at least until he returns for the next sequel.

It's interesting to contrast Frank with Chaney's Phantom in the 1925 adaptation of Gaston Leroux's book, *Phantom of the Opera*, or Chaney's Quasimodo in *Hunchback*. In the latter, Quasimodo is referred to as a "slave" to the evil Jehan (Brandon Hurst). However, Quasi isn't the happy, good-hearted character in the animated Disney version of the '90s. He's angry and bitter at being outcast from society, hanging off the belltower and sticking his tongue out at the citizenry. As an intertitle card says, "To townspeople he was an inhuman freak," so they might have had it coming. Frankenstein searches the countryside seeking friends though *The Unknown* and *Hunchback* show off an entire disabled underworld. The Court of Miracles in *Hunchback* is a safe space for all people, including those who see disability as a gimmick to con others. It's a world where Alonzos of all stripes converge. When *The Hunchback of Notre Dame* was remade in 1939 with Charles Laughton in the role, the tone was more analogous to *Frankenstein* than to *The Hunchback*'s 1923 predecessor. Laughton's performance is tragic, and the physical makeup on his face is softened—aided by Laughton himself having a rounder face—to make him look more pitiable.

Remember, per Victorian and eugenic thinking, these physically disabled characters are genetically flawed, so someone like Blizzard in *The Penalty*—whose evil ways are given a narrative explanation—is still not perceived as worthy of passing on his genetic material via reproduction. You could say Chaney's characters were perpetually friend zoned. Quasimodo is good enough to save Esmeralda's life but not enough to date her (nor do they get together in Disney's family-friendly interpretation). Nanon in *The Unknown* doesn't like being touched but conjures up a reason to explain her preference for Malabar over Alonzo. The disabled characters are self-sacrificing and demonstrate how their outer face masks a kind heart, but that's it. The disabled can save you from a fate worse than death, but having sex with them *is* a fate worse than death. This has changed, somewhat, over the ensuing years. Quasimodo did eventually get a romantic partner in another Disney version of *Hunchback*, albeit the 2002 direct-to-DVD sequel. And when director Joel Schumacher remade *Phantom of the Opera* in 2004, he cast actor Gerard Butler in the title role, screwing up half his face which, while being a laughable decision, does at least allow the audience to lust after the character.

This isn't the same for disabled women, who are barely represented on-screen in general, less so if they aren't physically attractive. As innocent as they are beautiful, disabled women of this time in film are lovely and tragic saints in equal measure, in spite of the pre-Code era that later celebrated women as hedonistic vamps and flappers. The best example of disabled women in silents is found in Virginia Cherrill's blind flower girl in Charlie Chaplin's 1931 silent feature, *City Lights*. The blonde's beauty represents angelic purity and etherealness, and her blindness causes her to fall into another disability stereotype I call "pretty disabilities." Those with pretty disabilities are usually Deaf, blind, or nonverbal women, which lets a beautiful non-Deaf, nonblind, or verbal actress inhabit the role without affecting her sexuality and physical appeal. We'll return to this topic again in chapter 8. Cherrill's character is singular in personality; apologies to the Chaplin lovers here who think the Little Tramp can do no wrong. She's so lacking in characteristics that she doesn't even possess a name, referred to as "*A Blind Girl.*" That title isn't used in the definitive way, as Chaplin's character is known as "*The* Tramp." She is just a random blind girl while he is undeniably synonymous with his character, known to audiences as the Tramp.

Virginia Cherrill is the beautiful blind flower girl in Charlie Chaplin's *City Lights* (1931). Photo via John Kobal Foundation / Getty Images

Chaplin's Tramp meets the Blind Girl when she hears the door shut of a chauffeured automobile and falsely assumes he's a millionaire. The blind are historically depicted in film as having ultra heightened senses, like sonar, and in *City Lights* the blind girl can apparently smell money. Cherrill and Chaplin didn't get along during filming and it's said Chaplin didn't particularly care if the actress knew how to act blind. His only acting tip for her was to "look inwardly and not to see me." A Blind Girl is poor and at risk of losing her house, but despite being deficient in funds she's overflowing in good-heartedness. The audience roots for her because she's pretty, sweet, and so very lonely. She doesn't appear to have any friends outside her family, sadly waving to a couple outside as she sits in her room, alone, with her birds. The audience understands she will be rewarded with a happy ending that has to involve the Tramp somehow because, like Tiny Tim, she's defined by her blindness and, like Scrooge, the Tramp is committed to bettering her circumstances. When a doctor reveals she's suffering from a fever and an unknown illness—because disabled people in movies are riddled with one mysterious ailment or another—the Tramp is compelled to get a job to help her, much like Scrooge is moved to help the Cratchit family after hearing Tiny Tim will die. The Tramp's love for the Blind Girl certainly illustrates the idea that disabled women are attractive and worthy of love, but it's complicated by the question of whether he is drawn to her goodness or the fact that she is blind and dependent on others. Their first meeting implies he's fascinated more by her inability to see what he looks like more than anything else. Is this a fetishized relationship?

The Tramp not only saves the girl's house but also pays for an experimental medical procedure to cure her blindness using money gifted to him by a drunk millionaire. Said millionaire has no recollection of giving the Tramp the money and, after it's delivered to her, the Tramp is sent to prison for robbery. When he's eventually released, he rediscovers the girl—her sight now restored—and sees she's opened a successful business. Now that the pair are equally able, the (former) Blind Girl's soul is given a final test—because the audience must know she is worthy of the Tramp's love and suffering. She must be able to "see" that the downtrodden Tramp who enters her shop is her one true love. I love to see what would have happened had she turned him down. Would she have been immediately struck blind again? Of course the outcome is never in doubt because the blind girl's outer beauty is representative of her purity. All's well that ends well, and the movie concludes with the girl declaring, "I can see now!" To quote Shakespeare, there's a double meaning in that!

The 1928 film *The Man Who Laughs* brings the threads of this early time period in disability discourse together. Directed by Paul Leni, a pre-*Casablanca* Conrad Veidt plays Gwynplaine, a circus performer who, as a young boy, had a widespread grin permanently carved onto his face, otherwise known as a Glasgow smile. Now grown, Gwynplaine works in a traveling circus alongside his beloved, the blind Dea (Mary Philbin, post–*Phantom of the Opera*), whom Gwynplaine saved when she was just a baby. When it's discovered that Gwynplaine is the heir to a fortune, the evil Duchess Josiana (Olga Baclanova) plans to marry him for his money.

With Universal on a hot streak adapting popular literature connected to the horror genre, it wasn't surprising that in the wake of their success with 1923's *The Hunchback of Notre Dame*, they'd turn to another Victor Hugo–penned book. Chaney was initially slated to star in the film, but for various reasons, he left the project and did *Phantom of the Opera* instead. To watch *The Man Who Laughs* is to see everything previously crafted by Universal brought together for a heartbreaking presentation of a man desperate to be loved in spite of his hideous disfigurement, which was committed against his will. Veidt is a master of expression, with the ability to convey a multitude of emotions with his eyes. Like Chaney, the chronic grin on Veidt's face illustrates the magnificent craftsmanship of Universal's makeup and prosthetics department, as well as Veidt's desire to endure hardship for authenticity. Veidt was fitted with dentures containing metal hooks to pull back the corners of his mouth. As with Chaney, Veidt was praised less for showing a touching and authentic depiction of disability and more for being able to make the audience sympathize with him despite how grotesque (for the time) he looked. A 1928 review in the *New York Times* read, "Mr. Veidt dexterously conceals the lower part of his face during some scenes, so that the sympathy in his eyes, the sadness at his plight, cause one to forget, momentarily, his awful mouth." The Victorian correlation of monstrousness and tragedy is the focus.

Gwynplaine ended up inspiring pop culture somewhat, with *Batman* comic artist Bob Finger alongside Bob Kane and Jerry Robinson allegedly using the character as inspiration for the supervillain the Joker. When people learn that fact and then watch *The Man Who Laughs* they're shocked that it isn't an out-and-out horror movie. Gwynplaine looks monstrous, but he is another tragic character like Quasimodo. His fruitless hope that something will, or can, fix him comes through in a scene where Gwynplaine tries to wipe his smile off after another circus performer jokingly says to him, "[You're lucky] you don't have to rub off your laugh." The fact that Gwynplaine is descended from nobility seems like as good a solution as he can get. His extreme wealth gives him power that will help him transcend his disfigurement. His elevation in status should, in theory, lead to greater social acceptance because of his money and rank. But because Gwynplaine has made his living as a clown—interestingly enough not exclusively because of how he looks but because his surrogate father was interested in it—the House of Lords continues to look down on him, regardless of rank. No matter what, his disability or his low-status job will always leave him an outcast. So Gwynplaine rejects his inheritance in order to stay true to himself, declaring, "A King made me a clown. A Queen made me a Lord. But, first, God made me a man." Gwynplaine's rejection and finding of his own self-worth is revolutionary in an era where disabled autonomy was either ignored or seen in the negative. He decides to carve his own path in life. He may possess a kind and noble heart, like the other characters referenced in this chapter, but he's given an added sense of power by rejecting societal acceptance and maintaining his personality.

Giving us another fun twist to highlight the character's independence, Gwynplaine rejects the beautiful, able-bodied Duchess. Gwynplaine is hot to go and the ladies are responding, so that alone is fantastic, but Dea and Duchess Josiana represent his two life choices. Dea, the Madonna, represents disability, kindness, and acceptance; Josiana, the whore, represents acceptance by the abled world, wealth, and a hiding of his true self. Olga Baclanova's old-world Josiana is similar to the 1920s liberated flapper that would disappear by the end of the decade with her highly sexualized, independent manner. She's nearly nude in her first scene, the camera focused on her bare legs. Her husband, the Duke, is uninterested in her and queer-coded, so once Gwynplaine is revealed as being of noble stock, her marriage to the Duke is hastily annulled.

When Josiana sees Gwynplaine perform, she's repulsed yet aroused by him. Her seduction of him is akin to Christine Daaé's reveal of Chaney's Phantom in *Phantom of the Opera*. But with Phantom the reveal is more for shock value to the viewer. Christine stands behind the Phantom and takes his mask off so the audience can witness his face before she does. She is alarmed and cowers in fear. Josiana is more straightforward. She wants to see Gwynplaine's grin close up but also wants to experience it in a sexual manner by having him kiss her. Kinky. The camera watches her tease and play with the scarf that covers the bottom of Gwynplaine's face, the barrier between his mouth and society, before pushing it down to reveal his grin to the viewer. It's a sexually charged moment that shows she's aware of his disfigurement and is still turned on by it. (This is *definitely* a fetishized relationship.) But we also see Gwynplaine's shocked and overwhelmed reaction to having someone *want* him. He falsely believes that Josiana cares for him, but he's more interested in using his disfigurement to validate his own love for Dea. After meeting her, Gwynplaine explains, "A woman has seen my face and yet may love me. If such a thing is possible I may have the right to marry Dea."

Gwynplaine believes Dea is too perfect, too untouchable for him because of his appearance. "Dea, I haven't even the right to love you," he says. Gwynplaine's surrogate father, the philosopher Ursus (Cesare Gravina) tries to dissuade him from pursuing Josiana with this backhanded compliment: "Forget such nonsense. Dea loves you—and she'll never see your face." Not words of comfort, my dude! What Ursus means is Dea's love is (literally) blind and unconditional, so Gwynplaine's heart truly lies with her.

Dea is reminiscent of Chaplin's blind flower girl. Her relationship to Gwynplaine has similar beats, though it's a mutually disabled relationship. Born blind, Bea's big blond curls and diaphanous gowns are reminiscent of a princess or angel. She's also able to "see" Gwynplaine's inner torment. "It's wonderful how my Gwyn makes people laugh—even when he's sad," she says and later explains that "God closed my eyes so I can see only the real Gwynplaine." Her disability is ordained by God to make her a saintly, virtuous woman! As an intertitle explains, "In the sightless eyes of Dea, the image of Gwynplaine stood out always in a shaft of light." Her relationship with Gwynplaine is chaste in contrast to Josiana, with Gwynplaine treating her like a father would a child. You're hard-pressed to watch them show any outward displays of affection short of one brief kiss that moves quickly across the frame; Dea later kisses him, equally as quick, on the cheek.

Unlike the tragic disabled characters Lon Chaney played, Gwynplaine gets a happy ending. He's reunited with his created family of Ursus, Dea, and their dog, with everyone bound for greener pastures. Though unspoken, the romantic celebration of Dea and Gwynplaine's love implies they will have everything that makes for a happy marriage, including children—another slap in the face of eugenics—as they go off to live a life of their choosing.

We started this chapter with monsters and you can't close out a chapter about this early time in cinema without talking about the ultimate depiction of disability cinema (and nightmares): 1939's *The Wizard of Oz*. Disabled people were presented as childlike entities in need of care and protection, so what better way to illustrate this than by using them as objects commonly associated with children: dolls. My thoughts on the Munchkins in *The Wizard of Oz* are mixed. They're the first disabled characters people see when they discover movies for the first time. But for those who don't have dwarfism but may have other disabilities that stunt their growth, being compared to the Munchkins happens frequently. As I wrote in a 2017 article for *Pacific Standard* on the subject of disability, I have a vivid memory of being in a shopping mall bathroom when a small child asked her mother what was "wrong" with me. Her mother replied I was special, "like the Munchkins in *The Wizard of Oz*"— because anything short and disabled equals a resident of Munchkinland!

As author Robert Bogdan discusses in his book *Picturing Disability* about the disabled typecasting the Munchkins represent, they are "characters whom a viewer cannot take seriously." Little people have historically been used as comic relief going as far back as the court jesters of medieval times. One example is Billy Barty's character in the musical *Gold Diggers of 1933*. Barty plays a baby (or a man masquerading as a baby; it's unclear) with a lecherous eye and a penchant for peeping at women undressing. Audiences don't take him, like the Munchkins, seriously because he is small, cherubic, and nonthreatening. There's nothing sexually violent about Barty, just gross. Even today, little people actors are left to play roles like dwarves and elves, while movies like Damien Chazelle's *Babylon* and Martin Scorsese's *The Wolf of Wall Street* find opportunities to use them as shock value, mocking and putting little people in dehumanizing situations or as the butt of jokes for hedonistic abled leads.

As *The Wizard of Oz* sells them, the Munchkins are children who live in flowers, carry lollipops, and wear little bonnets and short pants. These aren't adults paying taxes but breathing porcelain dolls with shellacked hair and rouged cheeks. Look at the Lollipop Guild. They have extremely rosy cheeks and a mechanical gait that makes them look robotic, like they're playing at being human. This is why the audience finds the Munchkins simultaneously cute and terrifying: They appear as able-bodied people shrunk down to doll size. There's an "uncanny valley" element to them, particularly if you know little about dwarfism. Some have proportionate features, wherein all parts of the body are small to the same degree and appear like a body of average stature. Others, nonproportionate, might have average-sized torsos and shorter or longer limbs. In the case of *The Wizard of Oz*, there was a desire to specifically find those with proportionate dwarfism to create the idea that these are living dolls. Viewers see proportionate, doll-like versions of themselves rather than actors displaying overt depictions of dwarfism, like being disproportionate. Because of my disability I am disproportionate, with an average-sized torso and smaller legs. If I can't pass like they do, do I not exist? Am I, as a person whose body isn't proportionate like them, something to be reviled? To the actors portraying the Munchkins, many had never seen anyone else like them before and didn't know how to handle it. As Munchkin actor Jerry Maren said in the MGM documentary *When the Lion Roars*, he was "flabbergasted" at seeing 124 little people on a set, having grown up being the only little person in his family.

One can only imagine how disabled audiences of the 1910s through the 1930s reacted to seeing Lon Chaney's performance in *The Penalty* or Boris Karloff as Frankenstein's monster. It's doubtful many saw movies to begin with, as those with disabilities so often lived their lives on the streets or in medical institutions. These movies weren't made for them though. Movies like *The Penalty*, *Frankenstein*, and *The Wizard of Oz* were made for mass able-bodied consumption. They laid the foundation for what disabled movies would focus on for decades to come: presenting the disabled as cute, simple-minded, overly pure, monstrous, slaves, clowns, or bitter cripples who sought their vengeance however they could get it. Disabled characters in films were in need of care and protection because disabled people on the streets were in need of care and protection. They couldn't be trusted to get jobs, control their money, get married, or have children. Let's look at a disabled movie that showed humanity at its worst and what real disabled bodies looked like while helping to usher in the Hollywood Production Code.

2 "ONE OF US"

I'm regularly asked what my favorite disabled film is and I regularly cite a small handful of movies, several of which are explored in this book. The earliest one I mention is director Tod Browning's 1932 film *Freaks*. *But, Kristen, how can a movie made in the 1930s be one of the best movies? Didn't you just lay out how the 1930s had disabled characters mired in outdated stereotypes?* Yes, I did. *Freaks* deals with several of those outdated tropes, more as the result of an ableist studio system than as a bad script. But what *Freaks* did through its storytelling and authentic casting—it remains, to this day, the biggest disabled cast in an American film—is revolutionary, then and now. And while the disabled community remains divided on its legacy, its mere existence, and how home studio MGM sought to destroy it, shows how deeply ingrained systemic ableism is in Hollywood.

The cast of Tod Browning's *Freaks* (1932). John Springer Collection / Corbis via Getty Images.

Freaks follows a group of circus performers—many of whom were actual circus workers employed in sideshow freak shows at the time—as they live, love, and work. Little person Hans (Harry Earles), a member of the troupe, falls in love with able-bodied "big woman"/trapeze artist Cleopatra (Olga Baclanova, post–*Man Who Laughs*), at the expense of his long-suffering girlfriend and fellow little person, Freda (played by Earles's own sister, Daisy). But Cleo is only interested in Hans because of his large fortune and decides to marry him and quickly kill him off so she and her lover can share the spoils. This doesn't sit well with the rest of the circus performers, who discover Cleo's plan and enact the "code of the freaks" to get retribution for their friend.

There's no one unified opinion on *Freaks*. It's controversial for audiences, both abled and disabled. For every person who loves it, you'll find another who thinks it's exploitative. Some say it's a groundbreaking story about disabled agency, while others say it depicts those with disabilities as murderous, vengeful monsters. I see both sides but always reiterate that *Freaks*, for better or worse, is a unique narrative that dares to have so many disabled performers in one space. If you think that isn't reason enough, consider a story disabled comedian Maysoon Zayid told during a 2020 panel focused on disabled storytelling. Zayid explained she pitched a sitcom based on her life and wrote a secondary character who was gay, Jewish, Black, and in a wheelchair. "I had producers tell me he can be gay and Black; he can be Black and a wheelchair user. But he cannot be a gay, Black, Jewish wheelchair user." So while able-bodied characters are multiple things at once, disabled characters are perceived as disabled, period. *Freaks* doesn't make every character completely nuanced, but stray scenes of the everyday lives of the "freaks" opens a door toward showing who they are in private, the mundanity of their lives, the high points and the low.

Freaks started out like any other movie: as an attempt to capitalize on the success of another highly successful film. That other movie was Browning's previous 1931 horror feature, *Dracula*. Already a master of the horror genre during the silent era, Browning helmed several successful features alongside his favorite actor, and our chapter 1 friend, Lon Chaney Sr. The pair did ten movies together, including the arm-ripping good time that is *The Unknown*. Once Chaney died in August 1930, Browning was adrift, professionally. He started working at Universal and found success with Bram Stoker's titular vampire. He was soon courted by MGM, where the studio's head of production and "Boy Wonder"—so-called due to his success—Irving Thalberg, offered Browning carte blanche to make anything he wanted. Thalberg came to regret that decision.

Browning read the Tod Robbins short story "Spurs" in the 1920s and wanted MGM to buy it as a vehicle for Chaney. I can only imagine whom Chaney would have played had this been done in the 1920s—maybe the Hans character? The original story holds several commonalities with what eventually ended up on-screen. It focuses on a man, a little person, who marries a woman who is only interested in his money and plots to kill him. When MGM lured Browning back in 1931, he saw it as his opportunity to make his passion project. It's said that when screenwriter Wallis Goldbeck showed Thalberg the finished treatment for the story, he declared: "I asked for something horrifying . . . and I got it."

Browning was fascinated by circus performers from a young age. At sixteen, he quite literally abandoned his family to run off and join the circus, working his way up from roustabout to spieler (otherwise known as a barker), before crafting his own acts involving contortionism. He was billed as "the living hypnotic corpse" in a live burial act. Browning was drawn to those who worked in the sideshows, mostly disabled people, who found the circus to be the only place that offered them a living. Several freak show performers saw international stardom; most famously among them was Charles Sherwood Stratton, billed by circus impresario (and badass musical biopic subject) P. T. Barnum as General Tom Thumb. But it was a hard road that saw performers struggle to balance stardom with the knowledge that they were participating in their own exploitation. To paraphrase Julia Rodas, the freak show performer and the colonized subject were one and the same, not just because both were billed as exotic others but also because both were compelled to work under the guise that their oppressor was caring and protecting them.

First-time viewers of *Freaks* take note of the able-bodied characters' abject cruelty against those with disabilities, starting with the carnival barker who opens the movie proclaiming to the audience around him and, by extension, those watching in the theater, that they are about to witness "living, breathing monstrosities" who, "if not for an accident of birth," could be any of the able-bodied people in the audience. By othering the circus performers the barker reminds the audience that disability can strike at any time. They're positioned as monsters whose disease is contagious and can infect good, abled Americans. He directs everyone's attention to a nearby exhibit. It's not known who, or what, is on display, though he describes it as someone who isn't one of those "accident at birth" freaks. This average, able-bodied person is someone whose disability has changed by violating the code of the freaks and thus our cautionary tale begins.

Unlike the doll-like Munchkins, the disabled performers of *Freaks* aren't aesthetically pleasing to the audience's eye. Their disabilities are overt and extreme to an extent that audiences, even today, struggle to accept them. As Smith writes in *Hideous Progeny* about Browning's film, "Viewers could not bear to see a 'candid' representation of 'physical abnormality' [in *Freaks*] without the kind of framing that could distance them from and help them explain or make sense of such bodies." Thus the need for an able-bodied buffer for the audience to identify with. They exist here, embodied in the kindhearted but basic Venus (Leila Hyams) and Phroso (Wallace Ford), friends to the circus performers, but these characters aren't the movie's central point of view. Their characters aren't nearly as memorable compared to the visually distinctive Hans and Frieda, "half-man" Johnny Eck who walks on his hands, or Prince Randian, the "Human Caterpillar," whose very cool ability to roll a cigarette is shown on-screen.

Browning eschews the able-bodied buffer and forces the audience to empathize with the disabled characters by telling a sensitive story about circus performers trying to make their way in an unfeeling world. Seeing Hans, Prince Randian, and Johnny Eck move around on-screen was shocking to me upon my first viewing. Disabled people raised in an unaccepting environment, whether familial or societal, can be filled with self-loathing and internalized ableism they need to unlearn, and I'm a prime example. Their bodies scared me because they were similar to mine. They couldn't hide their short sizes and missing limbs. They were so obviously disabled. It's one thing to look in a mirror and wish you were someone else. It's another to be confronted with how others might see you. John Thomson once wrote that "we are horrified [by *Freaks*], but we are simultaneously ashamed of our horror; for we remember that these are not monsters at all but people like us." There's a collective need to rewire one's brain to see disabled people outside of this internalized horror. Seeing so many disabled people on-screen is a helluva start.

Cleopatra is the story's villain, but Browning makes a point to depict the casual ableism espoused by every non-disabled character. Cleopatra isn't one bad apple in a pristine orchard. She's representative of how the whole batch is rotten, even if they think they have good intentions. There are those who show their callousness, like a scene where a group of performers born with microcephaly innocently play near a river. When a man passing by sees the group, he says they should be "smother[ed] . . . at birth or [locked] up." Even presumed allies like Phroso, Madame Tetrallini (Rose Dione), and the beautiful Venus fall victim to ableism of the time. Phroso and Madame Tetrallini infantilize the performers by referring to the microcephalics as "good girls" and "children." Venus later uses the word "freak" to represent all the disabled performers, as if it's their identifier. This is what writer Meira Cook calls "the systemic monstering . . . of the so-called normal characters" showing who is truly monstrous, and how a so-called normal exterior can hide a dark soul. It's an obvious but effective trope in this time period, when eugenic thinking so often placed disability as something to avoid.

What shocked the audiences in 1932, and surprises them today, is not only the sheer abundance of disabled people on-screen but the pride they take in their disabilities. Frieda tells Hans that the unified love and respect of the performers for each other allows them to see Hans for the person he truly is. "To me, you are a man, but to her [Cleopatra] you're only something to laugh at." None of the actors can pass for abled, yet Browning takes time to focus on how they're no different from the abled people around them and films them doing everyday things. The bearded woman gives birth to a baby girl, shocking in itself since disabled characters are usually perceived as asexual and, again, eugenics was opposed to them procreating. There are numerous allusions to disabled people having sex in *Freaks*, and not in ways that are titillating. The bearded woman's baby aside, Hans checks out Cleopatra upon seeing her for the first time and conjoined twins Daisy and Violet (played by long-time circus stars Daisy and Violet Hilton) have an entire subplot wherein each one loves a different man. During a romantic moment when Violet kisses her fiancé, Daisy reacts as if she is experiencing pleasure, through her sister, also. Other scenes include a woman who doesn't have arms enjoying a casual meal with her feet. These aren't the social parasites the eugenics movement sold disabled people as being. They have the same domestic situations and life events as able-bodied audiences, and they are healthy, kindhearted, and articulate though their bodies aren't aesthetically conventional. These moments could be easily cut, and no doubt MGM tried, but they illustrate the simple fact that the lives of disabled people are no different than anyone else's. They sleep, they eat, they have relationships and children.

Browning asserts, time and again, that the circus performers aren't just people, but adults. Hans gets angry when Frieda brings up his cigar smoking, seeing her concern as though he were a child being scolded. Later, Frieda, upset that another woman is trying to take her man, talks about being no different from abled women. She, too, can be cheated on. Frieda holds a lot in common with Dea in *The Man Who Laughs*. Frieda is threatened with losing her beloved to an able-bodied person, also played by Olga Baclanova. But where the Man Who Laughs sees Gwynplaine reject the sighted woman in order to return to the "good woman" who stood by him, it takes Hans almost dying for him to realize the error of his ways. His fear of infantilization returns when Cleopatra eventually shows her true colors to Hans on their wedding night. She calls Hans a baby and puts him on top of her shoulders, galloping around like he's riding a toy horse. Hans may have the wool pulled over his eyes with Cleopatra, but it's never implied that his childlike height is a signal that he has poor judgment. No, he is blinded by love. Hans doesn't see Cleopatra's villainy right away, but his friends do, and it is their unity and love for him that saves him.

The movie isn't unimpeachable, however. The critiques thrown out by disabled critics are valid. *Freaks* is bound up in the remnants of the Victorian-era freak show (because it always comes back to the Victorians, doesn't it?). The story is a horror spectacle that involves real circus oddities for an able-bodied audience to revel in. They are on display in the circus landscape of the movie, with the added layer of exploitation of being sold to an audience of paying customers in a movie theater. As Cindy Lacom writes, the freak show was the primary way people with disabilities could make money. "Those who displayed themselves in freak shows at least participated in a capitalist economy." Capitalism, the great uniter! Victorian freak shows also attempted to thread the needle between offense and spectacle by relying on the mundane. "On the Victorian freak-show stage, that meant titillating the audience with the wonderful and grotesque without offending them," says Lacom. "Performing difference in ways both sublime and familiar."

Olga Baclanova and Harry Earles in Tod Browning's *Freaks* (1932). Donaldson Collection / Getty Images

Audiences of the Depression didn't take well to seeing disabled people on a big screen. As J. Hoberman explains, "*Freaks* is asking a Depression audience to identify not with the Beautiful People who were going to make it in Hollywood, but with sideshow mutations, a total underclass. As a reflection of the time, it's almost revolutionary." That it is. *Freaks* doesn't trade in pity. The characters' ability to thrive is an act of defiance. I hold more in common with Hans and his friends than the porcelain, pristine Munchkins of Munchkinland. Audiences in 1932 let their antipathy toward the film be known. With many of the stories around the making of *Freaks*, it's unclear which are true and which were crafted during the film's release to sell it as a horror feature. Story editor Samuel Marx claimed that the disabled actors were required to eat in a separate mess hall so that the Beautiful People, as Hoberman calls them, in the MGM commissary could "eat . . . without throwing up." Bet that story killed with Marx's friends. Even acclaimed writer F. Scott Fitzgerald was thrown into the *Freaks* legend. Marx went on to say Fitzgerald "turned pea-green and, putting his hand to his mouth, rushed for the great outdoors" after meeting Daisy and Violet Hilton. Costar Olga Baclanova said, "Every night I felt that I am sick because I couldn't look at them."

Freaks was advertised as a movie "not fit to be shown," though how that was defined in the pre-Code era is not clear. The cinematic hedonism of the day apparently didn't extend to disabled characters being shown as people. The movie's marketing played *Freaks* up as exploitative and prurient in its themes, with posters asking, "Do the Siamese Twins make love?" or "Can a full-grown woman truly love a midget?" (That word was okay in the 1930s.) A review in *Variety* at the time said the film was completely unbelievable because "it is impossible for the normal man or woman to sympathize with the aspiring midget." There's a pull quote for ya! When the movie hit theaters, the *Los Angeles Times* reported that spectators fled their seats and the movie's production manager claimed "a woman . . . tried to sue the studio [MGM], claiming the film had induced a miscarriage." Nothing else is known beyond that, so take it with a grain of salt. Regardless, MGM cut thirty minutes of footage from the movie, which totals sixty-two minutes today. The original version is unfortunately lost. *Freaks*'s existence, coupled with some other Hollywood indiscretions, is cited as a reason the Hollywood Production Code—a list of regulations Hollywood studios had to adhere to for distribution—was implemented. MGM quickly withdrew the movie from theaters soon after release. and it took thirty years before *Freaks* saw a revival and critical reevaluation. If not for the film's rediscovery on the midnight movie circuit, *Freaks* might have disappeared into obscurity, a strange oddity known for its casting and nothing more.

Because Browning practically abandoned the source material for *Freaks*, especially the ending, Robbins's original story has yet to get that same reexamination. In the film, as the circus travels through a raging thunderstorm, the other performers decide to take their revenge on Cleo for her attempt to murder Hans. It's hilarious to watch the "freaks" look at Cleo askance, aware of what she's doing. *They* are the ones judging *her*, not the other way around. The group chases her through the rain, crawling and clambering in the mud. What the barker from the beginning was showing to the curious crowd is soon revealed: Cleopatra is now transformed into some type of chicken woman. None of this happens in Robbins's original story and yet, for as strange as the ending of *Freaks* is, the end of *Spurs* is weirder. In the book, Jeanne Marie (the character the viewer knows as Cleopatra) drunkenly tells her new husband Jacques (renamed Hans in the film) that she can carry him on her shoulders from one side of France to another . . . for reasons. One night, she ends up at the doorstep of her lover, Simon, to tell him Jacques has taken that promise literally and she is trying to hide from him. Jacques shows up astride a wolfhound and brandishing a sword to kill Simon and force Jeanne Marie to keep walking with Jacques on her back.

Jacques becomes a literal burden on Jeanne Marie's back but, not gonna lie, I wish Browning did something similar. Who wouldn't have wanted to watch Harry Earles ride a wolfhound with a sword? It makes more sense compared with questioning how the circus performers have the ability to put a woman's head and torso on the lower half of a chicken and have everything move independently. I appreciate the ending for showing the ride-or-die community Hans has at least. We see his friends pull out switchblades and guns to protect him. But the ending reiterates to the able bodied the horror of disability. Cleo was a woman once famous enough to have a prince try to kill himself over her beauty which is ruined because of the violent nature of the "freaks." The audience presumes that the worst punishment Cleo can face is being disabled and placed on display in a sideshow that, for the last sixty-two minutes, the movie has shown as a warm, tight-knit community of people who want to be there. Cleopatra is doomed to a life of spectacle, lacking in agency, dehumanized, and exploited seemingly without her consent. How is this different from Hans and his friends' lives?

What *Freaks* pulled off in 1932 by giving us a large disabled cast and characters who are relatable, funny, and charming and who, most importantly, don't die at the end balances out the criticisms of the film. But because the production didn't utilize professional actors, an unfortunate stigma was cemented that we still see today: that disabled actors can't act or that they are only cut out to play disabled characters similar to themselves. The movie's notoriety also prohibited the disabled cast from capitalizing on the film or finding any success in Hollywood. Several cast members went on to have careers outside of the movie, however, though relegated to the circus world. Harry and Daisy Earles, who play lovers Hans and Frieda, were brother and sister, so you understand why their relationship in the movie is as chaste as can be. The pair were well regarded in the circus field as part of the famed "Doll Family," along with two sisters who were also little people and three additional siblings who did not have dwarfism. Harry, along with his other sister Gracie, were billed as the "Smallest Dancing Couple in the World" in the 1920s, while Daisy was touted as "the midget Mae West." Harry had previously worked with Browning on the 1925 Lon Chaney vehicle *The Unholy Three* and was featured in *The Wizard of Oz* (no surprise) as a minor member of the Lollipop Guild. The lack of opportunities in movies for little people, coupled with their thick German accents, saw Daisy and Hans retire from the screen soon after the movie's release. Daisy did return in 1952 with a memorable role in the circus-centric drama *The Greatest Show on Earth*. The Earles clan lived together in Sarasota, Florida, where Daisy died in 1980 and Harry five years later. The last member of the Doll Family, Tiny, passed away at the age of ninety in 2004.

Daisy and Violet Hilton, who play the conjoined twins in the movie, have a story that's fascinating on its own. Dean Jensen's 2006 biography, *The Lives and Loves of Daisy and Violet Hilton* is a must-read if you want the full look at the wacky adventures of their life. Daisy and Violet made a second film in 1952, an exploitation feature called *Chained for Life* (not to be confused with the Aaron Schimberg feature of the same name). The movie is a difficult one to watch, not only because of how cheaply made it is but for how it actively looks down on the sisters. *Freaks* presented Daisy and Violet as beautiful, vibrant young women—they were just twenty-four years old—who capture men's desires. *Chained for Life* sells the twins, now forty-four years old, as a joke. It's best remembered for one unique camera shot where the twins are separated. The sisters ended up becoming more famous for a series of gimmicks involving multiple fake marriage proposals and weddings, eventually overstaying their welcome in the public eye. They retired and spent their golden years working in a grocery store before dying in 1969 of the flu.

According to Johnny Eck, the boy with no lower body, Tod Browning took him under his wing and promised Eck a second film that Browning would direct. Whether this deal was real or not Eck moved back to his native Baltimore with his brother and opened a penny arcade. When *Freaks* was revitalized on the midnight movie circuit in the 1980s, Eck would regale those who visited his Baltimore house with stories about the movie. Unfortunately, after a brutal home invasion in 1987, Eck and his brother went into seclusion. Eck passed away at the age of seventy-nine in 1991.

And what happened to Tod Browning? The man so determined to tell the story of *Freaks* in the beginning that it became his passion project? His career never recovered after the release. He directed four more films afterward, two of which left him uncredited, before leaving Hollywood (or Hollywood leaving him) in 1939. *Variety* even accidentally printed his obituary in 1944 only to discover he wasn't actually dead. Browning eventually died in 1962 at the age of eighty-two.

Freaks is not a perfect depiction of disability but, as you'll come to see in this book, nothing is. However, *Freaks* is one of the best depictions for the fact it was made by a major studio with a predominantly disabled cast. It's bananas to think it still boasts the record for having the most disabled cast members in 2025. It should have been broken several times over by now. The movie is shocking, frank, and, at times, exploitative, but it doesn't hide anything about disability. It presents its characters as they are, as they lived. They aren't to be pitied. They love, they eat, they have friends. Those who see them as "less than" are misguided villains. Watching *Freaks* is to actually *see* disabled people who aren't ambulatory or conventionally attractive on-screen. They aren't meant to make an able-bodied audience comfortable. Maybe this is why *Freaks* speaks to me. They represent (and look) so much like myself, and to be uncomfortable with them is to prove why we need more disabled performers in movies. The fact it exists is still a miracle.

3 DISABLED ACTORS
AN ALL-TOO-BRIEF HISTORY LESSON

I grew up as the central disabled character in my life story for a long time. No one else in my family was disabled. Until eighth grade, none of my friends was disabled. During my high school graduation I was one of two students who had, according to my principal, "overcome adversity" during the four years I attended and, apparently, touched the lives of the students. Why he felt the need to call this out is beyond me, and, if anything, I was more indignant about being placed in the same category as another student. *You didn't have to argue with the principal about putting a ramp on the stage, did you, Ryan?* Part of the reason I wanted to write this book is that I wonder how differently I'd view myself as a child, teenager, or young adult, if disabled actors—not disabled characters played by able-bodied actors, but actors *with* disabilities— and disabled directors were on-screen and well known at the time. A 2024 study by USC Annenberg listed that of all the speaking roles in film in 2023, just 2.2 percent involved a character with a disability, a 0.3 percent increase from the previous year. It doesn't mention whether any of the characters found within that 2.2 percent were played by disabled actors, nor does it chart stats on disabled directors, screenwriters, or below-the-line talent.

Because film is a global medium the characters viewers see reflect the best (and, in several instances, the worst) of ourselves, affecting how we perceive ourselves and others within the world. As mentioned in the previous chapter, there is a stigma that disabled people are not good actors, unable to read lines or emote as necessary. Most people struggle to think of a physically disabled actor routinely working today. And if one is working, they are usually playing a disabled character. The belief being that disabled actors are only required to tell specifically disabled stories, so it's thought that they can strictly play facets of themselves, ignoring what an actor actually does. As the Annenberg study shows, just over a third of disabled characters were inconsequential to the plot.

It scares me to think of how today's disabled children, disabled girls in particular, feel about themselves, because I remember how I felt about myself growing up. Kids and teens learn so much from movies and TV, so not seeing yourself depicted has, as multiple studies have shown, long-standing implications. As film industry professional Alice Tofi says in a 2021 study, "When people feel like they aren't represented well on screen, the effects are damaging." Of the fifteen thousand people surveyed by Tofi, 44 percent of those with disabilities said poor representation affected their mental health. I certainly understand that feeling. I grew up thinking the rites of passage espoused in teen movies weren't open to me, because I never saw someone even close to myself engaging in them. I compartmentalized my viewing as a kid, as most people who belong to a minority group do, and identified with characters who weren't disabled but had elements of who I felt like inside. Hilary Duff in *A Cinderella Story* might have felt awkward and ignored, but she seemed to have a helluva better shot at making her dreams come true (and getting the guy) than I and my wheelchair did. In the movies, the experience of prom or losing one's virginity are straightforward and authentic as they can be to able-bodied teens but, as a disabled girl, especially in the fashion-conscious, diet-loving '90s, I wrote these things off completely because I didn't see how disabled girls experienced them.

But there have been disabled performers and directors out there, and it's worth looking at a couple of them to see what their journey through Hollywood looked like. Disabled performers worked as far back as the silent era. Comedian Harold Lloyd lost the thumb and forefinger on his right hand in a bizarre accident involving a papier-mâché bomb he was holding during a publicity photo shoot. Actor Lionel Barrymore was a prominent wheelchair user starting in 1938 due to arthritis and a broken hip. Actor Herbert Marshall, the English-born star of films like 1932's *Trouble in Paradise* and 1941's *The Little Foxes*, lost his leg in WWI after a bullet shattered his knee and left him to rock a wooden leg for the rest of his life.

Each actor responded to their disability in different ways. Lloyd hid his damaged hand throughout his career, while Barrymore's wheelchair was thought to be a prop for his characters because so many of them were old men. Marshall didn't talk about his leg frequently, but the story was well known to those around him. In a 1945 interview for *Motion Picture* magazine, a soldier wrote about how Marshall inspired him after the soldier became newly disabled. He wrote, "Herbert Marshall gave me my life back. When I found out I had a metal claw instead of a hand, I was completely broken. While I was in the hospital, we were told Herbert Marshall, the film star, was coming to talk to us. I was disgusted with the idea [of him] coming in to give us a Pollyanna speech. It turned out to be anything but that. Mr. Marshall talked real sense into us. Before he left, we were convinced that if he had been able to lead a normal life, we could do the same." Seeing Marshall and hearing how he understood them resonated with the soldiers. That's the power of disabled representation.

The power of disabled representation in film is what first inspired another soldier, Harold Russell, to take up acting. Russell lost both of his hands on June 6, 1944, when a defective dynamite fuse detonated some TNT he was handling, making him one of sixty-three bilateral amputee vets in the country during WWII. Because of his injury he had prosthetic hooks in place of his hands for the rest of his life. (Fun fact: When the Army found Russell's wristwatch, it was still ticking.) The 1944 short film *Meet McGonegal* followed a bilateral amputee named Charles McGonegal, who illustrated to disabled vets how to do basic things without their arms. It was this feature that gave Russell the inspiration to help other vets transition to a new life with a disability. As Alison Macor writes in her book *Making the Best Years of Our Lives*, detailing the creation of the 1946 feature that made Russell a star, it wasn't solely Russell's desire to act that broke him into Hollywood. Former Army trainer Major General Norman T. Kirk, who you might call the P. T. Barnum of this story, decided that Russell was the perfect specimen to help show the United States the value of disabled people. Kirk believed that "if they [veterans] were to see someone like Russell ... demonstrating how he had learned to use his steel hooks, that might provide the inspiration they needed." Russell wanted to find a way to use his privilege to help veterans understand that they could lead fruitful lives, but Kirk saw him through the prism of the dreaded "I" word: inspiration, a term fraught with conflicting emotions to the disabled community. Remember Tiny Tim? Tiny Tim's job was to inspire Scrooge to be a better person, and that's still how the word is taken by the disabled community today. So, if you learn anything from reading this book, it's to stop calling disabled people inspirational. Not all of us are, I promise you.

Russell himself didn't see himself as an inspiration either. He had a hard time accepting the loss his hands. Russell felt shame at his injury, particularly because "he had been wounded during training and not in combat." We see this in *Forrest Gump*, when Lieutenant Dan becomes angry at Forrest for saving his life because he didn't die in the field "with honor." That feeling didn't go away once Russell was given his prostheses either. Having hooks terrified him. "That would mean I'd be openly advertising the fact that I was a cripple and a freak," he said. He originally demanded prosthetics that looked like human hands but he had trouble working with them as they required a lot of strength and dexterity to move the individual fingers. He eventually resigned himself to using the hooks. This is a poignant story replicated throughout the book because medical equipment like hearing aids, wheelchairs, and prosthetics are perceived by the able bodied as fun shortcuts through life or intended to mimic the exact function and experience as the ability *they* are born with. Wheelchairs can't give the same functionality as walking, so the able bodied personify them like cars ("don't speed in that thing"). Hearing aids should make your hearing the same, if not supersonically better, than the hearing person's, but they don't. The 2019 film *Sound of Metal*, discussed in chapter 10, does a great job of explaining this dichotomy and how expectations and reality don't mix when it comes to disabled equipment.

While Russell was being an inspiration for the Army, producer Samuel Goldwyn, himself inspired by an article in *Time* magazine, was trying to make a movie about returning war vets. He enlisted the help of director William Wyler. The pair used a short story written by war correspondent MacKinley Kantor as the basis for a script that eventually became *The Best Years of Our Lives*. The movie focuses on three returning WWII vets challenged with various problems associated with reintegrating into society after their discharge. Two of them deal with psychological trauma and financial instability while the other, Homer Parrish, tries to acclimate to life with a physical disability. Kantor's original short story was . . . problematic, to say the least. In the original story Homer, given the unappealing last name of Wermels, is described as a "spastic," a medical term generally applied to those with cerebral palsy or muscular dystrophy but which can be found in anyone who has a form of brain or spinal cord damage. As Kantor describes him, Homer is "alive on its right side, and dying and jerking on its left / it walked with pain and twisted muscles." You aren't misreading that: Homer is written in third-person "it" language. He's not a person, he's a nondescript creature. Unsurprisingly, Russell called this conception of the character "a gargoyle in human form."

Director William Wyler wanted to cast an actual disabled veteran for the role, but Kantor wanted the able-bodied performer Farley Granger instead. When Wyler saw Russell in the 1946 short film *Diary of a Sergeant*—the film

Kirk made with Russell to inspire other vets—he knew he'd found his Homer. Russell believed it was a hoax when he was offered the part. Once he accepted he was given $5,000 ($85,671.39 in 2024 dollars) for his performance. Wyler and Russell were kindred spirits; both men were disabled by the war and fought to be taken seriously in spite of it. Wyler was deafened during the filming of his 1944 war feature *Memphis Belle*, making him one of the few disabled directors working in the studio era (if not the only one).

Harold Russell (middle) holds his two Academy Awards next to producer Samuel Goldwyn (left) and director William Wyler (right). Bettmann / Getty Images

The Best Years of Our Lives is one of the best disabled narratives because of Russell and Wyler's awareness of how the world treats those with disabilities and, in turn, how disabled people see themselves. Fellow vets Fred Derry and Al Stephenson (Dana Andrews and Fredric March, respectively) deal with everyday struggles like money and job placement, but Russell's Homer is the perpetual outsider whose own family can't accept him because of his hooks. Every interaction Homer has is colored by the feelings of others, whether that's his mother hiding a cry when she sees him for the first time or how Al drunkenly tells everyone in the bar that Homer has hooks for hands and it doesn't bother him, so it shouldn't bother anyone else. This bar scene, in particular, personifies what Russell no doubt thought every time he entered a room: that his mere presence automatically acts as a magnet for stares.

When Homer gets ready for bed, he requires his father's help to unbutton his shirt and take off his hooks. (This was actually something Russell could do on his own but acted out for the movie.) Wyler uses these opportunities to capture the way the able bodied infantilize those with disabilities, and the feelings of helplessness and guilt the disabled experience alongside it. Homer says at one point that "all I know is I want people to treat me like everyone else and stop pitying me. I guess it's hard for them to do that. I've just gotta learn to get used to it and stop paying attention." Russell had a hard time with this himself and it's one of many things the script translated from his own experiences. As Macor says in *Making* The Best Years of Our Lives, "Russell found himself ill-prepared to deal with the 'inquisitive questions of well-meaning strangers, the naked stares of barflies and the self-conscious embarrassment of everyone I met.'" Almost every interview Russell gave leading up to and after the release of *Best Years* was about his disability and how others, through seeing the movie or meeting him, realized his hooks were real and not a prop. During a prerelease screening, Russell was seated next to a woman in the theater. "When the theater lights went down and she reached for Russell's hand in the darkness, she recoiled in horror, screaming 'He's got an iron hand.'" This still happens with the few disabled performers working today. In a 2021 article I wrote for IndieWire I interviewed *Fear the Walking Dead* actor and wheelchair user Daryl Mitchell, who admitted fans didn't believe he was actually disabled.

As much as I love *Best Years*, it set up some tropes that continue into other disabled movies in the future, particularly with regard to characters' finances or the lack thereof. Homer says he receives $200 a month from the government (the equivalent of $3,163.25 in 2024 dollars) and in the immediate aftermath of the film's opening, he seems content living with his parents. Unlike Al and Fred, Homer's story doesn't involve him trying to work but, instead, dealing with a romantic plot through his relationship with a woman named Wilma (Cathy O'Donnell). Homer has a fair amount of privilege, being a white, ambulatory man who is still aesthetically pleasing to the audience's eyes, an issue whose significance we'll discuss more in chapter 8.

With his can-do attitude and easygoing personality, Homer (and Russell by extension) is a symbol for disability in America at the time. If he can do it, so can you. The fact that he's a veteran—and Russell was a poster boy for the War Department's rehabilitation campaign—situates him as a man who sacrificed for his country and should be celebrated for it compared to the regular disabled Joe who happens to be born disabled. *He's lost something, dammit. You can't be sad for something you never had.* Eugenics was out of vogue at this point, but Russell is a Tiny Tim of sorts whose disability is patriotic and his patriotism is founded in his disability. That's not to say Homer isn't a nuanced character but that the nature of patriotism can't be divorced from it.

Unlike the folks at MGM who played up the horror aspects of *Freaks* in 1932, there was a fervid desire to portray Homer's disability with a sense of authenticity and zero salaciousness. Joseph Breen, the head of the Motion Picture Producers and Distributors of America and overseer of the Hollywood Production Code, judged what type of content in movies could be seen by audiences. Breen had no problem with Homer's hooks or how they were depicted, even though as recently as 1943 the media avoided publishing images of wounded vets and their injuries during the entirety of WWII. In this case, the movie was sold as having a grander purpose than showing off the horrors of war. The movie was a balm to the soul and a teaching tool to prepare abled audiences for the surprise of seeing and interacting with disabled veterans. Dr. Howard A. Rusk called *Best Years* "a training film for all of us . . . its message is even more important for the veteran's family, the general public and particularly the hundreds of thousands of non-veterans who suffer from physical disabilities."

Because of the disabled community's marginality, it's left to allies to watch movies like this (or read a book on the subject, wink wink) to learn what they don't know. It's also why film literacy, when it comes to disabled representation, is so important. Bad representation leads to embarrassing faux pas when actually interacting with disabled people; I have numerous examples I could share! *Best Years* has the audience see the microaggressions people inflict on the disabled firsthand and that frequently the only response the disabled have is self-deprecation. When a bar patron says, "Can I ask you a personal question?" Homer cuts them off at the pass with "You want to know how I get these hooks and how do they work?" This is replicated in contemporary cinema. In Aaron Schimberg's 2024 film *A Different Man*, the physically disabled character Edward (played by Sebastian Stan) has an interaction when a random passerby waves at him in a diner, for no other reason than Edward is disabled. The embarrassed Edward explains to the woman he's with that it happens frequently.

Alongside the microaggressions, *Best Years* also illustrates the tiny nuances of disability that come from the lived experience of its star and director. When

Fred and Al go to shake Homer's hand in the opening scene notice how they grip his wrist—to get skin-on-skin contact—as opposed to shaking the end of his hooks. This is one of several moments where Wyler pulled from Russell's own experience. But even with this sensitivity to the actor in mind, shooting the feature wasn't easy for Russell. He said, "There were times during the shooting of the picture when I thought I was reliving all the miserable, agonizing days after I lost my hands." There was an air of what we now know as PTSD for Russell having to re-create the early days of acclimating to his disability—even though Russell, by this point, was proficient at taking care of himself.

Once *Best Years* was released Harold Russell became an overnight sensation. "I went to bed on Thursday just another guy and woke up on Friday to find I had become more or less famous." Russell went on to win two Academy Awards for playing Homer Parrish, one for Best Actor in a Supporting Role and an honorary Oscar for "bringing hope and courage to his fellow veterans." It's hard not to call that latter one the Inspo Award, especially since it was given under the belief that Russell wasn't going to win the main award, for Best Supporting Actor, because he didn't go to the film's premiere or engage in any significant prefilm publicity. This wasn't Russell's fault. Producer Samuel Goldwyn wanted to keep him and actress Cathy O'Donnell under wraps to sell them as hot new discoveries. The Samuel Goldwyn Company eked out every ounce of publicity from Russell before sending him on his way, however. When the *Los Angeles Daily News* published an article about a handless soldier using his hooks to put the wedding ring on his WAC fiancée's finger, Goldwyn pushed for Russell to marry his girlfriend, Rita as a publicity stunt to promote the movie. "Rita and I were practically reduced to playing bits at our own wedding," Russell said.

In his Oscar speech, Russell said, "I'd like to accept this trophy in the name of all those thousands of disabled veterans who are laying [sic] in hospitals all over the country." After the movie's successful theatrical run, and the Oscars that accompanied it, Russell said he didn't want to make more films because "nothing could top his experience with Wyler." In later years it was uncovered that Russell tried to turn a sow's ear into a silk purse. In a 1996 interview, Russell said Wyler, who died in 1981, actively discouraged him from continuing in movies. "Wyler told me I should go back to college because there wasn't much call for a guy with no hands in the motion picture industry. I figured he was right." Wyler, himself living with an invisible disability as a Deaf man, continued to work—winning another Oscar in the process—until the early 1980s.

After *Best Years*, Russell got an offer from William Morris to participate in a touring variety show. "I knew that a lot of people wanted to see the fellow with the hands who had won two Oscars in Hollywood," he said. After the first two appearances, Russell realized the decision was a mistake. "In a sense, I was merely a glorified freak being exhibited in a high-class sideshow," he said. In a way, Russell's life somewhat paralleled the cast of Browning's 1932 movie *Freaks*, if only in the sense that he didn't walk away with the career he anticipated. Russell left Hollywood to work for the President's Committee on the Employment of People with Disabilities in 1948, and became the National Commander for AMVETs, a nonpartisan, vet-run organization that advocated for veterans post-WWII. Russell was also a key proponent of the passage of the Rehabilitation Act of 1975, which prohibited discrimination of disabled people by federal agencies. He returned to the screen one final time for a brief appearance in the 1980 Richard Donner–directed film *Inside Moves*, which tells the story of a man acclimating to life after becoming disabled after a botched suicide attempt. Russell plays the supporting character Wings, one of a group of elderly disabled men who hang out at a local bar and befriend the main character, Roary (John Savage). Russell is the only disabled character in the movie played by a disabled actor. *Inside Moves* shows a different side of Russell's acting. He isn't the stoic example of patriotism but rather a charming, fun elderly gentleman who appreciates life. To watch him in this is melancholy, as it shouldn't have taken this long for him to grace our screens again. Russell did a few TV appearances before retiring from performing for good in 1997 and passing away in 2002. Curious to know what happened to Russell's Academy Awards? He kept his honorary Oscar on the mantle of his Massachusetts home until he died, but the one he secured for Best Supporting Actor was sold to a fan for $60,500 to pay for his beloved wife Rita's medical bills.

Harold Russell was sold to the American public as the epitome of "strength, courage and great faith in the future," according to Samuel Goldwyn. And while audiences celebrated that, it's hard not to feel that Hollywood chewed him up and spit him out. There's a stereotype I notice in disabled narratives, wherein a disabled person must be of use to an abled character—we'll talk about this more in chapter 5—and Russell is the off-screen equivalent. He sold *The Best Years of Our Lives*, both the actual movie and the film's message, but once it was over, Hollywood told him adios. He was no longer useful to them. I'm happy to see Harold Russell went on to have a pretty remarkable life, even without the bright lights of Hollywood, but it should have been his choice and not because someone told him he couldn't make it.

Actresses have struggled for better representation on-screen, but there aren't nearly as many examples of disabled actresses to pull from. Where disabled men play characters who are brilliant, flawed, courageous, and desirable, disabled women and the characters they play are couched in terms of their sex appeal or lack thereof. A great example of this is found in the life and career of Susan Peters. Never heard of her? Not surprising. Susan Peters was born Suzanne Carnahan in Spokane, Washington. She only made twenty films in her entire career, but she left an imprint on the history of disabled women in film. Prior to her accident, Peters made her mark in prestigious feature films like 1940's *Santa Fe Trail,* opposite Errol Flynn and Olivia de Havilland, 1941's *Meet John Doe,* and 1942's *Random Harvest.* It was in *Random Harvest* that Peters earned her only Oscar nomination for Best Supporting Actress. Her mounting success set her up to become one of MGM's most promising stars. What could have been.

It was on January 1, 1945, that Peters's life changed forever while on a duck-hunting trip in the Cuyamaca Mountains with her husband, director Richard Quine, and extended family. Peters was shot in the abdomen when she accidentally dropped her gun and was left paralyzed from the waist down. She spent the rest of her life as a wheelchair user. Peters was still a bankable star in the aftermath of the accident; her performance in the wartime drama *Keep Your Powder Dry* was released three months after. Because of this, her home studio of MGM offered to keep her on retainer and sent her scripts for consideration. None of the roles led to any work and it's unclear whether MGM was truly thinking of putting Peters in anything. We do know Peters was not happy with the films MGM was sending to her, similar to Harold Russell in *Best Years.* As you should know by now, studios liked to make their disabled characters overly happy, optimistic, and inspirational. Tiny Tims all around! But Peters was having none of it. "Metro-Goldwyn-Mayer kept sending me Pollyanna scripts about crippled girls who were all sweetness and light, which I kept turning down. Two years after my accident, I gave up and broke my contract. I won't trade on my handicap," she said at the time. Whether MGM didn't see any money in it, or because Peters refused to play ball, they shelved one of her final films shot prior to her accident, *The Outward Room,* which, for me, is a cinematic holy grail. Peters found work in radio, a medium that didn't care if you were disabled or not.

She was regularly urged by friends Lucille Ball and Desi Arnaz to continue making movies. (No disrespect to my beloved Lucy and Desi, but why didn't they offer Peters work or film a project with her if they still thought she should be in movies? Food for thought.) Friend and fellow performer Charles Bickford brought Margaret Ferguson's novel, *The Sign of the Ram*, to her attention. Intrigued, Peters pitched it to Columbia Pictures, who purchased it for her to star in. Directed by John Sturges, *The Sign of the Ram* follows a woman named Leah (Peters), the second wife of the wealthy Mallory St. Aubyn (Alexander Knox). Leah is beloved by her husband and stepchildren but, because this is a disabled movie, things can't be happily ever after. When Mallory hires a new assistant named Sherida (Phyllis Thaxter), Leah starts to wonder if she's going to be replaced by this newer, younger (and abled) assistant, causing her to interfere in everyone's lives in order to keep them closer to her.

It's unfortunate, because of the rarity of disabled performers on-screen, that *Sign of the Ram* is so groundbreaking simply because Susan Peters stars in it, despite how it plays on outdated stereotypes regarding women and the disabled. That Peters was able to get this project made at all is amazing, and she gets top billing to boot. Through the compartmentalization that comes from being a disabled person watching flawed disabled characters there are elements of Peters's performance, and of *Sign of the Ram* in general, that I love regardless of how they devolve into stereotype. She gives Leah such a hunger for love and companionship. It's understandable why she so fervently wants to keep her family intact and, without drawing attention to it, the audience understands that as a disabled woman Leah feels lesser compared to Sherida. Pop culture in Peters's day, no doubt, told her that any man, if given an opportunity, wants an abled woman, so ableism fuels many of her actions. But in spite of her desire to avoid playing "crippled girls who [are] all sweetness and light," the character is controlling and manipulative, falling some way into feminine stereotypes of the time. Two women in one movie . . . clearly they despise each other.

There is a lot about the movie that feels progressive for 1948. Leah's close-knit relationship with her husband and stepchildren illustrates the codependency that accompanies families with disabled people in them. As much as Leah worries about being replaced, or erased, by an able-bodied woman, her stepchildren have their own issues with identity and are unable to find a healthy balance between being child and caregiver. Leah is praised for bearing her disability without complaint. As her husband says, "Instead of being defeated by her handicap she's risen above it. And it's her drive and vitality that's brought the family unity." Leah bears her struggles with a pretty smile, which her family takes as proof of her strength and resilience. Leah feels obligated to feign happiness. Whether we're inspirational, brave, courageous, or whatever word you choose to use, disabled people are told that the pressure to suppress their feelings and showcase themselves as an example of disability with grace is pervasive. Her family has unified around a common issue: Leah and her disability.

Because Peters was a disabled woman, even when she's playing on stereotypes it still has an air of authenticity to it, no matter how small. Case in point: her wheelchair. The first thing that takes me out of a movie with a disabled character is whether the wheelchair user's wheelchair is one you'd find in a hospital (one of the large, foldable ones with zero support for one's back or legs). No one who uses a wheelchair would live their life in those. They're extremely hard to push and are uncomfortable in the long-term. It's unclear whether the chair Peters uses in this was her own, but it certainly looks more like a regular, everyday chair, albeit one covered in some unfortunate chintz-looking fabric. It may look like an armchair with wheels but, hey, that's better than a big, boxy hospital one.

The audience reads Leah's continued use of the word "content" as false. She's placating herself when she's anything but content. The movie does a fine job showing the unique tightrope between a love for one's family and catering to them for fear they'll throw you away. It's the sense of loss and lack that disabled people who live with able-bodied families feel. It's something I've felt a time or two. How would life be different if the people around me didn't have to deal with my disabled issues? Because of this perceived comfort, her family falsely assumes she's happy with her lot in life. At one point it's said that "it's so brave of her . . . to have created a whole new world for herself." Because of their own internalized ableism her family doesn't see Leah as adapting to an unforgiving world that doesn't prioritize disability. They believe that, like magic, she's created a happy world for herself that gives her control. For a disabled viewer, it's easy to empathize. The belief is that, as a disabled person, we should avoid being a burden to our loved ones. Leah regularly reminds everyone that her domestic life is a pleasant one and that she appreciates her family's love.

Leah's husband, Mallory (Alexander Knox), talks about how she had "so much vitality" prior to her disability, but it's unclear what this means as Leah is still vivacious and full of life when the audience meets her. Mallory shows his ableism by seeing Leah through the prism of what he thinks she's missing. She, too, knows what she's missing. Part of this is because Leah is disabled later in life after years of being able bodied. Most disabled representation on-screen comes from formerly able-bodied characters who are made disabled at some point, because audiences won't understand anything else. Movies focus on how the characters navigate this newfound lack of ability. While Susan Peters was disabled later in life, it's doubtful the movie would have changed anything if she was born that way, because that is the only disabled story told. Everyone is aware in *The Sign of the Ram* that something is off, even Leah. But since she is motivated by a fear of replacement—and Hollywood reminds us that able-bodiedness and a pair of fully functioning legs are critical for pure happiness—Leah is driven to sabotage her family to maintain her position.

Leah brings us back to the disabled villains of Lon Chaney's Alonzo the Armless. But since she's a disabled woman, she is bound to the strictures of sexism that women of the 1940s dealt with. (Gotta love how the patriarchy screws over all women equally.) As with Homer in *Best Years,* Leah worries that her husband's love is conditional. She tells him, "I've given you a pretty rotten deal." There's a reason marriage vows don't say "in sickness and in health, and in disability." When Leah thinks Mallory no longer loves her she decides to commit suicide. Homer represented hope and perseverance to film viewers, but a disabled woman like Leah can only showcase love, marriage, and extreme fidelity. Without love, ability, and a husband, she has no purpose. Here's one of the greatest lessons I can impart to you right now: Representation in Hollywood is littered with the bodies of disabled characters. Since there's nothing idealized about being disabled in the Hollywood dream factory, the greatest kindness a disabled character can do on-screen is die beautifully and make way for the ableds to live happily ever after. It's a win if they make it to the end credits at all! So poor Leah, a character who didn't exhibit any prior suicidal ideation outside of the immediate aftermath of her accident, decides to end it all rather than lose her status in the family.

It's worth reading Margaret Ferguson's phenomenal novel on which the movie is based. It suffers from unfortunate ableist language, but the reader understands everyone's motivations for how they act, including Leah's. Leah feels like she is a burden but we see her family sabotage her by chronically hovering around her. Each person is responsible for what happens because of how they let ableism get to them. It's a worthy read, especially in comparison to the feature.

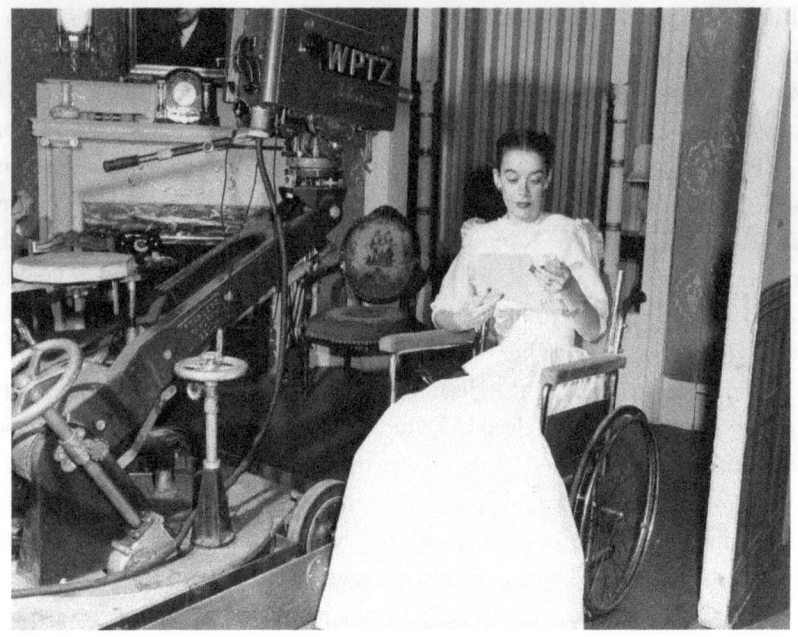

Susan Peters relaxing in her wheelchair on the set of *Miss Susan*. Keystone Features / Hulton Archive / Getty Images

Harold Russell saw his life translated to the screen through *The Best Years of Our Lives*, but Susan Peters was a disabled woman who tried to remain a working actress. As we saw with Russell, Hollywood didn't think there was much work for her outside of playing disabled. The actress divorced husband Richard Quine soon after *Sign of the Ram* was released and, with no other film offers, retired from the screen. She turned up onstage, starring in a touring production of Tennessee Williams's *The Glass Menagerie* and playing Elizabeth Barrett Browning in *The Barretts of Wimpole Street*. In 1951 she followed her friends Lucy and Desi to the burgeoning world of television and became the first disabled actress to appear on the new medium. Peters starred on the NBC series *Miss Susan* as an attorney who uses a wheelchair. Peters loved that the series wasn't a melodrama and, as writer Cary O'Dell writes in a 2023 look at the show, "Being a wheelchair user is treated as a complete non-issue. Susan Martin is not portrayed as a character to be pitied or one in need of help or one whose life is restricted in some fashion." Unfortunately, critics claimed NBC was exploiting Peters's real-life tragedy for viewers, which sounds like a BS way of saying they didn't want to look at a disabled woman living her life. The series was quickly retitled *Martinsville, U.S.A.* to focus less on Peters and more on other, abled, characters. The decline in ratings, coupled with Peters' own deteriorating health, saw the series quickly canceled within a matter of months. What's sadder is that because many of the episodes were filmed live in the early days of television the majority of the series has been lost to time. Only two episodes of her performance in *Miss Susan* survive today, and both are housed in the Library of Congress.

Peters started suffering from depression around 1948 and moved to the small town of Lemon Cove, California, where she lived in seclusion on her brother's horse ranch. On October 23, 1952, she died at the age of thirty-one. Her official cause of death was a chronic kidney infection due to her paralysis, coupled with bronchial pneumonia. Her doctors later admitted that she had lost interest in eating or drinking in the final weeks of her life, implying a possible suicide. We'll never know for sure. Either way, Susan Peters deserved a lot better than she got, and disabled actresses owe her a debt of gratitude. It would be nearly forty years before another disabled woman was seen on movie screens. Thankfully, that same woman is still working in the industry today, with an Oscar to prove it.

There are two performers whose names I knew before I formally started writing about disability in the movies. One was Marlee Matlin. Before the pandemic, I made the sad confession that I didn't have much of an opinion about Matlin's career because I'd never seen the movie that garnered her the Best Actress Oscar: 1986's *Children of a Lesser God*. Because the history of representation is so haphazard, much of my avoidance of the movie was fueled by my belief (which I now know to be false) that the movie's Oscar success was indicative of another derivative take on the subject. That, as the lone Deaf person to win an Oscar there had to be a level of pity involved in her depiction. It's such a sad state of affairs to see how internalized ableism leaves those of us with disabilities uninterested in supporting other Deaf and disabled creatives because of how Hollywood has shown them. Seeing *Children of a Lesser God* left me blown away by Matlin's performance, the character she plays, and the sensitivity of the story itself.

Matlin's rise to fame is as fascinating as those of Harold Russell and Susan Peters. Deaf from the age of eighteen months, Matlin was discovered by actor Henry Winkler while performing onstage for the International Center for Deafness and the Arts. Her rise to fame was quick: She was just twenty-one when her debut film, *Children of a Lesser God*, came out, and by twenty-two, she won an Oscar for it. What makes her stand out from the likes of Russell and Peters is that, outside of her continued work in film and TV to this day, she's been candid about what being a Deaf and disabled individual is like. Like anyone, disabled people are flawed and Matlin has talked openly about being an imperfect person. Movies situate the Deaf and disabled as saintly characters but they can be addicts and endure traumas outside of their disability. In her 2009 memoir, *I'll Scream Later*, Matlin talks in detail about the drug addiction that saw her spend some time in the Betty Ford Clinic, as well as the physical and sexual abuse she suffered as a child and during her romantic relationship with costar William Hurt while making *Children of a Lesser God*. The fact that Matlin has been willing to discuss those things has done a lot to erase various stigmas about disabled people.

Phyllis French played the lead role when *Children of a Lesser God* premiered onstage, and though it's probable that Matlin would have had a career without the movie, it's impossible to talk about her career without it. Based on the 1980 stage play of the same name, the film follows speech pathologist James Leeds (William Hurt), a teacher at a New England school for the Deaf. James meets Sarah (Matlin), a rebellious young Deaf woman who refuses to engage with others or physically speak, happy to live in silence and exclusively use American Sign Language (ASL). The pair embark on a relationship, though James as a hearing man and Sarah being Deaf create various obstacles in their relationship.

There's something different about *Children of a Lesser God* almost immediately and it's the different experiences of the Deaf students found within it. This is Sarah's story, but the school is composed of Deaf people of all genders and ethnicities—important, considering that stats show disabled characters remain predominantly white and male. Sarah is as complicated a character as any Deaf or disabled male character on-screen. She is described as brilliant, troubled, and a "pain in the ass," anathema to the disabled women talked about in chapter 1 with their overly angelic countenances. More often, the brilliant, troubled genius is a trope reserved for men, like Russell Crowe's John Nash in *A Beautiful Mind*. In this case there's a male microaggression in the idea that Sarah needs the right man to get underneath her international-woman-of-mystery demeanor.

Because of this quality Sarah's physical allure is increased. Ellen Stohl, the first disabled woman to pose nude for *Playboy*, once said disabled women are seen as asexual brains and not bodies. Sarah is sexual, having a promiscuous past as a teenager because she thinks it's the one way she has power over men. This is in marked contrast to Leah in *The Sign of the Ram* who, in spite of her physical beauty, is in a chaste marriage with Mallory. Sarah also wants children and tells James she specifically wants Deaf children. (Compare this, again, against *Sign of the Ram*, where Leah is explicitly said to be barren.) This is a movie I've experienced a few times now and this scene between Sarah and James always hits me. When I tell people I want to see disabled equality, I don't think about disabled people wanting their children to inherit their disabilities since it's always presented as a negative. It's worth holding this comment by Sarah against the scene in *Forrest Gump* wherein Tom Hanks's title character gets emotional at discovering his son doesn't have the same mental disability as him and is, in fact, "the smartest in his class." It's an amazing moment of acting by Hanks, but it tells audiences that disabled people should feel relief knowing they haven't passed on the burden of their disability to an innocent child.

Sarah is born completely Deaf, an important distinction in disabled representation that goes unnoticed as we've already mentioned. Making Sarah Deaf from the beginning tells the audience they have to relate to Sarah on her level, screw your abled comfort. It also places Sarah at odds with James, who acts as the audience surrogate. We'll get more into inter-abled relationships in chapter 9 but there are remnants of the relationship between the Tramp and the Blind Girl in *City Lights* from chapter 1 lingering in how James sees his relationship with Sarah. James refers to her as "beautiful, mysterious [, and] angry," and while there isn't the high level of fetishization as between Gwynplaine and the Duchess in *The Man Who Laughs* there's a question of dependence and what the power dynamic is between the couple. James is a teacher at the school while Sarah is a janitor, so financially and professionally, he holds the cards. There is also the imbalance of him being a hearing person and her being Deaf.

Sarah doesn't need a man to complete her or guide her through the world. As with Leah in *The Sign of the Ram*, Sarah remarks she's "content" with her life but the audience believes her a lot more than they do Leah. Sarah routinely reminds James about how *he* isn't on the same level as *she*. She calls him out for his attempts to be her savior. You can get good and sloshed by taking a drink every time James tells Sarah to "let me help you" or how much he wants to "take care" of her. (I don't recommend this drinking game, by the way.) She also makes fun of how slow and amateurish James is at sign language, which is saying something because he's working at a school for the Deaf. This scene has another funny bit of business that comes from rendering deafness accurately. Matlin's signing is so rapid-fire that you can see her in a 1930s screwball comedy. She signs fast because it's second nature to her, whereas James has to think out his words and sign them as he's saying them, like a person thinking of a sentence in a foreign language and translating it before finally speaking it aloud.

But Sarah, and Matlin, have a high level of disabled privilege. Matlin is conventionally beautiful and can pass for able bodied, if needed. A character goes so far as to verbalize this, saying, "If you didn't know there was a problem you would have thought she was normal." Disabled viewers are reminded that able-bodied people require us to look conventionally pleasing while having disabilities. These stray comments do a great job to illustrate how well-meaning people filter things through an abled lens. During a poker game Sarah, and the audience, notice how many people compliment her for interacting with them by saying "very good," as if she's a dog who's pulled off a trick. James makes Sarah feel guilty by reminding her that he can't enjoy music because Sarah can't. Though the audience sees this as his own guilt at having hearing ability that she can't experience, because Sarah is the more interesting character it's another mark in his inability to understand what brings *her* joy in life.

Children of a Lesser God's biggest flaw is in the overreliance on getting Sarah to speak. In a film that has stuck to telling Sarah's story through her own voice (i.e., via ASL), it's a jarring way to get her to bond with the abled audience. Sarah's mother, played beautifully by Piper Laurie, explains that Sarah's voice, altered by her deafness, made Sarah "look awful. She sounded awful." Her mother relies on aesthetics to justify Sarah's need to be silent but also to set stakes for Sarah to eventually speak and prove her wrong. James, at one point, asks Sarah, "Don't you want to be able to get along in the world?" Sarah, to her credit, says something that disabled people think all the time: "They couldn't learn to speak my language, yet everyone wants *me* to speak" (emphasis mine). Essentially, why should disabled people always have to be the ones to conform? Why is it so often on Deaf and disabled people to get along with the able bodied instead of the other way around?

Marlee Matlin was the first Deaf woman to win an Academy Award, a distinction that has yet to be repeated as of 2025. Matlin gave her speech in ASL with her own interpreter by her side and, much like Louise Fletcher's signing during her Oscar speech—her parents are Deaf—it showed off sign language to audiences who might not have ever seen it. (It was only within the last few years that the Academy has had regular sign language interpreters in use at the ceremony.) I hope another Deaf or disabled woman wins it in my lifetime. But Matlin's Oscar win was a contentious topic, personally and professionally. It continued a pattern, to be discussed further in chapter 10, about the myth of playing Deaf or disabled yielding an automatic Oscar. Matlin even heard directly, by her own boyfriend of all people, that winning the award was a fluke. As she recalled in Dave Karger's book *50 Oscar Nights*, Matlin worried about how her boyfriend and costar William Hurt would react to her win after he lost the Oscar for Best Actor. "After the ceremony, Bill held my hand, and we found our limo," she said. "We got inside, sat down, and he was just staring at me. I could see him thinking. He was very quiet. And he said, 'So you have that little man there next to you. What makes you think you deserve it?' I looked at him like, What do you mean? And he said, 'A lot of people work a long time, especially the ones you were nominated with, for a lot of years to get what you got with one film.' I didn't even dare argue with him. I thought to myself, Is he right? I mean, he was. But was he not happy for me?" Deaf and disabled performers hear so often that they can't act, so the fact that Matlin's win was undercut by a man who claimed to love her is disheartening. Even worse is that this mentality still mars Matlin's win. I've heard my fair share of responses to her win being boiled down to "she was playing herself" because of the continued false belief that disabled actors aren't acting.

Sarah is an independent woman who doesn't die or repent for anything. She may not verbally recite lines of dialogue, yet she is constantly speaking. Her expressions and energy illustrate how a silent performance *is* a performance. Matlin in *Children of a Lesser God* was a game changer for how Deaf and disabled women were shown on-screen. When I interviewed Matlin for the first time I was intimidated because she was an actress who led the way for so many other Deaf and disabled performers and made Deaf and disabled audiences see their life experiences as normal. To see her was to witness the representation we still crave today. Though others have tried to diminish her accomplishments, she still keeps crafting unique characters, so much so that she is one of the most name-dropped Deaf and disabled performers in film.

I mentioned there were two performers I prominently heard about in the disabled movie world. The other was Christopher Reeve. It would be impossible to close out a chapter like this without discussing Reeve, the global impact he had on disabled acting and directing, and how Hollywood kind of screwed him over. Best known for playing Superman in the 1978 film of the same name, Reeve became a quadriplegic on May 27, 1995, after a horseback riding accident. His accident brought disability into the forefront of the lives of people who had never even considered the word before and, to this day, Reeve is the most famous disabled person in existence, more than twenty years since his passing.

Reeve was frank in discussing his accident and how it affected his family and mental health. It's unsurprising that, as the documentary *Super/Man* lays out, Reeve worried his life wasn't worth living. When someone doesn't have any interaction with disabled people, and watches movies as a means of seeing them, it's not surprising that becoming disabled induces fear and apprehension. In his autobiography, *Still Me*, and the documentary, Reeve discusses considering euthanasia in the immediate wake of his accident, which movies erroneously sell as the real means of freedom for disabled individuals. When a movie sells disability as a death sentence, those who enter the community see a foregone conclusion. Reeve admitted in an interview later in his life that he felt terrified and removed from the disabled community. "There is a period of shock, and then grieving, with confusion and loss. After that, you have two choices. One is to stare out the window and gradually disintegrate. And the other is to mobilize and use all your resources, whatever they may be, to do something positive." Said resources, and the goal of doing something positive with them, caused a divide in how the disabled community saw Reeve. He started engaging in an expensive exercise regimen, using machines to stimulate his muscles to prevent atrophy and, he hoped, stimulate his nervous system to make his body strong enough for whenever a cure for paralysis was discovered. He sought to bring attention to the nature of spinal-cord injuries, though this led some to conclude that Reeve was only interested in curing his own disability as opposed to helping others cope with theirs. It's easy to understand why Reeve went this route since movies assert disability as something to triumph over, and the idea of a magic cure is a disability narrative trope because writers assume that the ultimate dream for anyone with a disability is to have it disappear.

But Reeve and his wife, Dana, did use their activism to help those with all manner of disabilities. Reeve supported bills to raise lifetime caps on insurance as well as legislation that allowed the disabled to continue receiving disability payments after they returned to work. Dana Reeve, understanding the backlash against her husband's desire to cure disability, made a key part of the Christopher and Dana Reeve Foundation focus on helping disabled people live full lives and advocate for more inclusive spaces. Reeve's disability worked against his career in Hollywood but he put a face on inaccessibility and how those with disabilities are treated in society. There's a scene in *Super/Man* wherein Reeve is honored at the 1996 Academy Awards and is filmed going through the bowels of the venue to access the stage itself. To an abled audience, this scene hypes the anticipation for his debut at this ceremony, but to a disabled viewer, you roll your eyes at the fact that there's no accessible means for him to get from A to B. Reeve was lauded at that Oscar ceremony by numerous actors and directors, but it didn't give him any significant opportunity to keep acting after his paralysis.

In 1998, he decided to take a chance and star in a movie, a TV remake of the 1954 Alfred Hitchcock movie *Rear Window*. In the original movie, Jimmy Stewart plays L. B. Jeffries, a man with his leg in a cast who witnesses a murder across the street. The basic plot beats between 1954 and 1998 are the same. Reeve plays Jason Kemp, a man who becomes paralyzed after a car accident, the result of driving while talking on a cell phone. (The film almost functions as a PSA against cell phones, a new thing in 1998, in cars.) Reeve's ultrawealthy tech character gives viewers a specific look at disability. Jason has 24/7 care, lives in an expensive loft (with an elevator), and has a voice-activated housing system that would make Alexa blush. When Jason asks, "Do you know how expensive it is to be disabled in America?" it's hilarious coming from a man with the ability to pay bills and order a pizza with a voice request. In 1998! At the same time, he calls out issues inherent in being disabled in this country: that it costs a significant amount of money to just exist, and most people don't notice that. The character parallels Reeve somewhat. Jason repeats that his situation is "temporary," and sections of the movie focus heavily on Jason's rehab routine to show he's still strong.

The 1998 *Rear Window* isn't particularly good, but it's far from the worst remake in the world. It's highly unique and illustrates that disabled actors are actors, first and foremost. Watching Reeve move in a motorized wheelchair—and the day-to-day life of being a quadriplegic shown so starkly on-screen—is amazing. I can only imagine how things might have been different had he been allowed—yes, allowed—to continue acting. As I wrote in 2022 when I first saw Reeve's *Rear Window*, the movie is a remake of Hitchcock's film and an advertisement from the actor that Hollywood should continue working with him. Reeve wanted to use this as a makeshift proof of concept for him to retain his career, thus why Kemp seems so much like Reeve. This was Reeve's attempt to remind Hollywood that, while he may be disabled, that was no reason to avoid casting him.

The film didn't yield much critical or commercial response upon release and was the last feature of Reeve's acting career (outside of a few stray TV roles later on). Though he did eventually turn to directing, it was out of necessity, the one job where he could still work. And even then the jobs were limited. If you ask a person today to name a disabled director, it's doubtful they'd think of him in that context. People didn't want to see Superman in a wheelchair. Not even Superman was safe from ableism.

These are just a few of the disabled creatives who have existed in the industry. There are others, and we'll talk about a few more as this book continues. But whether you're talking about Harold Russell, Marlee Matlin, Susan Peters, Christopher Reeve, William Wyler, Peter Dinklage, or Neal Jimenez, the fact is that film history has not given disabled actors and directors the opportunity to thrive in this industry. Most are one-offs. Those who continue to work today are still labeled "disabled actor/director" despite trying to focus more on the work and less on their disability. This only stymies the conversation of what needs to change to promote true inclusion.

4 WAR AND THE RISE OF THE BITTER CRIPPLE

As I've mentioned, the first wheelchair user I ever saw in a movie was in *Forrest Gump*. I was six years old and probably shouldn't have been watching the movie at all, but I was fascinated by seeing someone like me in a wheelchair. On the surface, I had nothing in common with a thirtysomething Vietnam veteran with anger issues, but watching him use a wheelchair showed there were others like me out there. It also established an emotion I realized later in life to be common in movies about disabled men: anger. Lieutenant Dan, the legless Vietnam vet content to be a shrimp boat captain, is hostile to everyone. Who can be hostile to Tom Hanks? Dan explains to Forrest in the movie that a preacher at the VA hospital told Dan that God is listening to him and that if Dan just opened his heart to God, then the disabled man could "walk beside him in the Kingdom of Heaven." This makes Dan angry. "*Walk* beside him in the Kingdom of Heaven, well, kiss my crippled ass." I interpreted his anger, as a child, as pointed out at the world, at people's interpretations of Dan as a disabled man. To me, it seemed similar to my own anger at what I couldn't do because of my disability. Yes, I did put my desire to be a ballerina on the same pedestal as coming back from war. I go back to the God scene a lot when I talk about my love (yes, I said it) for *Forrest Gump*, because I've had my fair share of conversations with people who subscribe to a religion of some kind or those who believe that a version of the afterlife includes a cure for my disability. Dan's anger at this moment is relatable. He isn't angry at his newfound disability. He's angry at people who believe he's not a whole person because of it. Two things are true at once: Lieutenant Dan is angry at being disabled, and he's angry that people can't accept him for who he is as a disabled man.

Animosity isn't a trait common to disability in general, but it often is. This tends to be found most often in war-centric movies involving disabled people, a trope I call the "bitter cripple." The bitter cripple is seen in movies about the post-WWII era, when disability was at the forefront of daily life due to the wide swath of vets returning home with various physical and mental infirmities. As

Stephen P. Safran writes, "Popular 'moral wars' such as WWII project patriotic metaphors and feature returning service people facing concrete challenges." These characters endure war and are disabled in the process only to come out the other side resentful at their changing circumstances, as well as how the war robbed and left them without a sense of cathartic valor.

We talked about *Best Years* in the previous chapter but Harold Russell's performance, coupled with him being an actual disabled person, deepened audiences' connection to the character and taught them how to handle being in the presence of disability, which was the movie's ultimate goal. Homer valiantly fights for his country and faces the challenges of reacclimating to how others perceive him as a disabled man. His patriotism exists on two levels. Audiences watching *Best Years* learned how to interact not with Homer Parrish but with their neighbor, brother, or father. This also gives the character an additional sense of purpose, of use, to the abled characters and the audience, to educate them on how to be better people for having known a disabled person. As Bosley Crowther wrote in his initial review of *Best Years*, "By demonstrating frankly and openly the psychological blocks and the physical realities that go with prosthetic devices they [the filmmakers] have done a noble public service of great need." Note how Crowther didn't cite Russell as having any involvement in the creation of this "noble public service." He devotes two lines to Russell, calling him "incredibly fine." Homer Parrish was leveraged less to help disabled people find acceptance with themselves and more to make able-bodied viewers avoid embarrassment. That Russell's performance is fantastic enough that the audience connects with him as a person is just an added bonus.

The WWII-era movies that focused on disability didn't diminish how veterans gained their disabilities and instead emphasize them as a sacrifice for the good of the country. Simply existing is enough to illustrate the patriotic offering of joining this man's army. In the 1945 feature *Pride of the Marines*, John Garfield's Al Schmid finds purpose as an inspiration for other blind veterans, while reiterating that disabled vets can have normalcy by accepting and adapting to their new circumstances. Based on Al Schmid's life story, *Pride of the Marines* is Disabled Vet Film 101. It sets up Al's idyllic life before the war and, over the course of the runtime, shows how being disabled sends him through the stages of grief before he comes through to become a productive member of society and gain societal acceptance thanks to the individual love of one woman. Because this is the Baby Boomer era, even the disabled were told they could have the American dream that includes sex and children. Take that, eugenicists!

Pride of the Marines spends a significant amount of time establishing Al's relationship with the sweet, all-American Ruth (Eleanor Parker). The idea of a girl waiting back home, for disabled characters, is a means of possessing abled support and proof that someone will vouch for your good-heartedness. If your girl is willing to overlook your disability, you're worth giving a job to, is the mentality. (Note: This does not work for disabled women.) Ruth is Al's reason for living, to remind him that he doesn't need to be a hero. It takes nearly an hour before Al is blinded after a grenade goes off in his face and causes him to lose all vision in one eye and near total blindness in his other. To say that Al doesn't take it well is an understatement. When he's handed something in Braille in the days after his accident he derisively says, "This is for blind people! I don't want any of this stuff!" Later, a particularly overwrought Al asks, "Why didn't God strike me dead?"

Homer Parrish meets the audience in *Best Years* after his medical rehabilitation is complete. Similar to *Freaks,* and how circus performers understand each other, WWII movies about disability claim the truest sense of community is found in the VA hospitals and rehab centers among other disabled people. It's there that disabled vets can educate and commiserate with each other in a landscape that's both insular and accepting. Community found in hospital settings or support groups is a common trope to this day, seen in later movies like *The Waterdance* and *Sound of Metal*.

Pride of the Marines uses its hospital sequences to illustrate how many men are in the same boat as Al. But if the goal is to help Al transition into his new life, his friends and doctors don't offer much help. His friends preface their conversations with Al by saying their names, because apparently he's no longer able to tell who anyone is by hearing their voice. Several also try to get on his level by comparing his situation to other people they know, making for some unintentionally cringe-inducing strawman arguments. A doctor tells Al that "people have the wrong idea about blindness" before talking about a friend of his who is blind, married, and has three children. It's hard to believe this friend truly exists, not because blind men can't be married and have kids but because the scene reads as if he conjured a person out of thin air to make his point.

Al's best friend, Lee Diamond (Dane Clark), is the worst offender of this technique. He compares Al's situation to the discrimination Lee faces as a Jewish man. While the issues disabled people fight in this country are analogous to certain minority groups, they aren't the same. Each minority group comes with different entrenched histories. But too often this concept of "You think you've got it bad because you can't get into your house? At least you're not [insert minority here]" becomes a cheap game of one-upmanship in film, as if it's a competition between all minorities to be heard and have their needs addressed.

Lee's argument erases the BIPOC disabled people who were living in this time and dealing with struggles related not only to their disabilities but to their race as well. We'll get to Hollywood's erasure of disabled people of color in chapter 6. All arguments like these do is create a false equivalent while reminding those with disabilities to bear their problems silently, with grace and dignity because it can always be worse. *Forrest Gump* does something similar in a scene where Lieutenant Dan, after having his legs amputated, pulls Forrest out of bed in the middle of the night to berate him for saving Dan's life. Dan asks Forrest if he knows "what it's like not to be able to use your legs" to which Forrest responds that he does. No disrespect to Gump who, true, wore leg braces before literally breaking free of them at the beginning of the movie to become the human equivalent of the Road Runner, but his response is kind of BS. There's a world of difference between having one's legs straightened and confined, temporarily, by a brace and completely losing both limbs forever.

Al's main fear is that Ruth'll reject him because of his blindness. As so happens in movies about disabled men, if you can't be with the one you love ... might as well jump in front of a bus. (Is that not how the song goes?) Al doesn't want Ruth "to be a seeing eye dog" for him, which Ruth contradicts when, upon discovering Al's blindness, she proclaims, "I didn't fall in love with his eyes ... I fell in love with Al." Full disclosure as a ride-or-die John Garfield fan, there's no masking the man's hotness. Sighted or blind, fine is fine! Ruth's actions are commendable, but her stoicism presents female partners of disabled men in two categories. Ruth is the pure-hearted saint kind enough to see past Al's disability, similar to Homer's fiancée Wilma (Cathy O'Donnell) in *Best Years*. When Homer brings Wilma into his room to show her his nighttime routine and what is required of her if she marries him, it's a test as to the purity of her soul. As G. Toles writes, the scene focuses on "the art of humiliation, stressing that Parrish hopes to show his girlfriend how grotesque his body and stumps have become. . . . It is up to Wilma to save their love through empathy and understanding." Women who can't see past disability or who abandon their man because of it, like Beatrice Alexander (Hillary Brooke), in 1945's *The Enchanted Cottage*, or Lily (Julianna Margulies), in the 2017 film *The Upside*, are painted as bitches or cold-hearted shrews.

The depiction of disability in *Pride of the Marines* is another example of a "pretty disability," a nonthreatening and invisible disability that allows a nonblind actor, like Garfield, to play the character while still retaining the actor's good looks and his ability to pass for conventionally normal. It's impossible to think Ruth will reject Al because he still has that beautiful face. It's also amazing that a grenade only manages to affect his retina, not the cornea or any of the surrounding soft tissue near the eyes. Photos of the real Schmid show physical changes to his eye area that was erased in the finished product. There ain't anything wrong with Garfield's eyes in this movie. (Okay, I'm done fangirling.) When Al and Ruth are reunited, Al tries to push her away by reminding her and his other friends that he's blind while simultaneously showing how he doesn't need their help. It's great to see the stage business that shows Garfield's research into blindness, like how he puts his finger into a glass of water to feel how full it is. These moments show the authenticity behind the camera for disabled viewers, whether through screenwriting research, an actor's preparation, or blind/disabled consultants.

Ruth soon tires of Al being a Debbie Downer and tells him, "You want to be lonely. You want to feel sorry for yourself. You want to be helpless!" You might assume Ruth is cruel, but she sees Al's blindness as a personal problem for him, not for anyone else. But his blindness takes on an added, symbolic layer. While Al Schmid was a real person, like Homer Parrish his disability is a metaphor for American perseverance. Ruth's comment is the kick that Al and all American disabled vets need: to get up and not pity themselves or expect it from others. In a moment of pettiness, Al says, "I don't see any of those things God made. I don't see a thing." If Al lets his bitterness consume him he won't see and appreciate the sacrifice he's made for his country. He must open his eyes, literally and figuratively, to appreciate his country and the new lease on life he's been given. It's trite as hell, but that was the 1940s for you. Thankfully, Al is able to move forward and the movie ends by rewarding him with the ability to see color. The audience is left to think that, off-screen, Al eventually gets his sight back completely. There's no addendum that says that while the real Al Schmid did regain partial sight in one eye, he was still legally blind for the rest of his life. For the time, it was more important to leave audiences with hope than to rely on facts.

Disability during WWI and WWII in film was a patriotic maneuver to show and celebrate not only Americans' commitment to the war effort but also how fantastic the country treated its returning vets. *Pride of the Marines* and *Best Years* focus on disabled communities in the military and rehab system. For all the positivity in movies of this time, veterans still faced a bevy of personal and professional hurdles. These movies claim that it is the outside world where men face their biggest issues. The hospitals in these movies are remarkably clean and well organized, which was not the case as the decades wore on. The goal was to make veterans' lives easier with the GI Bill opening a path for them to buy homes and get jobs, but it ignored the rampant employee discrimination that existed. It feels like a smoke screen, particularly when the most powerful person in the United States, President Franklin Delano Roosevelt, was a disabled American. But the American people didn't know this at the time. Roosevelt had been a wheelchair user since 1921 after contracting polio. As Safran notes, it was presumed that Americans would not accept a person with a disability running their country: "Rather than bringing pride to the disability community, the 'Great Deception' [the term crafted for hiding Roosevelt's disability] was fabricated so that the U.S. public never saw their leader as a wheelchair user. Pictures of a vibrant and strong President were seen as vital to leadership and thereby counter to the image of weakness associated with paraplegia." While there has never been a president with a physical disability since Roosevelt, Hollywood has used him to promote American pride since his passing in 1945. When Michael Bay's *Pearl Harbor* hit theaters in 2001— just four months before 9/11—several scenes showed Roosevelt (played by Jon Voight) in his wheelchair and struggling to stand up in front of an audience of government officials. As the film implies, his disability was well known. It's funny, because while film remakes so often erase disability, this unintentional bit of revisionist history actually leans into it.

Homer Parrish and Al Schmid show the noble sacrifices soldiers made in WWII and how Americans came together to share their appreciation. So it makes sense that the bitter cripple type is more commonly found in Vietnam veteran stories. Unlike WWII, which Western audiences see as having a very clear-cut enemy and understood stakes, Vietnam remains politically, divisive, and Hollywood took its time illustrating that. The first film to focus on Vietnam was John Wayne's *The Green Berets*, released in 1968. The film was highly positive on the war, with the Pentagon reportedly donating $1 million dollars ($9 million as of 2024) to the production. Once the war ended, and filmmakers were more honest about Vietnam, the movies transitioned vet characters into angry and alienated men dealing with substance abuse and railing at a hostile world they felt didn't understand them. It wasn't until 1986, with the release of Oliver Stone's *Platoon*, that Vietnam was depicted with a sense of realism, showing audiences the horrors of war and the antipathy against those who fought in it. Vietnam vets like Luke Martin in *Coming Home* and Ron Kovic in *Born on the Fourth of July* are on their own, questioning whether they have been sold a bill of goods. They rage against a world that doesn't appreciate their sacrifice or the war they fought, and leaves their characters forging a path through life that throws out American patriotism in favor of individual identity and acceptance.

Coming Home isn't just one of the best Vietnam-era films about disability, it's the best disabled feature, period. Released three years after the conclusion of Vietnam, the movie is a groundbreaking exploration of disability that illustrates disabled autonomy and sexuality in a way that has never been bested. Set in California in 1968, Jon Voight (not a wheelchair user but giving a helluva performance) plays Vietnam vet and paraplegic Luke Martin. While recuperating in a local army hospital he reunites with former classmate Sally Hyde (Jane Fonda), whose husband is overseas. The two engage in a relationship that ends up affecting the trajectory of their lives and changes who they are.

Considering this chapter focuses on a trope called "bitter cripples," it stands to reason that most of these guys are terrible or at least hard to spend time with. This isn't a bad thing—disabled people can be rude, misogynist, racist, and so forth. The distinction lies in how regularly this is associated with disabled characters, and since Vietnam brought home a host of angry men it's unsurprising that Luke Martin is a bit of a dick at times. He can be unfeeling. His quote in the yearbook, according to Sally, says that he'd take a mirror to a desert island. His personality is also felt by other vets in the rehab hospital he's staying in where he is equal parts acerbic and funny. He tells one guy, "Kevin, I thought you died Wednesday, man." He's no Tiny Tim, not at all.

What makes Luke interesting is that he's a character who isn't explicitly angry about his disability but by how society and the healthcare system treat him and others like him. He's helpless in medical situations, reliant on nurses and doctors to provide his care. As in *Pride of the Marines*, there's a community of disabled men Luke is surrounded by who try to hype each other up. In this case, though, they aren't helping Luke make sense of his disability. Instead they're all trying to grasp the same strange new world they've returned to. The opening scene sees the men commiserate about the horrors they encountered in Vietnam. Luke says, "Now I'm paralyzed *and* I killed people" (emphasis mine). It's an interesting sentence, laying out what the audience should take away from Luke. He's a disabled man, yes. He also did horrible things in the name of his country, and now he lives with his changed circumstances and the knowledge of what he's done.

As previously mentioned, movie audiences meet disabled characters who have lived their lives as abled. The narrative that focuses on them is about learning how to be disabled, because they are perceived as so mysterious that an able audience won't otherwise be able to relate to them. *Coming Home* does something different with this and the romantic relationship between Luke and Sally. Sally is oppressed as a woman, pre–Second Wave feminism. It's not the same as Luke's situation, though the pair have a lot in common as they both feel unseen and undervalued. Sally is *not* an able-bodied buffer because the audience doesn't come to love Luke by *her* loving him, nor is she the central protagonist of the movie; her and Luke are co-leads. Since Luke is a fleshed-out character, there's no need for Sally to aid in the audience's connection to fill the gaps. Voight's magnetism and cinematographer Haskell Wexler's camera keep Luke in the frame or position Luke and Sally in the same space so the audience sees each character as a couple and on their own. Where disabled characters are judged by their desirability, or presumed lack thereof, it's easy to understand Sally's physical and emotional attraction to Luke. He's smart and good looking and appears to have his life somewhat in order. The movie illustrates that their relationship is no different than a love story in any other movie, with the pair eventually having sex. Sally and Luke have two disparate identities and motivations. Luke can't easily acclimate to a new life as disabled, while Sally tries to reconnect with her husband (Bruce Dern) as well as deal with her feelings for Luke.

Voight spent five weeks in a wheelchair to learn how to function as a full-time wheelchair user. He also lived in a disabled rehabilitation center for nine weeks. It's clear Voight has an awareness of how to move as a wheelchair user via this training. I can usually tell when someone has sat down in a chair that very second and starts wheeling it, but Voight knows when to actually push the chair and when to let gravity take over. He's working smarter, not harder. The union between his performance and Hal Ashby's direction makes everything sing. Ashby, like Tod Browning before him, takes care to show the audience how Luke moves through life. Not just the narrative beats but the day-to-day moments that leave you asking, "How does a wheelchair user do that?" Sally is told by another patient that the VA doesn't prepare soldiers to acclimate to society, doesn't talk to them about how to handle changes in their sex lives or how to handle money. Ashby fills in those blanks. In a pre-ADA world, Luke is self-sufficient and appears in a good position to get a job. He has his own apartment and car. These are things it's safe to presume he had before, but he doesn't lose them and openly adapts them to work with his changed abilities. We watch Luke transfer from his chair into his car, and vice versa. We watch him drive said car with hand controls. His wheelchair is narrow, light, and customized to his person. We also see the everyday invisibility so commonplace to disabled lives, such as when Luke goes to a grocery store. When a woman blocks his path, he repeatedly asks her to move her own shopping cart so he can get by, but she ignores him. He pushes his chair and a shopping cart like a boss.

Ashby casts a harsh light on the able bodied in *Coming Home*, with his biggest critiques reserved for the American healthcare system and the treatment that returning veterans received at the time. With twelve million Americans currently using some form of military health insurance, veterans hospitals remain overburdened and underfunded in 2025. Staffers in Luke's rehab center are overwhelmed and apathetic. One employee is left to tend to a dozen men. The hospital is grungy and outdated. Though the US government funneled in millions to help movies accurately portray the military, *Coming Home*'s presentation of the nation's VA hospitals was a bone of contention. The Gerald Ford administration refused *Coming Home* producer Jerome Hellman's request to film in an actual VA hospital due to "political differences." It wasn't until Max Cleland, a Vietnam vet and triple amputee, was appointed to head the VA during the Jimmy Carter administration that the production was granted permission, though by that point the movie was finished.

Oliver Stone's *Born on the Fourth of July* shows a similarly taxed hospital system and while Stone's film is heavy-handed, it is the most accurate in its depiction of American VA hospitals in the Vietnam era. During that time, Charles Childs, a reporter for *LIFE* magazine (cited in Turner's "A History of Neglect"), ran an exposé in 1970 detailing the rampant neglect and mistreatment happening in these hospitals, including rats, overflowing garbage, and poor medical care. "Nobody should have to live in these conditions," paralyzed marine Marke Dumpert says in the article. "We're all hooked up to urine bags, and without enough attendants to empty them, they spill over the floor. It smells and cakes something awful. The aides don't commit themselves wholeheartedly, but with what they earn a year why should they? I've laid in bed on one side from 6 a.m. to 4 p.m., without getting moved or washed. . . . It's like you've been put in jail, or you've been punished for something."

Depictions of military hospitals changed as time pushed movies further away from Vietnam and into later wars, even if the medical care might not have historically changed. *Forrest Gump*'s release in 1994 was a rose-colored depiction of Vietnam and its medical system, the result of the thirty-year gap between the commencement of the war and the passage of the ADA. The hospitals on-screen are ultraclean, and the patients get one-on-one care.

Forrest and the group have so much fun in this hospital; it comes with Ping-Pong tournaments and unlimited ice cream. The continued financial incentives from the military leave questions about how much is sanitized to get funding. The 2006 film *Home of the Brave*, focused on vets of the Iraq War, sees Jessica Biel's amputee character, Vanessa Price, in Walter Reed Army Medical Center, the only named medical center in one of these features. When Vanessa is at the facility the doctors show off top-of-the-line physical therapies and prostheses to audiences, much of which is not covered by standard medical insurance. What's unintentionally hilarious about these scenes is how, for all the new tech Biel's character sees, she's saddled with a pretty terrible rubber hand prosthesis.

Alongside examining the VA, movies of this era are also open about government benefits for disabled vets. In *Coming Home*, a VA attendant tells Luke, "You get more for your disability than me and my old lady put together." Homer Parrish makes $200 a month on government disability benefits (around $3,200 in 2024) in *Best Years*, though he lives with his family and isn't financially unstable in the movie. Ron Kovic says he makes $1,700 from the government in *Born on the Fourth of July*, the equivalent of about $14,000 in 2024, though he considers it "charity money." Lieutenant Dan in *Forrest Gump* lives in a hotel and is happy "living off the government tit." Forrest Gump himself, generationally wealthy at the film's start, has zero financial problems. Homer and Ron live with their families in their respective films, although Ron is presumed to eventually move out. Lieutenant Dan, well, we're only privy to knowing that he lives in a hotel at some point before committing to living on an inaccessible shrimp boat as Forrest's first mate and then disappearing in the third act to return with "magic legs." Does he eventually get a house? An apartment? The movie doesn't really care to answer that. Just focus on the magic legs of it all.

All of these, unfortunately, contribute to the stereotype that disabled people are independently wealthy or financially secure. The stats indicate otherwise: Nearly 21 percent of people with disabilities live at the poverty line, and those numbers are higher for disabled people of color. The fact that this money is provided by the government through Social Security's Supplemental Security Income (SSI) and Social Security Disability Insurance (SSDI) system is also erroneously perceived by non-disabled people as "free" money. Most don't know the legal loopholes the government requires a disabled person to jump through to obtain and keep said benefits, all for, as of 2024, a whopping $943 a month for a single person. For that, the government can recommend you live in cheaper housing, restrict your ability to get married, and see you lose a dollar for every dollar you make at your job. Movies perpetuating this idea of disabled wealth manifests into the idea that we're being lavishly taken care of and that disability is a perk.

The passage of the ADA in July 1990 marks a demarcation in bitter cripple stories and disabled narratives in general. Not only had enough time passed for audiences to talk about Vietnam with honesty, but disability was on the minds of the American public after widespread protests leading to the eventual passage of the bill. Oliver Stone's *Born on the Fourth of July* hit theaters just six months after the ADA's enactment, and while it was filmed before the law passed, it highlights the pre- and post-ADA landscape the movie was made in and how that influenced films from here on out. You'll notice in *Coming Home*, pre-ADA, that Luke physically pulls himself and his wheelchair over stairs to get into people's houses. He builds his own ramp to access his own home. He even has to pop a wheelie to leave an inaccessible police station. The film is set in 1968 and filmed in 1978 when public locations could still get away with denying access to disabled people, and Ashby shows this. In *Forrest Gump*, released post-ADA, there are convenient ramps for Lieutenant Dan to use. Said ramps even become the source of comedy in a scene where Dan slides down an icy slope and seemingly crashes into something off-screen. (Boy, could I write a chapter about Hollywood's love of crashing or throwing wheelchairs into things. I see you, *Mac and Me*!)

Born on the Fourth of July is the prototypical bitter cripple movie because of how it illustrates society's ambivalence about the war at the time and the anger disabled vets felt about the war and their treatment by others. It also arrives smack dab in the middle of a renaissance of disabled stories, released the same year as *My Left Foot*, and two years after Cruise starred in the critically acclaimed—and today highly dated—*Rain Man*. Two years after *Born on the Fourth of July*, audiences saw Al Pacino play a blind man, and win an Oscar, in *Scent of a Woman*. Ron gives several speeches about being a disabled person, which no doubt looks great during the Oscar broadcast.

Born on the Fourth of July tells the true story of Vietnam vet Ron Kovic, a paraplegic anti-war activist. The movie heavily draws on the patriotism and determination of disabled vets in a way reminiscent of *Pride of the Marines*, specifically the high-stakes drama of its main character making sense of his new disabled life. Al Schmid and Ron Kovic would have gotten on like gangbusters. The movie's first scene gives off an air of foreboding as young Ron watches disabled vets from WWII assemble during a local parade, setting up disability as this unseen threat or silent invader lingering at the periphery of his life. Seeing these vets makes Ron assume that serving one's country brings similar rewards. Little does he know. His disability is practically fated.

Ron is set up as the living embodiment of America. His mother equates him to JFK in one scene. Like the war movies of the 1940s, victory and sacrifice go hand in hand here, and disability is the unspoken bond that unites the two. During a church sermon Ron's pastor says, "You've got to pay the price for victory. And the price is sacrifice." Sacrifice, victory, courage, and bravery are the buzzwords that get these characters into the war, and yet disability is at odds with every single one of those words.

Paralyzed and left in a wheelchair, Ron can't handle his disability and the political climate. His little brother tells him, "People don't want guys coming back like you," a dual statement indicative of society's feelings on the war and on people with disabilities. Stone's camera voyeuristically looks at Ron during his convalescence, where he's left wheeling around in a bulky hospital chair. He even has nihilistic platitudes like Al Schmid, saying things like, "God is as dead as my legs" and "I was paralyzed, castrated that day." Patriarchy is a helluva drug, as amputation and paralysis are aligned with physical castration in male characters. Since disability in movies is about what one lacks, if one lacks a limb, it's akin to losing the thing they think makes them a man. Eventually, as with *Pride of the Marines*, Ron finds community with a group of disabled vets hanging out in Mexico who engage in hedonism and debauchery, which culminates in Ron losing his virginity, so at least he's not angry, disabled, and a virgin. He eventually transitions from his "America, love it or leave it" mentality at the beginning and starts speaking out about how America has abandoned its people, specifically vets, to symbolize the new face of American patriotism.

We started this chapter with Lieutenant Dan in *Forrest Gump*, and it's worth returning to him now. Looking at the history of disabled vets so far, Lieutenant Dan adheres to many of those conventions. He's a legacy, having had a relative die in every American war ever fought. He doesn't want to live with his medals but wants to die with valor. His wartime duties are the equivalent of a glorious suicide mission. For him, disability equals failure, and because of this he resists the community of disabled people he's surrounded by, including the kindhearted Forrest. He doesn't see community, only isolation and depression. Forrest Gump is also a disabled veteran, though there's more to unpack regarding him as a disabled individual in chapter 5 than here. For him, being a veteran is a small part of who he is, whereas with Lieutenant Dan it's his entire identity. Referring to him as "Dan" seems odd. Forrest falls into a gray area. He's of use to the abled characters, having saved numerous lives in Vietnam, and is later recruited to be the face of the military's Ping-Pong tournament. He's a hero compared to the other vets. Yet because he can pass for abled, as his cognitive disabilities are invisible, he seems disjointed from the hospital community. He takes to hospital life, specifically the ice cream, and that's it. His war wound is played as a punchline—he's shot in the butt—and we don't see him in any medical situations like Dan being helped by orderlies to transfer in and out of bed.

Forrest Gump's fantasy depiction of war and veteran support is so positive as to look like a fairy tale. As previously mentioned, the American-run hospitals are clean and patients are so well cared for it's like a health spa. No one is screaming, doctors aren't overburdened. Doctors aren't even seen in the majority of these scenes. Without drawing direct attention to it the movie sells America's exceptionalism at caring for its veterans during Vietnam. When Forrest goes home, he's hailed as a hero, and any screaming protestors he encounters are written as violent or over the top, more tied into the nomadic, and perpetual victim, Jenny (Robin Wright), Forrest's wayward love interest, than indicative of the world at large. Forrest was disabled at the start. He didn't lose anything in the war. His disability, present from birth, is an asset to him. His low mental acuity makes him all but fearless, able to save his fellow soldiers at the expense of his own life.

Dan, like most of Forrest's close friends, is dichotomous to him. He physically lets himself go, rocking the Vietnam-era aesthetic of grungy hair and general frumpery. He becomes committed to a drunken, nomadic lifestyle involving casual sex. At least Dan is still seen as being physically desirable. The women might be sex workers, but, hey, it's something. When one of the women he tries to hook Forrest up with calls Forrest "stupid," Dan embraces some semblance of disabled community. Once this moment of clarity happens, Lieutenant Dan accepts being Forrest's sidekick. He is Forrest's first mate on their shrimp boat and appears to become Forrest's financial adviser—by implication, Lieutenant Dan also looks to have made himself ridiculously wealthy investing them both in Apple stock. Lieutenant Dan disappears for a large swath of the film's back half and the viewer doesn't learn anything about his life, whether he's self-sufficient or found a job and so on. He exists to live in the purview of Forrest's gaze. When he does return toward the film's conclusion, it's with titanium prosthetic legs that Forrest dubs "magic legs." Where previous disabled veteran movies hint at cures—Al Schmid regaining some semblance of color—they end with their characters remaining disabled. Dan is still an amputee, but his now being ambulatory is the granting of a wish. He's returned to wholeness, given the magic cure able-bodied people think every disabled person seeks. It undercuts a character who could have shown a progressive view of disability for the 1990s. But, for a young girl who was desperate for anything disabled, he certainly gave me something.

The passage of the ADA was supposed to solve every disabled problem in existence. The arrival of the new millennium expanded the public consciousness on disability, but the relative political stability of the 1990s and the lack of a full-scale war equivalent to Vietnam saw movies of the genre take a backseat until the US terrorist attacks on 9/11 sparked a new patriotic fervor. Thanks to changes in disabled treatment, the war movies post-9/11 tried to get at new facets of the disabled experience. It wasn't enough to focus on physical disabilities; psychological ones like PTSD demanded attention as well. The wars in Iraq and Afghanistan saw 36.9 percent of American vets come home with some type of psychological disorder. Whereas 21.8 percent of those were dealing with PTSD, another 17.4 percent dealt with depression. Gone were the shaggy-haired, bearded Vietnam veterans dressed in Goodwill clothes, and in their place were physically abled characters who could pass for non-disabled but held deep internal torment.

This was also an opportunity to showcase disabled women on-screen due to their increased presence in war zones. Of all active-duty military personnel enlisted in 2022, 17.5 percent of them were women. That number is not reflected in war films of the 2000s and 2010s, however. The one exception is the 2006 war movie *Home of the Brave* starring Jessica Biel and Samuel L. Jackson. An attempt to make a modernized version of *Best Years of Our Lives*, *Home of the Brave* is a *very* 2006 exploration of the Iraq War. It follows a group of characters dealing with psychological issues such as PTSD, grief, and combat trauma after their time in Iraq. Biel's Sergeant Vanessa Price is the only character with a physical disability after losing her arm in a bombing. Disabled women are nearly always presented through the prism of their looks, and Vanessa is no different. Her plot consists of the time-tested question all hot, disabled women ask when they're physically damaged: "Can a man ever truly love me if I don't have both arms?"

The question of whether she's still sexually desirable is all Vanessa Price deals with as a character, to the point that you start to wonder if the screenwriters hate her. Not to mention she's given the worst prosthetic hand in film history. (I cannot stress this enough. It's bad.) If Lieutenant Dan's magic legs are on one end of the disabled spectrum, these hands are on the far opposite end.

Remember how Harold Russell initially wanted a prosthetic hand that looked real but discarded it for hooks when the hands were too hard to manipulate? Vanessa Price doubles down on those hands, having a bulky fake hand/glove as her only option. This hand has zero articulation and is there purely to make her pass for aesthetically normal—although no one is gonna buy that, so what's the point? The audience watches the beautiful Jessica Biel flail around in situations where having one hand is an issue. Her day job is as a PE teacher, so when she's thrown a ball she can't find any way to pick it up. She isn't able to close her car trunk and gets angry when someone tries to help her. And in case you've forgotten how awesome having hands are these moments are cut alongside slo-mo flashbacks of her playing tennis with her long, perfectly normal arms. Disability is something to mourn, to miss, and to romanticize on the daily here!

Vanessa's bitter cripple anger causes her to distance herself from the boyfriend she had prior to her accident. Said boyfriend is understandably upset at her coldness, but because Vanessa is a woman, and a disabled one at that, it's not enough for her to end things with a man she no longer has feelings for. Disabled women are lucky to find a man who sees past their ugly disability at all, so if she's not going to be grateful she must be humiliated. Her boyfriend decides to leave her with the shittiest one-liner in Hollywood history: "Guess it only takes one good hand to push someone away." Why wasn't this nominated for an Oscar, ladies and gents? Vanessa's plot from here sees her finding a new relationship with another man. After their first date, Vanessa tells him how shocked she is that he's willing to date a woman with "one kid and one hand." The hand is a bridge too far, everyone! At least we get to watch her and her new man attempt to have a tenderhearted sex scene . . . punctuated by her getting her prosthetic stuck in her sweater. Homer Parrish and Wilma would never.

We've been through a lot of war in the last several pages, but I want to take us back to *Best Years of Our Lives* to end this chapter. In 1946, that film's goal was to educate an able-bodied public to see people with disabilities as people. That mentality was furthered through films like *Pride of the Marines* and *Coming Home*. The arrival of Vietnam transitioned that into showcasing disabled characters as lonely, isolated people angry about everything, including their disabilities. The perseverance of Lieutenant Dan and Ron Kovic was labeled a success story. They didn't let their disabilities stop them, but there was less discussion about society's continued lack of support and appreciation for people like them. That's all boiled down into something like *Home of the Brave*, which focuses on disabled pity and emphasizes that disabled people deal with too much while offering no real-world solutions on how to fix it. It's something we're still seeing today in a country that can't effectively implement the ADA and where veterans hospitals continue to be underfunded. Regardless of the politics of their respective eras, the bigger themes of these movies is the war between disabled integration into society and the stereotypes society imposes on the disabled.

5 "YOU NEVER GO FULL RETARD"

If you lived through 2008, you remember the controversy about Ben Stiller's *Tropic Thunder*. The film tells the story of a group of spoiled actors making a Vietnam War movie and, through a series of comic errors, ending up forced to become real soldiers when one of them is kidnapped by drug lords. It's a hilarious send-up of big-budget Hollywood filmmaking, but that's not what people latched onto upon release. Instead, the movie sparked a powder keg of controversy over a term one of the actors says: "Full retard."

Though I am not neurodivergent and do not have any cognitive disabilities, it would be ridiculous of a book like this not to look at the subject. And much of what is discussed in this chapter has been brought up by numerous disability scholars, those with and without cognitive disabilities. This is a broad swath, and I am not getting into the nitty-gritty regarding the authenticity of specific neurodivergent disabilities. This remains a launchpad for more writers to dive into those specific worlds.

The phrase is used as a derogatory description for actors who go overboard playing cognitively disabled characters. Actor Tugg Speedman (Stiller) discovers he falls into this category after playing a mentally disabled man named Simple Jack in a bid to be taken seriously as a dramatic actor. Scenes from the fictional movie *Simple Jack* are shown, including a Crayola-scribbled title card. Speedman's Jack speaks with a chronic stammer and sports large fake teeth and an unfortunate bowl cut. The performance is mocked and lampooned, the movie being more terrible than offensive; a faux *Entertainment Tonight* interview in the movie shows host Maria Menounos using Jack's affected speech to make fun of Speedman.

As Speedman walks through the jungle with costar and Method actor Kirk Lazarus (Robert Downey Jr.), an Australian white man wearing blackface for his role in the fictional movie they're shooting, Lazarus tells Speedman that his Simple Jack performance failed to bring in audiences because he went "full retard." He deconstructs how far is too far when it comes to playing a mentally disabled character, mentioning Dustin Hoffman's and Tom Hanks's Academy Award-winning performances in *Rain Man* and *Forrest Gump* as examples of characters who have mental disabilities but aren't so impaired as to be off-putting for an audience: "Dustin Hoffman, *Rain Man*, look retarded, act retarded, not retarded. Counted toothpicks, cheated cards. Autistic, sho'. Not retarded. You know Tom Hanks, *Forrest Gump*? Slow, yes. Retarded, maybe. Braces on his legs. But he charmed the pants off Nixon and he won a Ping-Pong competition. . . . You went full retard, man. Never go full retard. You don't buy that? Ask Sean Penn, 2001, *I Am Sam*. Remember? Went full retard, went home empty-handed." As Lazarus's speech lays out, *Rain Man* and *Forrest Gump* show their leads as high-functioning geniuses. Hoffman's Ray is a mathematical savant whose brilliance is hidden by his disability. Gump has a low IQ and becomes a hero and prophet for American pop culture. The audience watching these movies feels inspired and galvanized, not uncomfortable. There's a reason why imitations of Hanks's and Hoffman's characters are so pervasive: They're perceived as inoffensive and likable. And both films won Best Picture, giving them an air of quality.

The backlash against the phrase came fast. The Special Olympics and the American Association of People with Disabilities protested the film's Los Angeles premiere, holding signs saying, "Call me by my name, not my label" and "Ban the movie, ban the word." Dustin Plunkett, the global messenger for the Special Olympics at the time, said, "When I heard about it, I felt really hurt inside. I cannot believe a writer could write something like that. It's not the way that we want to be portrayed. We have feelings. We don't like the word 'retard.' We are people." The other actors, and director/cowriter Ben Stiller, were forced to respond. Robert Downey Jr. didn't take a side, saying at the film's premiere, "I think it's open to interpretation and that's the great thing. You know, if I want to protest something because it offends me, that's my right as an American, and it's also any artist's right to say and do whatever they wanna do." Stiller apologized for any offense taken but later said in a 2018 Twitter thread celebrating *Tropic Thunder*'s ten-year anniversary, "I make no apologies for *Tropic Thunder*. It's always been a controversial movie since we opened. Proud of it and the work everyone did on it." He went on to say, "Actually *Tropic Thunder* was boycotted ten years ago when it came out, and I apologized then. It was always meant to make fun of actors trying to do anything to win awards."

Society now understands the word is a slur against disabled people, but when it comes to how *Tropic Thunder* uses it, it's hard not to feel we're not seeing the forest for the trees. People were so quick to latch onto the use of the word that it overshadowed what the movie is discussing with regard to cinematic portrayals of those with mental disabilities and how those stereotypical uses are rewarded with Oscars. Recall the audience response in the 1930s to watching *Freaks*. As Angela M. Smith writes in *Hideous Progeny*, when discussing the physically disabled in *Freaks*, "Viewers couldn't watch 'candid' representations of physical disability without framing to distance themselves and help them explain and make sense of such bodies." The characters Kirk Lazarus references in *Tropic Thunder*, those which audiences *enjoy*, specifically Dustin Hoffman and Tom Hanks, are useful, charming, savantesque characters who don't have overt facial tics to show them as disabled. Their mental disabilities are quirky and fun enough to not make an audience uncomfortable watching them. If an audience doesn't have an able-bodied buffer to follow and is left to watch the disabled character solo, said disabilities must be hidden or otherwise entertaining enough for them to reconcile with the difference that disability creates.

John Steinbeck's 1937 novella *Of Mice and Men* is one of the most famous examples of how mental disabilities are portrayed on-screen. Steinbeck's book focuses on two nomadic ranch workers living in California during the Great Depression: brash leader George and the cognitively disabled Lenny. *Of Mice and Men* is considered one of the great works of American literature and Lenny Small one of the more recognizable disabled figures in pop culture. Steinbeck owes Charles Dickens a great debt for Lenny's creation, as he is the contemporary equivalent of Dickens's Tiny Tim (that guy, again). Lenny, like Tim, epitomizes the stereotype that the mentally disabled are innocent and pure. Since the mentally disabled don't always have the same kinds of limitations as the physically disabled—like Tim's reliance on crutches or the nonintimidating wheelchair user Clara in *Heidi*—they are perceived as gentle giants. Their childishness leaves them unaware of the consequences of their actions and enhances their persecution in an already unfeeling society. In *Of Mice and Men*, Lenny and George are forced to flee town after Lenny is accused of rape. He didn't attack anyone but refused to let go of a woman's skirt, thinking it pretty. George, Lenny's stalwart and non-disabled companion, tries his hardest to protect Lenny but to no avail. Not wanting Lenny killed by the encroaching lynch mob, George does what he perceives as a kindness and, at the story's conclusion, shoots Lenny in the back of the head. Disabilities lead to death in the movies one way or another.

Like any famous piece of literature, *Of Mice and Men* has been adapted for the screen several times. Odds are you saw it in school, whether it was the 1939 iteration starring Burgess Meredith as George and Lon Chaney Jr. as Lenny, or the 1992 version with Gary Sinise—Who else lurks in the credits of every movie with a disabled character but Sinise?—as George and John Malkovich as Lenny. Both movies are very good and lay the groundwork for the acting performances neurotypical actors give playing those with any type of neurodivergence: the repetition of words, looking into the middle distance, employing hand and head tics. Look for these bits of stage business in the performances of the characters we'll discuss throughout this chapter.

Let's break down the characters Kirk Lazarus uses in his speech and what they say about neurodivergence and cognitive disabilities. Autism in the movies is sold as an interesting mental eccentricity. As Alexandria Prochnow explains, "Although these characters are labeled as autistic, they are made out to be abnormal in behavior due to choice or personality, rather than their medical diagnosis . . . They fit in better with neurotypical people, because they embrace their 'different' traits and behaviors as inherent parts of themselves, instead of considering them symptoms of a disorder." *Rain Man*, the 1988 feature directed by Barry Levinson, is cited by neurodivergent and neurotypical people for its outdated stereotypes and its attempt to show what a "good" depiction of neurodivergence looks like—that is, what an audience should expect to see. The behavior of autistic character Raymond (Dustin Hoffman) is more a personality trait than a medical condition, meaning the audience embraces him because he is unique, not disabled. Don't let the title fool you, *Rain Man* is actually about the selfish Charlie (Tom Cruise), who bonds with his estranged autistic brother, Raymond. Charlie is a spoiled brat who kidnaps Ray after discovering his older brother is the heir to their father's estate. Charlie believes he's entitled to some financial incentive and thinks having physical ownership of Ray gives him some leverage to entice the hospital Raymond lives in to provide Charlie with a settlement.

Rain Man may be in reference to Hoffman's disabled character—"Rain Man" is the nickname Charlie gave his brother when he was little because Charlie couldn't say "Raymond"—but it's not 100 percent Raymond's story. It's about Charlie transitioning away from being an entitled schmuck into someone who genuinely cares for another human being. Never doubt the disabled community's apparent capacity for making people better. Through Charlie's crazed, illicit road trip with Raymond, the autistic man makes Charlie a kinder, better person. Charlie isn't just *Rain Man*'s able-bodied buffer. During the film's runtime he transforms into a parental figure and caregiver for Raymond as well as brother and kidnapper. There's something I refer to as "caregiver cinema," a storytelling device in disabled narratives that spotlight the stories of parents, teachers, lovers, or siblings who, through expanding the disabled person's worldview or perspectives, end up bettering themselves. Abled audiences see how the caretaker can't have a life of their own because of the intense 24/7 care the disabled person requires. *Rain Man* falls into this category.

Screenwriter Barry Morrow took inspiration for *Rain Man* from his friendship with intellectually disabled savant Bill Sackter and said in a 2018 interview for *The Guardian* that he was generally unaware of what autism entailed before this. Because of his lack of knowledge on the topic, Morrow decided to focus less on Ray and his disability and more on Charlie and Ray's relationship. Knowing a disabled person is a frequently used approach by creatives to utilize disabled lives as inspiration for a movie or TV project. It's also used to stave off criticism, basing the story in some way on a real person or connection. Often, but not always, these endeavors are not written or aided in any way by people with disabilities, nor are the main characters disabled. So when Morrow says that he didn't want to focus on Raymond and his relationship to his disability, I believe that, because Raymond's life as shown in the movie is quaint, simplistic, and highly organized. The institution Ray lives in is a sprawling location with rolling, well-kept green lawns. The residents sit quietly, almost catatonic, and watch game shows. Ray reminds Charlie, and the audience, repeatedly that he eats dinner at a specific time (and certain foods on certain days) and lives his life around when Judge Wapner is on. If his schedule is deviated from one iota he becomes overwhelmed and volatile.

Charlie's fight to "keep" Raymond makes the entire narrative come off feeling akin to Hoffman's earlier 1979 film, *Kramer vs. Kramer*. That film was about a man who learns to be a father and tries to maintain custody of his son. Charlie takes on the father role for Raymond and learns how to be a compassionate and patient parentesque figure while engaging in a similar custody battle over him. Making this a take on a parent/child relationship brings with it unexpected modern-day consequences. Charlie wants to put Ray in a conservatorship to safeguard his brother and, more importantly, Ray's money, which Charlie wants a piece of. Over one million disabled people in the US live under conservatorships either due to age or disability, and it's unclear how much exploitation takes place in these situations. In 2021, pop superstar Britney Spears put an eye on the exploitation and abuse that takes place in conservatorships as she attempted to get out of one herself. At the time, the conservatorship was said to be because Spears was physically and mentally unable to care for herself. She was eventually able to end the situation in November of that year.

Once Charlie flees with Raymond, the movie goes back and forth between how Charlie finds Ray annoying and not believing he is actually disabled. "You can't tell me you're not in there somewhere," Charlie asks, presuming Ray lives in the disabled equivalent of the Sunken Place from *Get Out*. Hoffman's performance is endearingly quirky with his head tilts and repetition of words and phrases, but it's Ray's prodigious math skills that make him of value to Charlie and worthy of the audience's attention. Ray's ability to instantly count a box of matches inspires Charlie to use his older brother to help him count cards in Vegas. The mathematical or scientific savant is a popular stereotype in movies and television despite a 2006 study that revealed only 20 percent of autistic people are "referred to as high functioning." The majority are of typical levels of intelligence. It's disconcerting that despite Raymond's ability to accrue $3 million in Vegas, doctors say he has no real-world concept of money and thus has no need for it. In testing this, he's asked what the price of a candy bar is, which, honestly, I couldn't tell ya either, doc. I'd no doubt turn into Lucille Bluth from *Arrested Development*. "How much can one candy bar cost? $10?" Like Forrest in *Forrest Gump*, money is seen as wasted on Raymond because he's comfortably taken care of and provided for by the healthcare community.

Raymond has lived in this fancy hospital/institution since he was a teenager, the result of almost scalding an infant Charlie in the bathtub. Since that time Ray is a burden passed down from father to (neurotypical) son. Luke in *Coming Home* showed disabled people as capable of living on their own. Sadly, the last thirty or so years of disabled narratives avoid the question "How do disabled people live independently?" and revert to letting able-bodied or neurotypical people inherit them like a fancy watch. The 1962 version of *Light in the Piazza* ends with Olivia de Havilland's Meg marrying off her mentally delayed daughter Clara (Yvette Mimieux) to a young man who finds her childlike demeanor cute. Leonardo DiCaprio's Arnie in the 1993 movie *What's Eating Gilbert Grape* lives with his older brother Gilbert (Johnny Depp) after the death of their mother. And the 2003 sports drama *Radio* ends with the entire town, in an act of symbolism, offering to take care of Cuba Gooding Jr.'s title character even though he ends up moving from his mother's home to his brother's. Even everyone's favorite kids film, *The Goonies*, ends with eleven-year-old Chunk (Jeff Cohen) telling the deformed, abused Sloth (John Matuszak) that he's going to live with Chunk and his family. Chunk doesn't ask his family if this is okay, but whose parents wouldn't be cool taking care of a grown man with severe disabilities they don't know?

Because movies use mental disabilities as indicators of intelligence, a character who is mentally disabled but quirky is simply hiding their brilliance. Charlie asks if Raymond is "in there" somewhere, and the movie responds yes, and what's in there is a genius! The schizophrenic tendencies of Russell Crowe's John Nash in *A Beautiful Mind* are the sacrifice he must pay for being a genius in the movie. This is something also explored in 1968's *Charly*, an adaptation of the 1959 novel *Flowers for Algernon*. Using the magic cure stereotype we see how intelligence and mental disabilities go hand in hand. Cliff Robertson's Charly Gordon is an intellectually disabled man given the opportunity to become a guinea pig for an experimental serum meant to boost his intelligence. The serum works as advertised but eventually turns Charly into a man so smart and cynical that he finds it hard to relate to others whom he sees as inferior to him.

Movies involving futuristic cures go back years and continue today. You can draw a line from *Charly* to the superhero film *Shazam!* wherein disabled character Freddy Freeman turns into a perfect superhero version of himself, one who is not disabled. Whether it's magic or science, finding a cure for disability (and not having the character ask questions about it) is a de facto default for screenwriters. Charly is a willing participant in the experiment, and why wouldn't he be? He spends his days playing on a playground with children and learns how to write using a small child's chalkboard. He is a literal man-child whom the audience watches with pity, hoping he will be fixed or otherwise taken care of. (*Tropic Thunder* hit it right on the nose with the number of movies, like *Charly*, that use backward, crayon-style fonts for their movies about the intellectually disabled. It's the Papyrus typeface for disabled films!) If that's not bad enough, Charly is mercilessly made fun of by his coworkers at the local bread factory. One uncomfortable scene has them put yeast into his locker so that when Charly opens the door the now rising yeast oozes out. Charly doesn't realize everyone is laughing at him and decides to join in by playing with the yeast.

The doctors are initially skeptical when Charly is referred as a candidate for the experimental serum. One even says, "Isn't it true that the retardate is overly sensitive and sometimes hostile?" We're definitely in a pre-ADA world. Charly is akin to *Of Mice and Men*'s Lenny, an overly emotional little boy in a man's body whose behavior the other, neurotypical characters in the movie perceive as dangerous when, in reality, it's a mark of his ignorance.

It's remarkable how many movies situate those with mental disabilities as dangerous, either intentionally or unintentionally. According to The Arc, an organization that works with the intellectually and mentally disabled, while 4 percent to 10 percent of the prison population has a cognitive disability, it is those with similar disabilities who are at a far higher rate of being victims of any type of crime compared to those without. They have the highest rate of violent victimization (83.3 per 1,000 people), according to a 2021 study by the Bureau of Justice.

Once the scientists put the hostility out in the air, the audience expects something to happen to prove their point. What's interesting is how it's the result of Charly becoming *more* neurotypical. Once he becomes more intelligent than the others around him, the serum starts to battle against his emotional immaturity. Because he is still emotionally a child, he ends up attempting to sexually assault his former teacher, Alice (Claire Bloom). Alice forgives him for . . . reasons, but the aftermath convinces Charly that he must go back to the way he once was. It's a bittersweet ending as the audience sees it as a reversion to sadness and loneliness rather than an act of agency and awareness from Charly that being smart/neurotypical and being a good person don't always go hand in hand.

When dealing with mental disabilities and the medicalized approach to them in movies, the mental institution is a popular setting. It wasn't always this way. Movies of the 1940s saw neurotypical people institutionalized with those with neurodivergence or other mental disabilities. Films like *The Snake Pit* and *The Lost Weekend* showed neurotypical people trapped in the horrors of the medical system, with the screaming, raving mental patient a call to solve mental illness for the protection of everyone. But when the onus is on the mentally disabled, a mental facility is only alluded to. Of all the movies consulted for this chapter, six feature disabled characters starting out or having previous experience in some form of institution or long-term care home. *Sling Blade* (1996) and *The Other Sister* (1999) are just two that have characters who lived in institutions. Some movies show them as safe spaces for those with mental disabilities to live among people like them, like *Rain Man*, and are akin to the disabled veterans communities discussed in the previous chapter. *Rain Man* and *Sling Blade* both end with their main characters returning to the institutions they started in, while *The Other Sister* and *I Am Sam* don't spend any time in mental facilities, and for the characters, they have zero wish to return. Any abuse claims are obliquely referred to in passing. According to a 2024 report, while there are far fewer intellectually and mentally disabled people living in US-based institutions today compared to the two hundred thousand living in them in the 1960s, there are still sixteen thousand developmentally disabled people institutionalized in the United States, period. There's little rhyme or reason as to what stories choose to focus on medical institutions or not, but it's possible that, in a post-ADA landscape, their limited use is a means of showing a fantasy version of how progressive America is regarding the mentally disabled. *See? Our disabled people no longer live in institutions! We let them live among you as long as they aren't too strange, are aesthetically pleasing, and don't live off the government.*

If the best place for mentally disabled people is in their own homes, with their families, movies don't show that in the best light either. Nearly every movie consulted for this chapter also has scenes of assault by able-bodied, neurotypical characters on neurodivergent characters, usually a family member, a reminder of the fact that the rate of violent victimization against persons with disabilities is nearly four times the rate it is for persons without disabilities, and family members are commonly the perpetrators. In movies where disabled characters are assaulted the audience sympathizes with the burdened family member. They realize this person is actually good because they regret their actions. Since the neurotypical person is often the protagonist, their moment of weakness is the result of frustration at their tragic circumstances. Regardless of narrative intent, the audience watches scenes of disabled characters in pain and distress, which can be triggering for disabled viewers. It's hard to find anything redemptive about Charlie's personality in *Rain Man*, even after all the time he spends with Ray. He's incredibly ableist, so much so that you can get drunk pretty quickly every time he says the R-word, and he also physically assaults Ray. But since Charlie is the audience surrogate and is Tom Cruise, that, coupled with Ray's quirks, makes the viewer understand Charlie's frustration.

The Johnny Depp–starring drama *What's Eating Gilbert Grape* gives us a more empathetic familial caregiver despite the movie being poverty porn to the hilt. Based on Peter Hedges's novel of the same name—Hedges is also the screenwriter—the movie follows small-town Midwestern grocery clerk Gilbert Grape (Depp) as he cares for his mentally disabled brother, Arnie (Leonardo DiCaprio), and his morbidly obese mother. *What's Eating Gilbert Grape* is an overwrought movie that hasn't aged well, whether due to DiCaprio's performance or the fat-shaming of Gilbert's mother, played by the late Darlene Cates.

DiCaprio secured his first Oscar nomination for the role of Arnie, and the character balances between the two stereotypes Kirk Lazarus talks about in

Tropic Thunder. DiCaprio's physical performance is uncomfortable for an able-bodied audience to watch as he wrings his hands and makes exaggerated faces with his mouth agape. Yet the character is a wide-eyed innocent, so simple that he decapitates a grasshopper with his mailbox only to have remorse in the next scene, sobbing about how he killed it. These are all Steinbeck tropes straight from *Of Mice and Men*. The audience roots for Gilbert to find his autonomy and become his own man, but that can't happen with Arnie making a public spectacle of himself and needing constant care, coupled with Gilbert's other family members being codependent on him. As the title implies, something is bothering Gilbert and the audience watches what *he* loses by caring for Arnie. When Gilbert goes off on a date, he trusts Arnie to successfully take a bath by himself. When Gilbert comes home, he discovers Arnie has stayed in the cold water for over a day, unable to figure out what to do. The death of Gilbert and Arnie's mother leaves the characters at a crossroads. Gilbert gets the best of both worlds. He stays with Arnie and becomes the family patriarch but is rewarded with a girlfriend and the ability to travel wherever he wants, with Arnie in tow. What does Arnie want out of life? Who knows, but it's obvious Gilbert is the one calling the shots.

Another mentally disabled character way too many people had imitations of in their back pocket is found in the movie *Sling Blade*. Everyone seemed to have thoughts about "french fried pataters" in 1996. *Sling Blade*'s Karl, Forrest from *Forrest Gump*, and Ray in *Rain Man* make up the holy trinity of mentally disabled impersonations. Karl (Billy Bob Thornton) has been institutionalized since he was twelve for killing his mother and her lover when he was a child. Now released, Karl attempts to go back to his hometown, where he befriends a young boy named Frank (Lucas Black) whose own mother is in an abusive relationship.

Though Karl's opening story details the double murder he admits he committed as a boy, the characters he meets after that have different interpretations of him based on how he acts. In Frank's eyes, Karl is a kindhearted friend and surrogate father figure who understands his problems. Frank's mother doesn't see Karl as a threat because "he's retarded" and lets him live in their garage. Thornton takes Steinbeck's Lenny and forces the audience to reconcile his performance with their preconceived notions about the character and, by extension, those with mental disabilities. Karl initially begs to stay in the institution, not just because the hospital is all he's known and he lacks few real-world life skills. His fear has to do with humanity's brutality and apathy. Karl killed the teenage boy his mother was with because he presumed she was being sexually assaulted, a wrong perception analogous to Lenny thinking a skirt is pretty and being accused of rape. But when Karl discovers his mother was dating the boy, coupled with the extensive physical abuse he endured at the hands of both his parents, her murder is motivated by the pure anger he feels. Karl is responsible for his actions and doesn't discount that, but there is necessary context. Karl's eventual murder of Doyle (Dwight Yoakam), the abusive boyfriend of Frank's mother, is justified because of Doyle's own violent anger. *Sling Blade* is interesting as the movie questions how much choice Karl actually has in his situation. He is either far smarter than he is given credit for or is placed in the same unfortunate circumstances he was placed in as a child. Are his actions the result of violence or ignorance? Is he a genius who found a way to dispense justice or a simpleton who doesn't know any better? Considering how much this movie grew on me, I gotta give credit to Thornton, who also wrote the script, for giving us that food for thought.

Thornton doesn't give the audience a specific able-bodied buffer; Karl is the fulcrum the entire ensemble circles around. They see Karl's mental disabilities as nonthreatening and turn to him as their witness and confidante, like a priest hearing confession. Frank discloses to Karl that he wants Doyle dead, while family friend Vaughan (delightfully played by John Ritter) admits to Karl that he's gay. Karl's killing of Doyle is an act of assertiveness that undercuts everyone's presumption of him as safe, yet Karl's kind heart remains intact due to how terrible Doyle is. Karl sacrifices his freedom after the murder and returns to the mental hospital. Karl doesn't give up his life but chooses to kill his independence because of how chaotic and cruel the world is, not just to him but to everyone. He finds safety and comfort in the hospital knowing he did something right. Unlike Lenny in *Of Mice and Men*, Karl doesn't die, but he bares his true soul to the audience. Looks may be deceiving, but Karl uses that to protect those he cares about.

If the audience questions Karl's true intentions in *Sling Blade*, then that leads down another road to a trope commonly found more in comedies than dramas: the mentally disabled fake out. This trope sees an able-bodied character pretend to have a mental disability under the belief they can either get away with something or gain an advantage from other people's pity or from their own thinking that disabled people are weaker. (The 2004 episode of *South Park*, "Up the Down Steroid," wherein Eric Cartman tries to win the Special Olympics by pretending to be mentally disabled is a must-watch example.) The best conception of this in film is 1995's *The Usual Suspects*. The crime thriller tells the story of a group of criminals all under the control of one man: a shadowy crime lord known only as Keyser Soze. Telling the story of Soze, and how the various characters came together and end up dead, is Roger "Verbal" Kint (Kevin Spacey), a disabled man with cerebral palsy. Kint controls the narrative and details a convoluted story that sees the other criminals underestimate or protect him due to his emotionality and condition. The twist—so famous it's considered the best-known ending of all time—sees the camera track Verbal's feet as he walks. His contorted limp transitions into a smooth, non-disabled stride with the audience's realization that he is Keyser Soze. The popularity of the ending saw several other movies emulate it, like the 2000 spoof film *Scary Movie*, a comedic send-up of popular horror movies of the time, whose ending reveals that the mentally disabled police officer, Doofy (Dave Sheridan), is the real slasher killing various teens.

The Farrelly brothers use the mentally disabled fake out frequently and, in the case of the 1998 comedy *There's Something About Mary*, to the best effect. The Farrellys use the disabled fake out to comment on the able-bodied idea that any disability creates a privilege, that the disabled get something able-bodied people don't. *There's Something About Mary* tells the story of lovable loser Ted Stroehmann and his enduring love for high school crush Mary (Cameron Diaz). Now a grown adult, Ted hopes to reconnect with Mary, but she has a score of suitors vying for her attention. One of them is accomplished architect Tucker (Lee Evans), who has cerebral palsy and uses crutches. Incredibly smart and said to have numerous successful businesses, Tucker is placed in situations at several points in the film where he can't reach stuff, with the audience watching him attempt to stay upright on his crutches while going through a series of comical contortions. The audience is meant to laugh at him, at least upon an initial viewing.

In Tucker's case, he is shown as a total fraud. Nothing is real about him, not even his English accent. He doesn't have a business, he isn't a successful architect, and he isn't disabled. He crafts an entire fake persona to get Mary to like him, thinking she wouldn't be interested in a lowly pizza boy who lives with his parents. Tucker, a.k.a. Norm, preys on Mary's goodness and creates a nonthreatening persona of a disabled character who rises above his disability. He isn't just a good man, he's a good disabled man. He crafts Tucker as accomplished and dashing with his disability his only flaw. He makes Mary believe he's seeking a partner, not a caregiver. He wants her to see him as needing protection and love because *he* believes everyone bends over backward for those with disabilities. He uses that as leverage to assert his own white male privilege because he thinks he's entitled to Mary. He's put on the biggest con of all the men in Mary's orbit and should be given his flowers for it, according to him. When you rewatch the movie knowing all this you realize how much Tucker exaggerates his movements to make Mary think he's charming and, most importantly, in need of her care. The audience laughs at Tucker because he has zero idea how disabled people live, move, and function.

The Farrellys have talked about their desire to be inclusive in their casting by peppering their films with actual disabled performers but such performers still haven't been in their leading roles and are often relegated to supporting. With *There's Something About Mary*, Mary has a mentally disabled brother named Warren (played by non–intellectually disabled actor W. Earl Brown), a childlike, mentally disabled gentle giant who doesn't know his own strength. The only actual disabled performers in the movie are background performers, seen when Warren participates in a program for those with mental disabilities. For a film that so skillfully sends up ableism it's disappointing that not one actual disabled performer gets a prominent role to balance the scales.

The 2005 film *The Ringer*, which the Farrellys produced, attempts to open the floor to more disabled characters to find a way to subvert disabled tropes. Unlike Tucker, though, there's little about this that works. (And it has the same plot as "Up the Down Steroid." Just saying.) Johnny Knoxville plays Steve Barker, who is desperate to raise the $28,000 needed to help his friend, who doesn't have health insurance, reattach the three fingers he lost in a lawn mowing accident. Steve's uncle, swimming in gambling debts, convinces Steve to enter into the Special Olympics by pretending to be a mentally disabled man so they can win the prize money. The inspirational sports movie is its own subgenre in disability cinema, filled with tropes of its own, and is a popular way to integrate people with disabilities as the ultimate underdogs. Steve is not an athlete nor has he done any training for it, which immediately puts him at a disadvantage against his competitors who, though mentally disabled, are actual athletes. If you are one of the over ten million people to tune into the Paralympics each year, you've seen the athletic prowess of these participants.

Because this is a comedy and Steve is our main character, the others aren't given much opportunity to shine and three of the actors playing Steve's Special Olympics friends are played by neurotypical performers. In *Something About Mary*, Tucker doesn't win Mary because he is nice to her. He is a liar and a fraud, and the movie emphasizes that his playing on disabled stereotypes makes him a horrible person. Steve in *The Ringer* is easily forgiven for everything he does simply because he's a nice guy. Never mind that he played on mentally disabled stereotypes or tried to defraud an organization. All is well because he tried to help a friend. *The Ringer* says that so long as one makes an effort to learn and befriend those with mental disabilities, things are fine. Go watch Bobby Farrelly's far better 2023 film *Champions*, about a disabled basketball team. It has some great characters, all authentically cast and is very charming.

Let's go back to *Tropic Thunder* for a second. Kirk Lazarus's entire speech revolves around the idea that if one hits the disability notes just right, they can win an Oscar. Is he right? *Sling Blade*, *Forrest Gump*, and *Rain Man* received Oscar nominations for their leading actors. The latter two films won in their acting categories. Thornton was nominated for *Sling Blade* but didn't win. *Rain Man* and *Gump* also took home Best Picture. *Tropic Thunder*'s point isn't entirely wrong. But what if you don't have the right combination of factors? What if you don't play mentally disabled well enough to sway a neurotypical audience (or Oscar voters)? For Kirk Lazarus, the de facto example of this is the 2001 drama *I Am Sam*, where Sean Penn plays the eponymous Sam, a mentally disabled Starbucks barista (bet the 'Bucks regrets that promotional tie-in) trying to raise his neurotypical daughter, Lucy (Dakota Fanning). When Lucy is removed from Sam's care due to his disability, he hires a firebrand attorney (Michelle Pfeiffer) to get her back.

Tropic Thunder says that Penn went home empty-handed for this role, but he *did* get nominated, just as Hanks, Hoffman, and DiCaprio did. The latter is the closest correlation to describe Penn's performance, and while correlation doesn't equal causation, it's worth pointing out that both nonwinning performances are overly reliant on exaggerated facial features, and the characters are of no use to their able-bodied counterparts.

Penn plays Sam as highly energetic, with his mouth perpetually open and a blank expression on his face. Yet Penn's casting makes the character come off as too aggressive and intimidating for what is supposed to be a simple and tenderhearted person. This is coupled with a movie that is already so self-serious that the audience misses an interesting story of how a mentally disabled man fights to keep a child who is intellectually superior to him. *I Am Sam* is worth giving kudos for not having an able-bodied buffer at least. Penn's Sam is the main character, and even when the movie transitions to its B-plot involving his attorney, Pfeiffer's Rita Williams, she's never set up as the protagonist of this story. The courtroom scenes in *I Am Sam* tend to focus on the highly ableist Rita, similar to Charlie in *Rain Man*, learning to grow as a character by interacting with Sam. I'd like to think her character discovers "what to call" Sam after using the R-word so frequently. And when you get down to it, there aren't nearly enough stories about disabled parenthood, let alone stories about parents with intellectual disabilities raising kids. They, of course, exist in reality. There have been court cases, in the US and abroad, involving disabled parents losing custody of their children because of the belief that their disability makes them unfit. One 2015 study of 5,256 households showed that in single-parent homes, 3.2 percent were identified as having a parent with intellectual disabilities, while two-parent households say just 1 percent identified as having one or both parents with intellectual disabilities.

Tropic Thunder points out there's something different in Penn's performance, though I don't believe he lost the Oscar because the character was too disabled. He lost because it's an overwrought part. Penn puts on a performance, and an inauthentic one at that. Audiences not used to disability don't want to see the struggles of a mentally disabled man working for subminimum wage at Starbucks. It doesn't inspire the warm fuzzies. However, the movie bucks conventions by not having an able-bodied buffer; the audience is left to identify solely with his mentally disabled character, who can't hide his disability, isn't of use to able-bodied characters, and wants the system to help *him* secure something *he* needs, in this case his daughter. You know what makes an audience happy? Seeing Tom Cruise rock some Ray-Bans while hanging out with a mentally disabled man who helps him win big in Vegas. Or Tom Hanks investing in Apple stock and telling everyone life is like a box of chocolates. Or Billy Bob Thornton eating biscuits and mustard before braining an asshole with a lawnmower blade. Honestly, that last one is my favorite.

I Am Sam is far from a classic, and its reputation precedes it. There's a collective remembering of movies like *I Am Sam* or 1999's *The Other Sister* as being bad for reasons people can't explain because they haven't seen the films. They just know it's terrible. This could be an act of solidarity now that there's more awareness of why neurotypical actors shouldn't portray neurodivergent characters. By not seeing the movies, no one has to feel complicit, especially if they like it. In cases where the characters are too disabled for an abled audience it's usually out of a fear of being uncomfortable, particularly around others. I, myself, am a victim of this. As a physically disabled person who is neurotypical, watching these movies is a painful reminder of where my own internalized ableism creeps through. I long believed several of these movies were terrible because I didn't want to be made uncomfortable watching mentally disabled people, even though it's a neurotypical character playing a stereotype of a mentally disabled character. However . . . *I Am Sam* is not a good movie. That has nothing to do with the character and everything to do with Penn's performance. What *is* a good movie worth watching to see how mentally disabled characters can be written well is *The Other Sister*, which tells a grounded family story about a neurodivergent woman who wants to live her own independent life.

Directed by Garry Marshall, Juliette Lewis plays Carla, a mentally disabled woman acclimating back into the lives of her affluent family after years of living in an institution. Carla seeks independence, but her mother, Elizabeth (Diane Keaton), is content to treat her like a child. Similar to Charlie in *Rain Man*, Keaton's Elizabeth is hard to redeem. She's similar to Keaton's other high-strung, perfectionist characters, but playing an ableist mother to a disabled daughter makes some of her reactions hard to swallow.

The movie starts with Elizabeth forcing her husband to sign Carla's commitment papers, a decision that makes him turn to alcoholism though it's never 100 percent clear whether this is a result of Carla's disability or Elizabeth's chronic nagging. In families where disabled children can't assert boundaries and find their own path in life, it's hard to want Elizabeth to reunite with her child, especially after having her committed. Elizabeth is no different from any other overprotective parent, telling others "Carla doesn't know what works for her" or some other variation on how her daughter doesn't know how to be an adult. She's content for Carla to run the family household after she dies and discourages Carla from going to school or getting a job. Thankfully, *The Other Sister* isn't about Elizabeth, but Carla. The movie's title implies that Carla is the burden, the sister that comes with far more baggage than her siblings do. The movie is honest about how families, particularly high-class ones, choose to hide their disabled relatives (the Kennedys and the Bushes are well documented to have done similar things with the disabled people in their families).

But Carla doesn't want to be a burden. She wants her own apartment and a job. She starts by trying to get her high school diploma and become a vet assistant. She also wants a relationship with Danny (Giovanni Ribisi), an intellectually disabled man she meets at school. Both actors are neurotypical, but the performances aren't showy. Lewis plays Carla as a quiet young woman always aware of what she wants and when. When she wants to talk to her mother about her life, Carla says, "I want to discuss my options now." When she decides to have sex with Danny, the audience watches her make that choice. The fact that Carla is sexual is unique for 1999, let alone that the movie goes through with the two actually having sex. Every motivation is justified and relatable. Even Carla's father and sisters are supportive of her and the choices she makes. It's not an us-against-them story. It's shocking in 1999 to see a movie where the family of someone with a mental disability wants their loved ones to find personal autonomy. It shouldn't be that way. *The Other Sister*, sadly, was a box office failure upon release, grossing just $27.8 million off a $35 million budget. The male audiences lusting after Lewis's Mallory Knox in *Natural Born Killers* weren't going to see that character. Since money talks in Hollywood, executives no doubt believed audiences didn't want to see movies about mentally disabled characters.

It's been sixteen years, at the time of this writing, since *Tropic Thunder* brought that infamous phrase into our lives, and little has changed when it comes to showing those with intellectual disabilities on the big screen. TV has been a bit more accepting of this, *Glee*'s Becky Jackson being a prime example, but it's only a start. If there's a need for a filmic counterpart, the 2019 film *The Peanut Butter Falcon* became somewhat of a box office success with authentic casting in a lead role. Produced by Zeno Mountain Farms, a company that crafts films starring and created by disabled people, it stars Zack Gottsagen as a man with Down syndrome who runs away from a nursing home to pursue his dreams as a wrestler. Though Gottsagen is surrounded by A-list actors like Dakota Johnson and Shia LaBeouf in supporting roles, the movie is his story 100 percent. Unfortunately, it didn't usher in a wave of films starring people with Down syndrome or any other cognitive disabilities. Successes like these are too often seen as a fluke, not indicative that disabled people want to watch stories about them.

Tropic Thunder may have been wrong for using the phrase, but the power behind what the phrase talks about remains. Audiences will only take specific viewpoints on mentally disabled characters. Maybe it's time to focus less on the word and look more at ourselves as audience members.

6   BLACK AND DISABLED

We've spent the last five chapters talking about a lot of white disabled characters and performers. That's not a coincidence. As the 2024 USC Annenberg study reminds us, 71 percent of disabled characters are white men and, like any historical look at film, racism plays a role right alongside ableism. The issues Black people face on-screen are not the same as what people with disabilities face, but there are some commonalities. Each group has endured stereotyping and erasure, and for all the time it's taken Black directors and characters to gain ground in the entertainment industry, the disabled community is still in the early days of shaking up Hollywood.

Intersectionality is a bad word in Hollywood. You can have a disabled person and a person of color in your movie. But you can't have a person of color *with* a disability in your movie. The stats prove it. As that same USC Annenberg study from 2024 shows, 54.6 percent of disabled characters in the films of 2023 were white. That's pretty staggering, considering that of the top one hundred movies of 2023, just 2.2 percent had a speaking role or named character for someone with a disability.

As a white-passing disabled woman, I acknowledge my privilege when it comes to writing on and discussing the topic of disability let alone disabled characters of color. I never worried before about seeing disabled characters of color on-screen when I was growing up. But it's impossible to watch these movies today and not realize the sheer abundance of white faces disabled audiences of all ethnicities are forced to identify with in order to form some kind of connection. As bell hooks lays out in her 1995 book *Killing Rage*, white people watch films with Black characters and presume that the positive relationships in the movies mimic current societal trends, ultimately depicting racial issues as existing in Black people's minds. This is similar to how able audiences look at disabled characters. Able-bodied audiences see disabled characters living in nice homes, not lacking for financial assistance, having their needs met, and assume they have no reason to complain. Whether you want to believe it or not, audiences think movies represent some element of reality. They set up the world we want, and it's up to us, the viewers, to figure out whether it's an authentic one or not. Sadly, most don't do their research. I can only imagine the struggles young disabled people of color face when watching entertainment in general, let alone adding in disabled stereotypes. Representation needs to be better for every marginalized group. But it's worth spotlighting, or at least acknowledging, the few films that have Black disabled characters and how disability tropes change when race is involved. If you didn't already suspect, it's bad.

The first Black disabled character I encountered was Ernie Hudson's Solomon, the kindhearted, intellectually disabled handyman in the 1992 thriller *The Hand That Rocks the Cradle*. Solomon exhibits a lot of the tropes we'll discuss throughout the chapter. Solomon is a Tiny Tim/saintly disabled man; his existence is solely to help the white family, the Bartels, who are the actual focus of the movie. As Rita Kempley wrote about the "magical Negro," a trope in pop culture where Black characters aid in helping white ones, the Black characters lack development and interior lives. Solomon lives within the confines of a scene. The audience is privy to nothing regarding him as a person short of him being a part of an organization that pairs intellectually disabled individuals with families looking to fill odd jobs. He has no family, friend group, or outside interests other than the Bartels. We don't even know if Solomon gets paid for his work, or whether it's some form of volunteer position or subminimum wage permalance job. (*I Am Sam* at least told us Sam made $8 an hour at Starbucks!) When the Bartels' precocious daughter asks what will "happen" to Solomon once he's done working at their house, her mother responds, "We'll just have to find something else for him to do." Now this sounds like a trap for indentured servitude. The Bartels are perceived as good people for hiring a Black man, with a disability and any fear of threat is mitigated by his childlike demeanor.

When Solomon discovers the Bartels' new nanny, Peyton (Rebecca de Mornay), has villainous intentions, she frames him as a child predator and gets him fired. It is here where race and disability crash into each other. We laid out in the previous chapter how characters with mental disabilities are depicted as nonthreatening, childlike characters whose actions are misinterpreted as dangerous. Black men have been presented in a negative light since the inception of film itself, going back to D. W. Griffith's racist portrayal of them as slavering rapists, played by white actors in blackface, in 1915's *The Birth of a Nation*. When race is included, a moment like the one in which Solomon is framed comes with the added history of false accusations by white people against Black people and cinematic depictions of Black people as predators. Stereotypes against Black men are thought to just attack Black men, not Black disabled men. The rise of Black directors and screenwriters coupled with changing views of race have moved us away from this as time has passed, but when it comes to disability the attempt to course correct leads to racism on top of ableism.

We see how this plays out in *Hand That Rocks the Cradle*. Solomon is removed from the Bartels' home, but the family never appears to reveal their fears about Solomon to the organization he works for. And because the audience knows he's been framed we keep rooting for him. When the heroine fights for her life in the finale, it is Solomon—who presumably lives in the Bartels' attic, I guess—who magically appears to save the day. (Seriously, does anyone else wonder why Solomon is just hanging out in their attic like Mr. Rochester's wife? No one?) The audience doesn't need to know where Solomon is or what he does outside of his scenes, so the ending stands as is. His kindhearted, gentle giant persona is proven right, and he receives the redemption he deserves. His race is not considered in this film to give off the impression of equality, but it ignores how detrimental and dangerous, in reality, the accusations are for him as a Black disabled man. It's difficult to believe the police would be so blasé to a Black man accused of child predation, especially on white children. And considering the movie was released about a year after the infamous Rodney King beating, the movie looks to utilize Solomon's disability to defang his race, in a way.

Contemporary views on race and disability are on people's radars, so there is an awareness to acknowledge and rectify the marginalization of minority groups. When Jordan Peele's *Get Out* hit theaters in 2017, it was lauded for its exploration of racism and white privilege in America. But it also takes a stark look at racism within disability and at the white supremacy within mainstream depictions of disability in film. Daniel Kaluuya plays Chris Washington, a Black photographer, who travels with his white girlfriend to meet her family for the first time. He discovers that her parents lead an organization wherein the brains of older white people are transplanted into young, Black bodies to obtain the host's physical traits. Through this process the Black person whose body is taken over is sent to the Sunken Place of their subconscious to live out the rest of their days. Chris's body is up for grabs and is coveted by white gallery owner Jim Hudson (Stephen Root), who wishes to inhabit Chris's body to cure his blindness, literally and metaphorically.

When the pair first meet, Jim claims his blindness is no different than the color of Chris's skin, citing them both as a genetic defect. Jim's blindness manifested later in his life so he's experienced the advantages of being able bodied alongside being an entitled white man. Since disability is situated as reflective of what a person lacks, it's unsurprising that a white racist like Jim would equate something like race alongside a disability like being blind. For him, both are inferiorities. Jim repeatedly mentions how good Chris's "eye" is, specifically his ability to capture pictures that have an impact and make him money. Jim, not having the same level of success, seeks to change this by co-opting Chris's body. Jim sees by appropriating Chris's body he won't just return to the able-bodied, sighted life he's lost, but he's also given a chance to take over what he thinks are Chris's excellent skills as a photographer. Jim takes the magical Negro trope a bit too literally. Peele shows how race and disability coexist in film while acknowledging the long-standing problems within both groups.

Many of the stereotypes Black characters fall into happen to Black *disabled* characters in film, but the addition of disability in a character of color forces the director and screenwriter to make a choice on what to prioritize. Is the viewer meant to denounce racism or ableism? *Because you can't do both, obviously.* In most cases, the choice is to avoid complex and politically wrought discussions of race, as they conjure up too much historical negativity for an audience—Nicole Kidman did tell us we go to the movies for magic, after all. Disability politics are perceived as simpler—who is against disabled people?—so it usually wins as the one social issue in the movie. But it's impossible to divorce race from disability, and it's ridiculous for movies to try. One in four Black people have some type of disability, according to the CDC, and in the United States 50 percent of people killed by law enforcement are disabled, according to a 2021 study. Prioritization of disability over race, as opposed to their interrelationship, implies that one or the other doesn't exist for these characters.

Let's return to our old friend *Forrest Gump*. When Forrest goes to Vietnam, he meets Bubba Blue (Mykelti Williamson), a Black man with a speech pattern and cognitive issues similar to Forrest's. Lieutenant Dan jokingly asks them if they're brothers because of how in sync they are. Bubba is coded as having the same low IQ as Forrest himself, though it's never explicitly stated that he has any type of mental disability. That being said, he is also a kindhearted man who takes things literally and has an obsessive love for shrimp. Unlike Forrest and Lieutenant Dan, Bubba ends up wounded in Vietnam and dies in Forrest's arms. It's jarring how the one Black character of significance who means anything to Forrest and has mental limitations strongly comparable with Forrest's, ends up getting killed. To break it down, Bubba is a Black man fighting in a war where 31 percent of ground combat battalions were made up of Black men. Black men also made up 24 percent of the US Army's fatalities, according to a Library of Congress report. This in spite of Black men making up 12 percent of the US population. So to a viewer watching the film, it's clear Bubba's race certainly was a factor of him being in Vietnam at all (and yet most of Forrest's battalion that he and Bubba travel with are white). But the film is content to not look at *why* Bubba is there or focus on his and Forrest's shared simplicity and the racial distinctions between them. The movie tries hard to rub elbows between race and disability, but not enough.

The Green Mile (1999) and 2003's *Radio* situate their Black male characters as equally nonthreatening, poverty-stricken men with childlike mental states to make the white audience feel comfortable with their race and disability. Each is the lone person of color in a lead or supporting capacity in their respective films, in largely white communities. Because of this isolation they are singled out for violence and gain the attention of the white savior, the true lead role of the film, who needs to save and protect them. The relationships in these movies are always quid pro quo: The Black characters have that special something that makes them of use, and the movie ends with some type of literal or figurative sacrifice from the Black character that changes the life of the white characters purely for having known them.

We've talked about the Tiny Tim principle numerous times already, but it's a stereotype we've seen through white characterizations. As previously mentioned, the magical Negro is a commonly utilized stereotype for Black characters wherein they are mystical, benevolent assistants to white performers. As Cerise L. Glenn and Landra J. Cunningham explain in "The Power of Black Magic: The Magical Negro and White Salvation in Film," "the debased Black role and glorified White hero are not only isolated roles for the viewer but symbolically used so that Whites do not have to consider the moral implications or validity of these roles." Akin to the Tiny Tim roles we've seen this type of performance makes a white audience comfortable watching subservient Black roles without reconciling with topics like racism and slavery. Those who come under the magical Negro umbrella aren't all disabled (Scatman Crothers's performance as Dick Halloran in 1980's *The Shining*, for example), but the integration of disability leaves the few Black disabled characters to fall into the same trap. The best example is John Coffey (Michael Clarke Duncan) in the 1999 adaptation of Stephen King's *The Green Mile*. King's 1996 novella tells the story of white prison guard Paul Edgecomb (Tom

Hanks) and his meeting with the death row inmate Coffey in 1935. The pair are brought together when Coffey, a Black man convicted of murdering two white girls, is brought to the Cold Mountain Penitentiary for execution. Once there, it's discovered that Coffey can perform miracles, curing Paul of a painful urinary tract infection and removing a deadly brain tumor from the prison warden's wife.

Michael Clarke Duncan is the magical John Coffey, with Tom Hanks, in *The Green Mile* (1999). Archive Photos / Stringer / Moviepix / Getty Images

Coffey's on-screen introduction is intimidating. All the viewer initially sees is his size. The camera doesn't show Coffey's face immediately, content to stay tight on his individual body parts, like his chest and arms, and how he dwarfs the white prison guards by comparison. This situates him as a gentle giant whose inner childishness is at odds with his outer strength, which he cannot control. But it is Coffey's blackness, not his mental disability, that makes him a supposed threat. Yet when Coffey speaks for the first time he speaks in slow, deliberate sentences and always calls the guards "sir," situating him as a respectful, innocent depiction of disability and blackness. He knows his place in the prison hierarchy, as well as in the world of race and disability.

The issues with the movie can't fall at the feet of its director and screenwriter as this is an adaptation of Stephen King's work. King is a frustrating writer when it comes to disability and blackness. When he's not falling into the magical Negro trope, he's using disability to emphasize the grotesque and burdensome.

King likened the horror genre to a freak show where "you look at the guy with three eyes or . . . the fat lady . . . or Mr. Electrical. . . . And when you come . . . you say, 'Hey, I'm not so bad.'" He makes use of disability to give able-bodied people a serotonin boost when looking at the disabled. His disabled characters fall into two categories: monsters like Zelda or benevolent martyrs like Deaf Nick Andros or mentally disabled Coffey or Tom Cullen in *The Stand*.

The Green Mile prioritizes racism by focusing on the hatred Coffey experiences from the local townsfolk, who presume he's a murderer, and from fellow inmate "Wild Bill" Wharton (Sam Rockwell), who spends most of his screen time calling Coffey racial slurs. Characters the audience assumes are on John's side showcase their own white privilege. Paul and the other white guards exert racial bias against John, even after he proves (1) he's of use to white people and (2) he performs literal miracles! Paul wants to learn more about Coffey's past so he travels to see the condemned man's attorney (played by none other than Gary Sinise) who outright says Coffey is guilty. The attorney tells a story about a "mongrel dog" he and his family had who, without provocation, attacked his son, leaving him partially blind. This proves to the attorney that a seemingly sweet demeanor masks inner brutality. He also weaponizes white disabled privilege, through his son, as a motivation for his racism.

John Coffey is like Lenny in *Of Mice and Men*, and his innocence makes Paul surmise, "I don't see God putting a gift like that into the hands of a man who'd kill a child." Characters who exhibit magical Negro traits are saints or noble, good-hearted characters who help white characters through a personal crisis. This is another way disability narratives leverage Victorian depictions of disabled people as saints, emphasizing that through their personal challenges, they are closer to God, and that rubs off on the average (white/able-bodied) person. It also creates the connection that Black people are more in tune with "folk wisdom and spiritual insight," as Glenn and Cunningham explain. Their saintly demeanor puts them on a morally equal footing with their white counterparts. Hanks's Paul, with his name and how he witnesses John Coffey's miracles, comes with his own apostolic connections, as if they are close cousins. By making John Coffey intellectually disabled with a similar path as Steinbeck's character, the white audience identifies that he is a friend. Their feelings are manipulated toward the idea that "this man is too pure for this world," and his death is a foregone conclusion even if he wasn't on death row because of how Christlike he is.

Paul, as the able-bodied buffer, sees the attorney's son and feels pity and empathy, but that's because the disabled experience is showcased through the lens of white disabled characters. The audience questions why they pity this white child and not the disabled Black man. As Glenn and Cunningham discuss, this is because the magical Negro may appear to be on the same footing as their white counterparts, but white supremacy always wins the day. A white disabled boy will always be prioritized over a disabled Black man. And this racial bias never goes away. When the guards illicitly extract John from his jail cell to cure the warden's wife, Paul and the other guards discuss how to safely neutralize John if he decides to escape or otherwise turn on them. There is still a clear lack of trust in his personal character despite his exhibiting no previous signs of violence. Also, *they're* the ones smuggling him out of prison!

But for all Coffey's goodness, coupled with the fact that he's an innocent man, like most magical Negro and saintly disabled characters, he goes willingly to his execution and forgives his accusers in a Christlike way. Coffey's execution is another moment wherein we shouldn't forget he is a Black and disabled man being executed. As Diana George and Diana Shoos say in "Deflecting the Political in the Visual Images of Execution and the Death Penalty Debate" regarding the death penalty in film, "The visual can deflect—even undercut— the political." So when executions take place in the movies, "the question of the death penalty itself remains untouched." A liberal audience watches *The Green Mile* and certainly fills in the social commentary behind King's story, but Coffey being a Christlike figure is what's tragic about his death, not that he's one of countless Black men executed for a crime he didn't commit. Since the audience is focused on Coffey's sacrifice, they don't think of how the death penalty might be used against Black and disabled people, or the inequalities to either group.

The 2003 sports drama *Radio* does the opposite of *The Green Mile* by prioritizing ableism. As mentioned in chapter 5, the inspirational sports subgenre is prime territory for disabled characters because the genre has a set formula to allow for characters to transcend or overcome obstacles tied to their disability. *Radio* is a period drama set in the 1970s and based on the true story of the friendship between a twenty-three-year-old mentally disabled man named James Robert "Radio" Kennedy (Cuba Gooding Jr.) and South Carolina football coach Harold Jones (Ed Harris). Harold attempts to integrate James onto the high school football team he coaches. By interacting with Radio, Harold and the entire town change and become better people. Everyone learns an important lesson at the end about tolerance for those with disabilities. Racism, on the other hand. . . .

The audience is privy to pieces of Radio's personal life. Radio has a mother who spends her days being a nurse and her nights being a nursemaid to her son. Radio fills his time walking around town collecting things and listening to the radio. Hmm, wonder where he got that nickname? Radio enjoys watching football and gets the high school team's attention after stealing a ball that's thrown over a fence. This petty crime is apparently an offense worthy of going to hell, since the team enacts revenge on Radio by abducting him, tying him up, and leaving him in their utility shed all day. *There's only one football, and it must be avenged!* This is meant to make the audience empathize with Radio as a disabled man, not a disabled Black man. Where Black disabled men are all too frequently harmed and killed in innocuous situations, the imagery of a sobbing Cuba Gooding Jr., bound and gagged for something as simple as taking a football is loaded and triggering imagery.

Radio is a period piece set in the 1970s as well as now being over twenty years old. But these problems with Black *and* disabled people have always existed, so to present this as a moment wherein a group of white boys simply pull a prank on a disabled man, divorced of race, is ridiculous. Adding insult to injury is *how* the other characters respond when they hear about it. Harold's wife chalks it up to "Well, I'm sure most of them [the team] have never done this before." *God, I hope not, but now that you brought it up. Boys will be boys, I guess.* A later scene sees Radio stopped by a police officer who thinks that Radio has stolen gifts he's found distributing to the townsfolk. In another triggering moment, Radio is thrown on the hood of a cop car and arrested, but since he is the only disabled man in town, as far as we know, let alone the only disabled Black man, a group of fellow officers recognize him and are appalled that the arresting officer doesn't know who Radio is. They explain that the officer is new to the force. He must have missed the meeting about Radio being a VIP. Radio is sprung from the jail and sits with the cops eating sandwiches and, yes, listening to the radio until he is bailed out in a moment that screams "not all cops."

Harold lets Radio act as the team's unofficial mascot, handing out towels and water bottles in the hopes that this makes up for Radio's treatment by the town. The only one who understands why it's inappropriate to use Radio as a mascot—just the phrase sounds like there's a double meaning—is the school's principal (Alfre Woodard), marked as the heavy of the school. She refuses to let Radio travel on the team bus for away games because he's "a severely handicapped Black man. What if he has a seizure?" If Radio's race doesn't factor into things, why does only this character emphasize it? The other white characters don't "see" Radio's color, but the principal understands that it does make a difference. It stands to reason that some towns, especially a Southern town in the 1970s, might be more hostile to Radio's presence than the one he lives in. It's also never said whether the school has any other disabled students or if the town has any other disabled people, so there's no basis for comparison. The viewer is left to feel sad watching Radio left behind on the football field and listening to the away game he was denied while standing in a torrential downpour. The moment is a little extra, to say the least.

Woodward's character and a few stray Black members of the football team are supposed to negate questions of racism because of their existence. As if to say things are progressive because it's the 1970s and a Black woman is a high school principal. The dichotomy of the debased Black man and the white hero are "not only isolated roles for the viewer," says Glenn and Landra, "but symbolically they are used so that whites do not have to consider the moral implications or validity of these roles." Radio is a unicorn to both the Black and white populace because he is treated like neither a Black man nor a white man. His disability is something beyond race despite how often he's called "boy," a term that, while common to disabled people as a sign of infantilization, is associated as a triggering, racist word for Black men. But, remember, the movie wants you to believe these characters only see him as a disabled man. Not a disabled man who is also Black. Harold, unconsciously, illustrates the power imbalance between them in the fact that he calls James "Radio." No one ever feels the need to show Radio respect by calling him by his actual name.

We're never given any insight into what Radio thinks about these moments, and the movie heavily implies he doesn't comprehend police brutality, racism, or injustice at all. These complex terms and emotions are lost on him. He doesn't even narrate a movie that's named after him, because he's too disabled. Debra Winger, playing Harold's wife in a small handful of scenes, gets the job for unexplained reasons. The team isn't punished for their antics, and it's hard to believe the cops are going to take it easy on the next disabled Black man, if one ever materializes in this town. Radio's personality is what we've seen numerous times already: He's sweet, naive, and overly trusting. Gooding Jr. also uses several of the same vocal patterns and exaggerated gestures that Sean Penn and Dustin Hoffman do and gets stuck with over-the-top fake teeth that look to have inspired *Tropic Thunder*'s Simple Jack.

Much of the love for Radio comes after seeing how much *he* loves the town. It's a purely conditional relationship. Harold's interactions with Radio are perceived as distracting and a contributing factor to the football team losing. Harold is the one to vouch for Radio by emphasizing what a blessing he's been for the town. Never mind that the populace, composed of white and able-bodied people, meets to discuss what to do with Radio after his mother dies, with the goal of putting him in an institution. Radio, despite being of majority age, neither is aware of this meeting nor gets a chance to defend himself. Harold is Radio's white savior, protecting him and finding a route for Radio to be cared for by others. Radio is not so much a person as a figurehead for compassion. He's the living equivalent of a "Kindness: Pass It On" commercial.

At the beginning of this chapter, I discussed how intersectionality is a problem when it comes to disability and race. The inspirational sports film opens up avenues for disability discourse and, in 2024's *Unstoppable*, showcases what good representation looks like. We've looked at films where either disability or race are explored, but never both. The story of Anthony Robles growing up in this world that acknowledges the existence of disabled people of color is unique. *Unstoppable* is the story of disabled wrestler Anthony Robles (Jharrel Jerome) as he tries to get on the Arizona State University wrestling team while navigating personal difficulties at home. Robles, an Afro-Latino man born with one leg, grew up in poverty in a community that struggled with drugs and crime. His mother (Jennifer Lopez) is involved in an abusive relationship.

Those in the crowd at Anthony's wrestling match immediately express their ableism and their underestimation of him in an early scene. "Is that guy missing a leg?" "Is this a joke?" *Unstoppable* prioritizes Anthony as the center of the story at all times from this first moment. The camera stays low to the ground during the wrestling scenes, showing off how Anthony wrestles with one leg, his body connecting and working with the floor in a way that's almost balletic. Anthony navigates locales that are seemingly inaccessible to him, like during a training montage wherein the wrestling team scales a rocky mountain. Anthony makes the entire climb with crutches, his hands bloody by the end. These moments are typical underdog sequences, but Anthony's disability doesn't just show audiences that it's possible for him to do it; disabled audiences watch how he traverses those spaces. Even if you aren't ambulatory, Anthony is not superhuman, nor is he someone to be pitied. He makes do with what he's got.

The movie's genre implies a certain level of inspiration, documenting how a character like him transcends his circumstances. This manifests both from a disabled perspective as well as from his desire to elevate his family financially. At a crucial moment Anthony tells his mother, "When people look at me they see what's missing." Anthony's mother, who is not an able-bodied buffer but her own fleshed-out character with a life and conflicts of her own, supports him and lets him come to his own realization that this isn't true. Society has made him feel he's not whole because of a missing limb. Anthony puts the burden of that lack on those that look at him and perceive him as being half-formed. To him and his family, who routinely crack jokes about his missing leg, it's something they know doesn't define him. By the end, *Unstoppable* isn't about Anthony showing the world that they've underestimated him but about showing himself that he can do it.

You've probably noticed we've focused exclusively on Black men. Black women remain severely limited in cinematic disabled narratives. Of the top-grossing films released between 2009 and 2019, Black women represented just 3.7 percent of leads and co-leads, regardless of disability. As of 2024, the number of films with women of color as leads or coleads decreased from 18 percent in 2022 to 14 percent in 2023. So finding a feature with a Black disabled woman of any type in a lead role is almost a lesson in futility. Thankfully, there's one worth shouting out, and it comes from the most unlikely of places: the work of director Kevin Smith. Smith's 2019 feature *Jay and Silent Bob Reboot* follows the eponymous stoners (played by Jason Mewes and Smith himself, respectively) as they go on a journey to win back the rights to their names after losing them in a copyright lawsuit. Along the way, Jay reunites with the daughter he never knew he had, Milly (played by Smith's daughter Harley Quinn Smith) who comes with her own Silent Bob facsimile, Sopapilla (Treshelle Edmond), who is Deaf. "Soapy," as she's referred to by Milly, doesn't have any superhuman powers, despite Smith's love of the superhero genre. Soapy lives in a commune with other Deaf people who grow the best weed in their state. She's a typical horny, pot-smoking, switchblade-carrying teenage girl who happens to be Deaf. Since this is Jay's story, the burden is on him to confront his own ableism, as he admits he's shocked to find out Deaf people smoke weed. His out-of-touch relationship with Deaf and disabled people dovetails with his misogyny, as he later freaks out about Soapy and Milly discussing sex, destroying another outdated stereotype that Deaf and disabled women are asexual. Jay has to get with the times and realize that everything he knows about women, let alone disabled women, is wrong.

When the film's villain, Shan Yu (Alice Wen) traps everyone at a comic convention, she demeans Soapy, saying Soapy needs to fill the void of "the solitude of silence." The joke is on Shan Yu, though, who, after abducting Milly and her friends, uses a KGB sonic disruptor that emits an ear-piercing sound to control them. Soapy's deafness leaves her uncontrolled and gives her the ability to punch Shan Yu and save the day, speaking her only verbal line in the movie: "Hearing is so fucking overrated." Unlike *Children of a Lesser God*, where the desire is to have the Deaf students speak so as to relate to hearing people, Soapy speaks because it's a callback to the previous films wherein Smith's silent character, Silent Bob, is usually the one who speaks a single profound line. I conducted an interview with Smith and his daughter in 2019, and the pair were surprised anyone wanted to talk about Soapy, let alone about her being a Deaf character. Harley Quinn Smith took the time to learn ASL because, while Edmond had an interpreter, it was easier for the two of them to discuss scenes through signing. This is reflected on-screen as Milly performs ASL when talking to Soapy, with Soapy's responses in subtitles. Even when Soapy isn't being directly spoken to, Milly always signs so she is never unclear about what's happening. Smith explained he initially wanted to create more intersectionality by making Soapy a Deaf and transgender character but couldn't find an actress who fit both. While Smith has yet to put another disabled lead in his films, he admitted the significance of representation on-screen: "If you see yourself on that screen, you're gonna tell everybody! Someone sees someone speaking with ASL they say, 'I speak ASL like that!'"

The only other Deaf actress of color of significance in a major film is Lauren Ridloff's Makkari in the Chloe Zhao–directed Marvel movie *The Eternals* (2021). The character is part of a wider ensemble but the Afro-Latina actress is the first Deaf or disabled actress to star in a Marvel feature. Her character doesn't die, though it's unclear if we'll ever see her in subsequent Marvel movies. Ridloff has been a vocal proponent about the need for better inclusion outside of feature films. She hopes that Deaf and disabled performers will one day just be praised for their performances and not for simply existing. "I feel that when people see me, they see a person who is more than just Deaf—I am also Black, Mexican and a woman. I champion for multiple communities. Don't get me wrong—I am proud to represent and advocate for marginalized communities, but I dream of the day when we can just act," Ridloff said in a 2022 interview.

It's incredibly easy to cast authentically and put disabled people of color in movies. This chapter focused on Black and disabled representation, but there are other characters of different ethnicities that exist outside the Black community. Disney's *Rogue One* cast Donnie Yen, a sighted actor, to play Chirrut Imwe, a blind warrior monk who becomes part of the Rebel Alliance helping the team blow up the Death Star. Like John Coffey, Imwe is a magical disabled character whose blindness is heightened, though not quite to the sonar levels of Matt Murdock, another blind superhero, in *Daredevil*. Imwe uses "the Force" to help him get through an area of heavy gunfire unscathed and becomes the sacrificial lamb by killing himself in order for the Rebels to secure the plans for the Death Star. Television is also somewhat more progressive when it comes to including disabled people of color. Actor Daryl Mitchell, a series regular on the AMC series *Fear the Walking Dead*, continues to act after a motorcycle accident made him a wheelchair user. Fans initially thought Mitchell's wheelchair was a prop, he shared with me in a 2021 interview. And actress Alaqua Cox is the first Deaf and Indigenous with a limb difference to lead a Marvel series, playing Maya Lopez in *Echo*. Proof that intersectionality on multiple levels *is* possible.

7 DISABLED HORROR AND THE HORROR OF DISABILITY

The horror genre has always been open to disabled characters and storylines, whether that's actual characters with disabilities or characters possessing significant disabled coding in the narrative. It's a genre that gives opportunities to craft an abundance of disabled characters on-screen, usually played by abled actors, when compared to other genres. However, the interrelationship between disability and fear sells the idea that disability is something to shun or kill and plays on the fears disabled people have about themselves. The silent film era through to the 1930s emphasized eugenics and the belief that physical beauty played a large role in describing a person's soul, but more contemporary horror films offer a greater sense of nuance in terms of characterization, representation, and disabled audiences' reaction where the viewer can at least chart the change in representation. The horror genre has given us disabled characters who are tragic heroes, saints, or grotesque villains, while widening the playing field to give us disabled characters who can be either predators or prey.

Isabel Cristina Pinedo writes in *Recreational Terror: Women and the Pleasures of Horror Film Viewing* that "much as the horror film is an exercise in terror, it is simultaneously an exercise in mastery, in which controlled loss substitutes [for] a loss of control." Watching a horror film isn't just a safe space to be frightened in, but to watch violence and horror from a safe and comfortable distance. This works with regard to the coding of disabled characters in the horror genre as well. An abled viewer watching a horror film looks at a portrayal of disability and safely sees the fantasy in it. They aren't disabled, so the fear is contained. As much as monsters don't exist, so, too, is the belief that disability cannot touch a healthy person. But disability comes with age, pandemics, and general health, so people are brought closer to it every day which puts the viewer on the knife's edge of fantasy versus reality as the remove of watching a horror movie gets blurred.

That being said, some of the most famous and enduring characters in horror films are coded as disabled, so a veneration of monstrosity becomes a veneration of disability. As educator and film critic Robin Wood says, "Normality is threatened by the monster," which, on the surface, implies literal monsters like serial killers Michael Myers in *Halloween* or Ghostface in *Scream*. And if one desperately wants to be normal, the concept of what is abnormal is frightening. But normality also stands for abled. Gwynplaine in *The Man Who Laughs* and Lon Chaney's Phantom and Quasimodo are perceived as monsters threatening "normal," abled society. However, the tragedy in Phantom and Hunchback, as well as Gwynplaine's humanity, turn the concept of who is truly the monster on its head. A horror character with a deformed face for an audience to shriek at is just as easily a pitiable, good-hearted character the viewer roots for. Screenwriters craft monsters, and it's in their hands that a character becomes good or evil, abled or disabled. In the world of slasher films, these pairings are clearly delineated: good = abled and evil = disabled.

Characters like Frankenstein's monster are placed in the villain position because they're different yet they garner the sympathy of the audience. Disability coded characters like Jason Voorhees in *Friday the 13th* and Leatherface in *The Texas Chain Saw Massacre* are villains the audience doesn't sympathize with, either due to a lack of backstory or the gruesomeness of their crimes. We get stray references as to whether the hockey mask–wearing Jason, of the long-running *Friday the 13th* series, is disabled. In the first film, Jason's mother (in case you forgot, the killer) says, "Jason should have been watched every minute," alluding to him requiring special attention. His drowning in Camp Crystal Lake is the direct result of the negligence of a group of horny camp counselors and sets off her need to gain revenge. Her motivations, to a disabled viewer, are somewhat understandable. She's a grieving parent avenging her disabled child. Other allusions to Jason's disabilities include the 1981 sequel, *Friday the 13th: Part 2*, wherein counselor Ginny (Amy Steel) psychoanalyzes Jason and mentions a potential mental disability. "What would he be like today? An out of control psychopath? A frightened retard? A child trapped in a man's body?" It says a lot that those are the three options she foresees: a murderer; a scared, mentally disabled person; or a man-child. More is revealed about this in 1982's *Friday the 13th: Part 3* when it's learned that Jason has hydrocephalus, a condition wherein fluid builds up in one's brain and the resultant pressure causes damage. A person describes Jason as being "so grotesque, he was almost inhuman." It's hard not to root for this guy with such antipathy toward him. If *Friday the 13th* were an '80s action film, the audience would root for Jason to get revenge like he was John Rambo. Even with all this potential explanation, the film hearkens back to the Victorian era to illustrate that a mentally disabled man with facial deformities is something to be destroyed . . . over multiple films.

Tobe Hooper's 1974 feature *Texas Chain Saw Massacre* puts disability in both killer and victim in different ways. Loosely based on the crimes of serial killer Ed Gein, the movie follows a group of friends traveling through Texas as they encounter a family of grave robbers who also run a slaughterhouse. The main muscle of this family is a man referred to only as Leatherface, a hulking figure who wears the skin of others over his own face. As cocreator Kim Henkel said in *The Return of the Texas Chainsaw Massacre: The Documentary*, the initial goal was to make the character more of a human, not a monster, because "the only genuinely frightening thing to people is [other] people." Leatherface is never explicitly called disabled, but his childlike demeanor coupled with his nonverbal abilities situate him as such. Leatherface is incredibly fearful of his family, who berate and abuse him. Because of their cannibalistic and unhinged personas, plus the lack of a backstory for him, Leatherface is a menacing depiction of disability as monstrous and dangerous. But there is still an undercurrent of tragedy found within him. As Henkel and Hooper discussed, early versions of the script gave Leatherface a detailed history and showed him as a torture victim who might have had his face skinned off. They also identified him as a character with mental disabilities. An attempt to make Leatherface somewhat verbal or more compassionate was thought to be "too rational" for a killer. Later sequels attempted to contextualize Leatherface's mentality or penchant for killing. As director Jeff Burr explained while making 1990's *Leatherface: The Texas Chainsaw Massacre III*, his depiction of the character is mentally impaired due to an injury that destroyed Leatherface's ability to speak or think, as well as his face.

Leatherface aside, *The Texas Chain Saw Massacre* has its most overt depiction of disability in one of its lead characters: the wheelchair-using Franklin (Paul A. Pertain). Franklin is the brother to the film's "final girl" Sally Hardesty (Marilyn Burns). In a 2024 social media post I declared that Franklin was the "worst disabled character on-screen ever" and was not surprised it took off online. People had opinions about Franklin. A lot of them. And why wouldn't they? Described in the opening narration as Sally's "invalid" brother, Franklin is slovenly and spends most of his screen time being obnoxious and whining. He's cut by a psychotic hitchhiker at one point and starts bawling to Sally, holding out his hand like a man-baby looking for comfort from his sister-mommy. He's stuck in a bulky hospital wheelchair that clearly isn't made for him, yielding no comfort or support. It probably came from a prop warehouse. (Directors, if it looks like it's from a hospital, it ain't hospitable to the body.) Franklin spends all of his time in his wheelchair, unsecured, in a moving van. How he's not sliding around is the definition of movie magic. As several people commented in response to my thread, "Don't we want to see unlikable disabled characters?" Sure! Franklin doesn't need to be likable. However, the complete absence of character development, even a sketchy one, leaves the audience looking at him purely from a surface perspective. There's little to him, so he's just unlikable for the sake of it. By failing to make him three dimensional, Franklin is unlikable because he is disabled. Plus, it's hard not to wonder whether the script, or Hooper, particularly likes Franklin since within ten minutes of meeting him, we find him peeing in a coffee can on the side of the road before being thrown down a hill and getting dumped out of his wheelchair. He's the Charlie Brown of disability.

I expected a lot of people to agree with me about Franklin. But I was more surprised by how many came to his defense, saying he was a sympathetic character and people should empathize with him. Some said he put a face on the ableism he received from Sally and her friends. It's something I hadn't considered before, and I started to wonder if maybe I'd misjudged him. Hooper and Henkel don't explain how Franklin ended up in a wheelchair. The only thing we know is his family once owned a slaughterhouse. But the post-Vietnam landscape of the movie, coupled with its release year, could imply his disability is the result of the Vietnam War. His constant "woe is me" attitude is similar to Tom Cruise's Ron Kovic in the Vietnam feature *Born on the Fourth of July*. *Texas Chain Saw* was released four years before *Coming Home*, marking the change in perceptions of those with disabilities. So Franklin's unlikability is a distinctive trait when looked at through the lens of disability history up to this point. He's far from a saint, and while he's obnoxious he isn't evil. He flirts with the line of being flawed four years before *Coming Home* gave us disabled characters who were just folks.

Once Sally and her friends settle into an abandoned house to search for gas Franklin is put into all manner of situations that, in any other horror movie, leave him with the word "victim" tattooed on his forehead. The house has stairs so Franklin wanders over dirt floors in his wheelchair screaming for Sally (or anyone) to keep him company. I've had personal experience with being left outside an inaccessible building while everyone else goes off to have fun (sans chainsaw killing), so this is a relatable moment for me. Sally goes in search of help to find out what's happened to her missing friends. Franklin, understandably, doesn't want to be left in the dark alone. People *are* disappearing, after all. He begs Sally to take him with her. Sally cries that she can't push Franklin's wheelchair, presumably because of Franklin's weight and the unwieldy nature of the chair itself. It's hard not to think Sally isn't just trying to dump him. A chronic agitation in movies about disability is the fear of being a burden to others. If you've ever questioned how long you'd survive in a horror movie, a disabled person is thinking, "I'd be the first to go for fear of slowing everyone else down." I think about this a lot (I also have a tendency to panic so I'd definitely be the first picked off). Franklin may be the most unsympathetic disabled character on-screen, but the lack of care or humanity offered by anyone else to him doesn't help. It only justifies Franklin's behavior. To answer the question of how long Franklin would survive in a horror movie, he makes it pretty far. He's the second to last character to die and the only one in a movie called *The Texas Chain Saw Massacre* to be massacred by said chainsaw.

The arrival of the 1980s brought more awareness of disabilities due to increased self-advocacy by disabled people and the eventual passage of the ADA. Horror movies expanded their repertoire of future victims to suit. It's unclear how much of this was motivated by altruism or the desire to create shock value through the killing of disabled people, but where monsters like Leatherface and Jason exist, disabled heroes or those who try to be are there to balance the scales. *Friday the 13th: Part 2* (1981) and *Nightmare on Elm Street 3: Dream Warriors* (1987) have disabled male characters putting disability in the hero role through their normality. They're one of the group: They neither possess unique abilities enhanced by their disability nor are they inherent victims because of it. There's also an egalitarianism in how the films depict their kills, with the disabled characters possessing no better or worse odds of making it out alive than anyone else does.

Nightmare on Elm Street 3 introduces us to Will (Ira Heiden), a wheelchair user and one of several teens living in the Westin Hills Psychiatric Hospital. Will is there after attempting suicide in order to escape the murderous serial killer Freddy Krueger (Robert Englund) who haunts his dreams. As with all the kids in Westin Hills, Will has one characteristic other than being a wheelchair user: He's a nerd who enjoys fantasy-based games. (*Dungeons and Dragons* was a big deal at the time.) Will is an average teen who happens to use a wheelchair. And because he's in a hospital we can excuse him using a bulky, noncustom wheelchair rather than his own. When *Nightmare on Elm Street 3* was in the script phase, Will was not originally written as a wheelchair user. When or why that changed is unknown, but it shows how easy it is to write a disabled character in any type of narrative. A disabled person doesn't have to exist strictly in a story about disability. Plop them into a horror movie and see what happens!

Once the teens band together to enter the dream world to destroy Freddy for good, the movie makes a fatal error by creating what they think is disabled wish fulfillment. The teens discuss what strengths they bring to the dream versions of themselves, advantages that could destroy Freddy once and for all. Will's dream strength is that he can do magic and walk. Many disabled people, myself included, will tell you they don't dream of themselves in their wheelchair. Not even Superman himself, Christopher Reeve, did. But tropes that involve cures or the mystical erasure of disability give viewers the idea that no matter how comfortable a disabled person is in their own skin, they will *always* wish they weren't disabled at all. This happens most often in disabled biopics or melodramas. *The Theory of Everything*, *Breathe*, and *Stronger* are perfect examples, featuring scenes where the mobility-affected person stands up or does something from their old life to remind audiences of what they used to be like. Fantasy features in which disability can be washed away also happen in the movie genre of make-believe. The 2019 comic book movie *Shazam!* has crutch user Freddy Freeman (Jack Dylan Grazer) become a grown adult/superhero through wizardry. The wizard's magic makes him reach his "full potential" which, in this case, means he's cured of his disability. No doubt the character, created in 1941, transforming from a disabled boy into an able-bodied superhero gave American men hope post-WWII, but in 2019 it says one's true self is achieved solely by being non-disabled.

It's ironic that *Dream Warriors* uses the magic cure trope at all because it doesn't increase Will's chances of survival once he's in the dream realm. Unlike Franklin and his chainsaw death, Will's demise isn't eventful nor is it connected to his disability. This in spite of Freddy joking, "It's the chair for you, kid!" At least Will doesn't die first. But because the horror genre is filled with disability so often, in a weird way Will's death is refreshing. He and the other kids are unified by death and fear. Freddy making the joke about Will's wheelchair, which isn't part of the scene nor his death, speaks more to Will's subconscious fears of confinement and the unspoken belief that society looks down on him because he's disabled. The fact that *Dream Warriors* is so blunt in its situating of Will—*he's in a wheelchair, this is how it happened*—is indicative of what good representation can be. A character is disabled, and that's it.

Friday the 13th: Part 2 is another example of inserting disabled characters into the horror world and situating them as no different from their cinematic peers. They all become bloody notches on a serial killer's belt. Mark (Tom McBride) is a good-looking, confident guy with an athletic build and, like any good-looking disabled guy, his disability is the result of him being a masculine daredevil. He tells one of the other Camp Crystal Lake counselors he was hurt in a motorcycle accident. But don't worry, "I don't intend to be in this thing [a wheelchair] all my life," he says. It's a throwaway line that stinks of ableism because of how unnecessary it is, as if to remind the audience that they should empathize with Mark because he doesn't want to be disabled and doesn't plan to be forever. God forbid he just be an athlete who uses a wheelchair and is fine with it. But I appreciate everything else about Mark so much this isn't a significant detriment.

What makes Mark different from Will is his sexuality. Disabled people are portrayed in movies as asexual or pining for love and intimacy that they never find. In a franchise known for its gratuitous sex scenes, *Friday the 13th: Part 2* is pretty chaste. Only one couple gets impaled while engaging in sexual activity! Mark's good looks, and the fact that horror movies of the 1980s sold themselves on the amount of teens having sex in them, put him in a position where he's able to be flirtatious and have desires that are reciprocated by others. He and fellow counselor Vickie (Lauren-Marie Taylor) get a solid make-out session and are on their way to having sex before that pesky Jason Voorhees comes a-calling. Mark dies before the sex is had, but it has nothing to do with his disability, it's just the hazard of being in a horror movie. If there's anything gratuitous in *Friday the 13th: Part 2* it's Mark's death. Cited by horror lovers as one of the most brutal demises in the franchise, Mark takes Jason's iconic machete to the face before falling backward, in his wheelchair, out the cabin door and down a huge stone staircase that's apparently been hiding off-camera the entire movie. It's a bit excessive. Why do horror films feel the need to go the extra mile on disabled deaths? Is it because the death of a disabled character is seen as edgy? Maybe it's an attempt to surprise able-bodied audiences or use the shock value to catch them off guard. The disabled's on-screen history of helplessness and victimhood puts them in the same category as children and animals: off-limits for slashers. They are an invisible line in the sand, a group of untouchables due to their perceived purity or the fact that they're easier prey. Mark, Will, and Franklin are on the same metaphorical footing as their abled friends. However, Mark and Will are relatable to disabled viewers because they understand their limitations and use what they have at their disposal. If death is the great equalizer, it's nice to see characters like them not depicted as overly weak or inferior.

Audrey Hepburn is a blind woman terrorized in *Wait Until Dark* (1967). Moviepix / Screen Archives / Getty Images

The final girl—the female survivor left to confront the killer at the end of a horror movie—is a familiar trope. When it comes to disabled final girls, there aren't many to choose from. Those who do exist mark a shift toward more contemporary looks at disabled women in general. The 1967 film *Wait Until Dark* stars Audrey Hepburn as Susy, a blind woman set upon by a gang of robbers who believe she's holding a doll filled with heroin in her apartment. Hepburn's character doesn't adhere to the final girl stereotype specifically, but her inclusion here sets the foundation for where disabled final girls have gone. *Wait Until Dark* is a brilliant movie but it suffers from the "pretty disabilities" stereotype: female characters who have invisible disabilities so the audience can still lust over the beautiful (and non-disabled) actress.

Hepburn, alongside director Terence Young, did her homework as best as she could. She visited a blind school and learned enough Braille so she could convincingly look as if she was reading and writing it. A scene wherein Susy writes her phone number down in Braille came directly from this research. But like the saintly sweet and nonsighted Dea in *The Man Who Laughs*, Susy is sweet and gorgeous and acts like a child, particularly in her interactions with her sighted husband Sam (Efrem Zimbalist Jr.). Lines like "I was the best in blind school today" or "I'll be the one reading *Peter Rabbit* in Braille" sound more like a child talking to a parent than a wife to her husband. Sam falls into the paternal role so aggressively that he comes off like a toxic partner, a stark reminder that disabled women experience intimate partner violence at a rate 40 percent higher than non-disabled women. Sam acts under the guise that he's helping Susy to become independent. Sam goes so far as to refuse to help Susy do basic things around the house. When she drops something on the floor, he makes her crawl on her hands and knees to find it. When a neighbor offers to help Susy take out the garbage, she tells them, "I'm supposed to be learning total self-sufficiency."

It's a blurry line between self-sufficiency and subservience. Susy and Sam's "don't help me" attitude manifests in the real world. I've had people watch me struggle to open a door or reach something on a high shelf. Their excuse: "I know disabled people don't like to be helped." Susy is told she has to be the "world's champion blind lady," setting the standard that all disabled people need to prove how accomplished they are at everyday tasks, that they've overcome their disability and/or it doesn't impede their ability to function. It's a means of showing they aren't a burden and, again, are of use. Susy reiterates throughout the movie how grateful she is for what little help she's given, or not given. When teenage neighbor Gloria (Julie Herrod) gets angry at her and starts breaking things, it is *Susy* who apologizes for her blindness, saying that it makes her angry. Never mind that this child trashed her apartment! Don't worry, Gloria's half-assed nonapology is that she threw things she knew weren't fragile.

Alan Arkin's villainous Roat brings *Wait Until Dark* into the horror world. He and his cohorts invade Susy's apartment, preying on her vulnerabilities and manipulating her. Roat wears different disguises throughout the film even after knowing Susy is blind. She's never going to notice he's the same person, but Roat enjoys playing with her. He also parallels Susy in being metaphorically blind by wearing sunglasses inside. Susy is physically blind while Roat tries to blind her to his intentions but fails to see he's underestimating her. When Roat decides to kill Susy she undermines him by removing every light source in the house, trying to place them on an equal playing field. This specific gimmick was promoted in ads for *Wait Until Dark* saying, "During the last eight minutes of this picture the theatre will be darkened to the legal limit, to heighten the terror of the breathtaking climax which takes place in nearly total darkness on the screen." Late-arriving patrons wouldn't be seated during the film's finale, and those who were smoking (which was allowed at the time) were urged to avoid lighting up during the scene. The climax is amazing and the film's highlight. The studios saw it as a means of putting the audience in the shoes of a blind person to sell the terror of being blind and threatened. Arkin himself knew audiences would hate his character, not because Susy is blind but because "you don't get nominated for being mean to Audrey Hepburn."

The 1962 feature *What Ever Happened to Baby Jane?* takes the opposite route as *Wait Until Dark*. Unlike the beautifully blind Audrey Hepburn, *Baby Jane* brings us into the world of hagsploitation, a horror subgenre featuring formerly glamorous actresses playing unhinged, and unattractive, psychopaths. The horror is derived from seeing two women over the age of fifty act. *Baby Jane* is also a frightening look at the power struggles in interabled (wherein one person is disabled and the other isn't) families and how this can manifest in disabled abuse. Joan Crawford and Bette Davis play sisters Blanche and Jane Hudson, respectively. Jane is a once-successful child star who has become the live-in caretaker to her wheelchair-using sister, Blanche. The pair have a river of grievances against each other. Jane was a spoiled child who received the love and attention of their father but failed to become a star as an adult. She resents her sister because Blanche grew into a successful actress. The film begins with a car accident, with Jane taking the blame for being behind the wheel and causing her sister's disability.

The disabled caretaking plotline and its true horrors flew under the radar. Abled audiences went to *What Ever Happened to Baby Jane?* to gleefully watch two once A-list actresses, Davis and Crawford, look grotesque and snipe at each other. The latter element was enhanced by a marketing campaign that heightened a real-life feud between the pair. Blanche is a victim trapped in a literal tower, the second floor of the house she lives in with Jane. Blanche shows gratitude and kindness to Jane, looking the other way at Jane's flagrant spending and alcoholism. Jane's alcoholism itself is fueled as much by guilt over the accident as by resentment for her dependence on Blanche for financial security. Jane, however, doesn't see Blanche as working in her best interest. She believes Blanche is selfish and uses her disability to control others. "Press a button, ring a bell and you think the whole damn world comes to you," she says. Jane is the caretaker from hell, a stereotype in itself, making a disabled viewer fear every caretaker is abusive. Elder abuse stats show two out of three caregivers commit some form of abuse. When Blanche makes plans to sell the house and live on her own, independently, she must "find a place for [Jane]" as if Jane is the disabled one.

Jane sees herself as Blanche's jailer and mother, with an almost godlike sense of her own power. She tells Blanche, "Now you have to depend on me for your food." Food becomes what Jane uses to torment Blanche, gaslighting her into thinking everything Blanche is served is tainted. Jane tries to feed Blanche a dead rat as well as Blanche's own pet parakeet. Blanche eventually stops eating altogether and becomes malnourished. Jane makes no bones about the fact that she's doing this to Blanche because of her sister's disability. Blanche says, "You wouldn't be able to do these awful things to me if I weren't in this chair" to which Jane responds, "But you are! You are in this chair!" The movie ends with the two eventually reconciling through Blanche's confession that she disabled herself by intentionally crashing her car, breaking her spin when the car slammed into the gates of her house and crawling out to stage her body near the gates to let Jane take the fall. It's presented as a balancing of the scales, but it only goes so far as it's unable to undo the abuse Blanche suffers.

Several years passed before another disabled heroine in the horror genre graced movie screens and we have Mark from *Friday the 13th: Part 2* to thank for it. Mark influenced director and screenwriter Don Mancini to create Nica Pierce, the final girl/leading lady of his 2013 features *Curse of Chucky* and its 2017 follow-up *Cult of Chucky*, spin-off sequels to Mancini's long-running series about Chucky the killer doll. "Since we were rebooting [the series] I needed to create a new leading lady, a new heroine for the franchise," Mancini said in a 2018 interview. "The initial thing was, 'How do I make this interesting and set it apart from the norm?'" Mancini thought *Friday the 13th*'s handsome and confident Mark was an interesting character who wasn't a "woe is me" disabled guy. Mancini used that to write a heroine who was like everyone else but happened to use a wheelchair. "My whole career people [have said], 'Oh, well, Chucky's not scary. You can just kick him,'" said Mancini. "So my initial impulse was, Okay, well I'll create a character who can't resort to that and she has to get bolder, braver and more ingenious in how she fights him."

It's easy to assume Nica (played by Fiona Dourif) is easy pickings, being a woman and disabled. Not exactly a group combo in this genre. She's a wheelchair user who's dropped out of college, not because of her disability but after being forced to care for her dependent mom. The two live in a large mansion.

Nica is similar to *Friday the 13th*'s Mark, particularly in her ability to be sexually desired *and* have those feelings reciprocated, but she is not a carbon copy. Nica doesn't have sex in this first film, but in the 2017 sequel, she has sex with a fellow patient in the hospital she's in, a scene Mancini said gave female executives pause for the fact that Nica has sex while in her wheelchair. A bridge too far, apparently. Fiona Dourif is able bodied, as well as conventionally attractive and aesthetically non-disabled in appearance, but the character sets a precedent for what is possible. It's an interesting return to the dichotomy between eugenics and sexuality. Disabled women don't engage in sex on-screen, because sex begets babies and eugenicists didn't want disabled children. Remember the continued reiteration that Leah in *Sign of the Ram* is barren. Everyone around Nica looks at her as something to either pity or control. Nica's mother, who struggles with depression and mental illness, shows her ableism immediately regarding her daughter's sexuality. She tells Nica that the mail carrier flirting with her is "just being nice." This undermining nature continues upon the arrival of Nica's older sister Barbara (Danielle Bisutti). The call, in a way, is coming from inside the house.

The set design and script do a lot to craft Nica's disability as authentically as possible. Nica's first scene sees her rock a custom wheelchair, which Mancini saw as a priority he wanted to get 100 percent right. "We learned so much about wheelchairs! Until I did this I didn't know anything about wheelchairs," said Mancini. If you look at the chair, you'll notice it's built for her specific body shape, offers back support, and is small and lightweight for her to self-propel and get around the giant house easily. It also comes in handy to quickly get away from a serial killing doll. The camera lingers on specific things that show the house is designed to accommodate her, from a shower chair in the bathroom to lowered counters in the kitchen. A massive elevator runs through the center of the two-story house to allow her full access—and create avenues for horror. Abled or not, who isn't afraid of being trapped, in the dark, in an elevator? Unlike Mark and Will, who mention they became disabled late in life, a flashback plays with the concept of Nica being disabled from birth. Chucky, in his human form (played by Fiona Dourif's father, Brad) kidnaps Nica's mom out of an obsessive love for her. Enraged that his feelings aren't reciprocated, he pierces her pregnant stomach with a knife. There's two ways to take this moment: The knife cut is what makes Nica disabled or she was disabled already. Nica will never know if she was born that way or not, though she tells Chucky, "I was born this way," proof that she accepts who she is. This moment is a rallying cry for every disabled person who has had to explain that an accident didn't change their life or that they were injured in some weird accident only rich people engage in.

This is a *Chucky* movie, but the script's true horror comes from how Nica's family think she's helpless and that their actions are a kindness to her. Barb tells Nica that their mother should have been the one taking care of her, not the other way around. Barb says everything with a smile on her face, truly thinking she's helping her sister while also showing her own resentment of her. But Barbara has ulterior motives in all this. Her goal is to convince Nica to sell the house after their mother's mysterious death and for Nica to live in an assisted living center. As Barbara explains, she doesn't want to "deprive" her own daughter of a good education which could be funded through the sale of Nica's home. Nica has no need for the money, according to her sister, especially since Nica has no children of her own and, as a disabled woman, is not expected to as far as Barb's concerned. Barb goes so far as to say that Nica must be jealous because Barbara is able bodied and "because I have a life" while bemoaning that "she [Nica] needs my help and she resents me for it." A disabled fear is laid bare: that all abled people see us as jealous, resentful, and bitter. That, deep down, the abled expect to "take care of us" in a way they see fit, whether that's being placed in a home or, in this case, massacred by a killer doll. For all of Barbara's control, the movie continues to show off Nica's independence, much of which Barb knows nothing about because she hasn't spent any significant time with her. She's surprised Nica knows how to cook, that she has interests, and is an average young woman.

In the 2017 sequel *Cult of Chucky*, Barb's attempt to take Nica's home, ironically, ends up succeeding. Mind you, Barb doesn't make it out of the first film alive. Regardless, Nica is placed in a mental institution after being blamed for the murder of her family in *Curse*. *Curse of Chucky* set up Nica as a character to tell a story of a disabled heroine who finds her own strength despite what others presume about her and her disability. *Cult of Chucky* continues to flesh out Nica as a character and situate her as a true disabled horror heroine à la Neve Campbell's Sidney Prescott in the *Scream* franchise or Jamie Lee Curtis in *Halloween*. Removing Nica's disability wouldn't affect the story one bit. This is what I'm talking about when people ask me what good representation looks like. Casting is simple. It's so simple that most directors and producers should just do it so we can shut up about it. There's no need to make disability central to the narrative, and nearly every narrative can have disability included.

Nica is surrounded by characters with different limitations in the hospital. Everyone's on the same level because they all have various flaws that make them prime victim material. It is Nica, however, who is the only one unable to hide her limitations. *Cult of Chucky*'s ending holds much in common with *Nightmare on Elm Street 3: Dream Warriors* although Mancini plays with consent and (literal) bodily autonomy. Nica is possessed by Chucky and, through him, gains the ability to walk. (Don't worry about how her bones or muscles would hold her up after decades of atrophy.) The magical cure is usually situated as being of benefit to the disabled character, transitioning them from disabled to abled because they desperately want to be. Here, Nica is possessed by a serial killer against her will who uses her body however he likes. It's body horror on multiple levels. Nica's body is invaded by an able-bodied person who can physically control her, as well as being a woman possessed by a man who would exploit her body for his own purposes. When the film series transitioned into a TV show in 2021 to continue the events laid out in the two movies, Nica is returned to her disabled body. It's not sold as a regression to a life she doesn't want but rather gives her back full ownership of her person and identity.

Disabled women in victim positions in horror movies if they're willing use their ingenuity and their adaptations to get the best of an attacker who presumes they're easy pickings. *Wait Until Dark* has Susy put her and Roat on similar levels by removing the lights in the apartment. Nica in *Curse of Chucky* takes an ax to her paralyzed legs to gain an advantage over Chucky that gives her an opportunity to stab him and end the movie. Mike Flanagan's 2016 film *Hush* picks up where Audrey Hepburn's Susy left off, creating a heroine who is self-sufficient and a total badass. *Hush* follows Deaf writer Maddie (Kate Siegel) who has placed herself in self-imposed isolation in a remote cabin in the woods as she finishes her latest book. When a masked killer, known only as The Man (John Gallagher Jr.), arrives intent on killing her, Maddie has to figure out a way to survive.

Like Nica in *Chucky*, Maddie is highly independent, a successful author, and has a home adapted to her life as a Deaf individual. She communicates via text and has smoke alarms that come with lights and noises loud enough to cause vibrations, an important plot device used later on. Maddie was deafened at thirteen after a bout of bacterial meningitis. This puts her in the able-bodied buffer position and allows Siegel to narrate Maddie's inner monologue as she writes her novel, and later attempts to conjure up a way to defeat The Man. However, as Siegel and Flanagan said in a 2020 article this decision was both a means to isolate Maddie further by placing her as an outsider to the Deaf community and also based on the limitations of the budget. And, considering how this book has laid out the fact that disabled movies aren't perfect, this is a concession I, personally, am okay with while understanding that Deaf people no doubt would feel differently.

The way The Man fetishizes Maddie's deafness and his way of toying with her makes him seem almost turned on by how defenseless she is. Think of it as if the dynamic between Chaplin's Tramp and the Blind Flower Girl in *City Lights*, or Gwynplaine and Duchess Josiana in *The Man Who Laughs*, were more disturbing. There's nothing romantic here. The Man doesn't see Maddie's blindness as something to celebrate but as something to use to torture her. The fact that the killer in *Hush* is named The Man also puts a point on the fact that he misogynistically believes he's superior to Maddie. The Man tells her at one point that he wants to "hear [her] scream," equating noise with submission and adding in an unspoken heavy note of implied sexual violence. But knowing all this, Maddie uses her deafness as a strength. "He's bigger, strong and faster," Maddie verbalizes. "And he has the advantage: He can hear you." As in *Wait Until Dark*, Maddie turns the adaptations she employs in her life into weapons. She uses the strobe effects of her fire alarm to disorient The Man. She isn't the world's champion Deaf woman, like Susy is for blindness, but works with what she has handy. *Hush* ends with Maddie sitting down with her cat and contemplating how she's survived. We don't root for Maddie because she lived *despite the odds*. We root for her because she's a woman who bested a man who thought she was prey. She doesn't express gratitude or any other distinct emotion but just sits in front of the audience as if to say "I survived." She's the Deaf final girl worth celebrating.

The *Quiet Place* franchise is another world where deafness is central to the narrative. Deaf actress Millicent Simmons and her character Regan are similar to Maddie from *Hush*. *A Quiet Place* integrates Regan's deafness into the narrative but flirts with making Regan a superhero whose deafness is a power used to destroy the alien creatures who are attracted to sound and have taken over Earth. Her being unable to hear is a great unifier since people are no longer able to make noise at the risk of attracting the aliens. But it's never clear if her family used ASL in their daily communications with Regan before the creatures arrived or if they only learned once her cochlear implant stops working. The fact that her father, Lee (John Krasinski), spends his time trying to fix the implant implies the latter. Lee assumes Regan needs her hearing in order to survive in the world they live in. That she'll have a better advantage if she can hear when things are happening. Regan may not need cochlear implants to survive, but they are something that will benefit her survival in the future. This in spite of his wife, Evelyn (Emily Blunt) telling him Regan knows how to take care of herself.

Strip away the aliens and the main conflict between Regan and her dad is the age-old ableist belief that she needs to have the same advantages as everyone else to "get along" in the world, to quote *Children of a Lesser God*. Caretakers of Deaf and disabled people in movies often think they know better than the actual Deaf and disabled person they spend their days with. In the end, it is the feedback from Regan's cochlear implants that repel and kill the creatures. Deaf advocates at the time criticized the movie's portrayal of cochlear implants, explaining that they don't make noise and the screenwriters simply conflated them with hearing aids. Microphones and speakers would, in theory, produce the same effect. Going this route of using Regan's deafness as a superpower riffs on the magical disabled trope, with Regan magically possessing the power to destroy the creatures, like the Deaf equivalent of the Ark of the Covenant.

The line between integrating disability into a horror narrative and using a disabled character to create horror is a fine one. Director Ari Aster utilized disability in two of his films: 2018's *Hereditary* and 2019's *Midsommar* with both films implementing a disabled character as a conduit for evil. *Hereditary*'s Charlie (Milly Shapiro) is a quiet young girl with unspecified mental disabilities who suffers one of the most gruesome deaths on-screen due to an allergic reaction to peanuts. As her brother drives her to the hospital, she attempts to get air by sticking her head out a car window and is decapitated when the car comes too close to a telephone pole. In a 2019 interview with Aster, he explained that it was never explicitly stated that Charlie was disabled. But actress Milly Shapiro has cleidocranial dysostosis, a skeletal disability. Regardless of directorial intent, the character is disabled coded. She's unable to communicate with her family and others, which is later revealed to be the result of her body being a vessel for possession.

Aster's follow-up, *Midsommar*, is more overt with its usage of disability in the character of Ruben (Levente Puczkó-Smith), a disfigured and mentally disabled prophet for a group of Swedish cult members. Ruben spends his time drawing alleged prophecies for the community and doesn't have any outside life. "Ruben . . . is a very important character," Aster said in 2019. "He's important more as a symbol, as an idea, than he is even as a character. There is politics woven into the film and Ruben is about as close as we get to that being articulated explicitly." There could be something interesting said about a cult taking the drawings of a mentally disabled man as divine gospel, but this is never unpacked nor is it used in a way to raise the character above being present for shock value. As writer James Moore said in a 2019 article, "Films like Aster's feed into the perception of disabled people as abnormal, subhuman and scary, and sadly people lash out at those which they find scary, even when they've no need to." Moore's statement that the perception of disabled people as scary and how that, in turn, causes audiences to lash out at those they find scary is true, especially if you're watching horror movies as a disabled person. A horror film's goal is to frighten and make an audience's heart race, but that same horror is bound up within specific fears for disabled viewers, turning the horror back onto them. Disability coding is a slippery slope. Directors who don't understand disabled history perpetuate unfortunate stereotypes.

I didn't have any other disabled people in my life, so movies about disability became my way into learning about who I was. As a child, horror movies about grotesque, disfigured monsters left me wondering if that was what adulthood as a disabled person looked like. I didn't realize it growing up, but while I was the only disabled person in my family and at my school, the ableism of others rubbed off on me.

The Man Who Laughs isn't a horror movie. It's a romantic drama. Yet there is something fearful in Gwynplaine's look that connects on a subconscious level to a disabled viewer because of how medicalized he is. His grin is illegally carved onto his face, reminiscent of the grand tradition of scientific experimentation on disabled bodies. It brings us back, yet again, to the world of eugenics and its desire to exterminate disabled people. It also puts a literal face on the idea that disabled people are perpetually happy and grateful for being allowed to exist in society. What's more frightening than having a literal grin pasted on you that masks your true inner anguish? Dea even comments on this: "It's wonderful how my Gwynplaine makes people laugh—even when he's sad." Dea even has her own internalized ableism because she can't see Gwynplaine's face due to her blindness. Instead, she thinks of how he brings joy to others through suppressing his personal pain. There are three other movies that terrified me as a child and crafted my self-conscious response to disability. Who knows how I'd take to these movies, or to myself, if I had more positive disabled examples to balance them out. With no good portrayals to counteract them, the physical shock of seeing disabled bodies, even ones coded as such, built a distance between myself and the character, to create its own type of terror.

The character who is the root of every fear and neurosis I have about disability is Zelda from Stephen King's novel *Pet Sematary*, and its 1989 film adaptation. The book and movie follow the Creed family who deal with a personal tragedy that sees patriarch Louis (Dale Midkiff) reanimate his dead son. Alongside this, there's a subplot that involves Louis's wife Rachel (Denise Crosby) and the trauma she endures from living with and witnessing the death of her disabled sister Zelda (Andrew Hubatsek). People forget how much aesthetics play into how we look at disability, whether a disabled person can hide it or pass for abled, or whether you're too disabled for others to feel comfortable. Zelda brings this all together. Zelda suffers from spinal meningitis and dies before the main events of the film. We meet her in flashback, practically a living skeleton with a deformed spine. A male actor plays Zelda to create an additional disconnect between the audience and the character. As I wrote in a 2022 article about my changing thoughts on the movie, "Growing up with a bone disability, Zelda utterly terrified me because I had no other disabled women, on screens large or small, to compare her to. I wasn't just scared of Zelda because the movie portrayed her as a villain. I was scared because I worried *this* is what disabled women ended up [looking] like. This is what I was going to end up [looking] like." Rachel feels she's haunted (or cursed) by Zelda because of Rachel's resentment at her sister's disability and the stress and trauma she caused in Zelda's life. Rachel's guilt at her ableism is apparent but is hard to empathize with as a disabled viewer. As she recounts Zelda's final hours alive, Rachel admits she hoped her sister would die to spare their family additional pain. When Zelda finally passes, Rachel declares, "They thought I was crying, but I was laughing." Can't imagine why she thinks she's haunted.

The 2019 remake of *Pet Sematary* treats Zelda worse by turning her into a CGI monster. The audience is meant to root for her death, which isn't a natural result of her meningitis but from being thrown down a laundry chute.

In talking through my own fears of Zelda, I realized how she and I were in the same leaky boat together, even though she is a fictional character. Rachel Creed is an ableist, and while the narrative sides with her I saw how Zelda was doomed to a life of death and sadness because her family let her down. After several years, I've come to sympathize with Zelda and appreciate her. She is a villain because of how an ableist society chooses to look at her. Zelda's worthy of love no different than Frankenstein's monster or Gwynplaine. I now lovingly refer to her as my dear disabled sister, Zelda.

Edward Scissorhands (1990) gives us a disabled fairy tale about a shy young man with scissors for hands. Sunset Boulevard / Corbis via Getty Images

Another disabled figure it took years for me to embrace was the title character of Tim Burton's dark, modern fairy tale, 1991 film *Edward Scissorhands*. *Edward Scissorhands* is not a horror movie per se but the tragic tale of the man with scissors for hands creeped me out because of how it juxtaposed Edward's disability with his outward appearance: the dark circles under his eyes and pale white skin, which are now the highlights of numerous Tim Burton–created characters. The extremely exaggerated appearance is a lot, particularly for someone who isn't seeing nearly enough good disabled representation. Edward in his all-black leather outfit with his wild hair is a visual culture shock, especially in comparison to the pastel world of the burbs he moves into. Johnny Depp, making another appearance in this book, plays the title character "born" with scissors for hands who comes down from his castle to live with the kindhearted Boggs family. Once there, he learns about the world and its prejudices and also falls in love with the Boggses' daughter, Kim (Winona Ryder).

Edward Scissorhands does an interesting job of enhancing its disabled coding by examining the little nuances of disability. Edward identifies as disabled, the camera capturing clippings he's saved from newspapers about other people like him. The headlines shout out things like "Boy without eyes reads with his hands." Edward starts the narrative with a sense of incompleteness typical of internalized ableism. He thinks he lacks something that will make him whole, that will make him abled. Edward tells Peg Boggs (Dianne Wiest) upon meeting her that he's "not finished," that his creator/father (Vincent Price) meant to complete him by crafting him a pair of conventional hands but died before they were completed. Edward tries to come to terms with this throughout the movie. Others offer him unsolicited solutions, including one person saying they know "a doctor who could help you," which excites Edward.

Edward shakes up the staid neighborhood because he's a newcomer, an invader of sorts, into their calm, organized suburban bubble. But like any good disabled character, he's of use to the abled residents, taking on various odd jobs like dog groomer, hair stylist, and gardener. There is a desire to put disabled people into categories, marking them as "good" disabled people—those who have something to offer—and those who are "bad" or are just average. I've been told I'm "unlike" other disabled people, that I'm somehow different because I'm articulate or because my appearance or intelligence doesn't make them uncomfortable. I'm the exception to other disabled people for them because they deign to know me.

The Boggses' neighbors don't want him to acknowledge or change his disability; they are fascinated with him because of it. They don't have any excitement in their own lives, so they put him on the same pedestal as the circus performers in *Freaks* or Gwynplaine in *The Man Who Laughs*. To them, he is something to gawk at while patting themselves on the back for "accepting" him. Joyce (Kathy Baker), one of the neighborhood busybodies tells Edward that he's not "handicapped" but rather that he's "exceptional." To her, one denotes limitation and the other shows that he's one of a kind (and worthy of her attention). Overly religious neighbor Esmeralda (O-Lan Jones) calls Edward a "perversion of nature," which the neighbors chuckle at and don't take seriously.

Edward's fame because of his disability makes his life appear fun. Standing out from the crowd, to the average person, presumably gives him benefits. When Edward goes on a TV talk show, someone in the crowd says, "But if you had regular hands, you'd be just like everyone else. You wouldn't be special." Never mind that he is dependent on others and struggles to find his place in society. When the world is designed to see you as the exception and not the rule, it leads to exclusion. Being special doesn't create access to businesses or integrate disability into society. More often than not, it's a way to keep the disabled out. Edward's exceptionalism opens the door for the neighborhood women, especially Joyce, the film's stand-in for the wicked witch, to fetishize and sexualize him.

Consent is questionably obtained in disabled narratives, if it's brought up at all. Joyce tries to seduce Edward when they're alone together. The scene concludes on a humorous note with the chair the two of them are sitting on tips over, but it's clear Edward has rejected Joyce and is unclear on what has occurred. She calls out to him as he leaves the shop, "Edward, you can't do that." Because sexual relationships with disabled characters are a rarity in modern films, and were nearly nonexistent in 1991 on-screen, Joyce telling Edward "[he] can't do that" hints at the idea that he should be grateful for her sexual interest in him. He should be happy she's willing to look beyond his disability and engage in a relationship with him. What disabled man, or disabled person in general, dares to reject an abled person who shows interest?

For as warm and welcoming as the Boggses are bringing Edward into their home, even they are not immune from using Edward. They just couch it as being in his best interest. In the hopes of fixing Edward's scarred face—the result of his accidentally cutting himself throughout his life—Peg calls the head of the Avon company where she works to get tips on how to fix his skin. Peg tells Edward she never had a reason to call the head of Avon before until she met him. Later, Kim coerces Edward to break into her boyfriend's house to steal some money. The Boggses see Edward as a child, and even though Kim and Peg aren't malicious in their use of Edward, their unconscious exploitation of him shows that even in the closest of families, the power dynamics between the abled and disabled are ever present.

The neighborhood starts to think Edward is a threat. Joyce goes so far as to feign "worry" about Kim's safety in the house, as if Edward is a sexual predator. She calls back to their previous interaction in the beauty shop, couching it as Edward having attacked her. Peg tells Kim that "it might be best if he goes back up there [to his castle] because at least up there he's safe." Edward, once perceived as exceptional, is now a dangerous monster. Everyone starts looking for Edward, like any good angry mob. An old man on his porch asks if they've found "that cripple." Where Edward was once accepted enough for the neighbors to use polite terms like "handicapped" or "exceptional," by the end they show how they really feel about him: They see him as a reviled cripple. Edward returns to live in his castle alone, a bittersweet conclusion that continues to situate two worlds: one for the abled and one for the disabled.

8 PRETTY DISABILITIES

I don't know who the first disabled woman I ever saw on-screen was. I'm sure there was one, and I'm also sure that she wasn't played by a disabled actress. My body was different from my peers. I was a teenage girl who couldn't hide her disability. So seeing realistic depictions of disabled women in the movies might have saved me thousands in therapy bills if they were out there. Seeing beautiful disabled women (played by non-disabled women) who were five feet seven and sitting down in a wheelchair made me believe that if I didn't look like that, I was doomed. I was a small, compact teen so if a proportionate, conventionally attractive woman like Susan Peters in *Sign of the Ram* can't keep the love of a man looking like she did, how could any disabled woman?

Like the world of fashion, Hollywood is an industry focused on aesthetics, and while people are aware of how media perceptions of body image affect abled children and teens, there's little written about how they specifically affect disabled teens. According to the 2024 Annenberg Initiative study, 71.7 percent of disabled characters on-screen are men, a 2.6 percent increase from the previous year. Movies teach us how to act around others. They also detail how we view ourselves. Being a teenager is riddled with judgment about one's self-worth and self-esteem, so movies teach us how to navigate rites of passage like dating, first kisses, first sexual experiences. As disabled girls and women remain limited in entertainment, it leaves generations of real disabled girls and women feeling more adrift than they already are. But disability in film is a man's game, and if disabled women are around their stories are couched in the romantic genre where the emphasis is on their looks. Those with invisible disabilities in movies have the opportunity to keep their aesthetic beauty intact (which allows them to pass for abled), like Marlee Matlin's Sarah in *Children of a Lesser God*. Those who don't conform are horror creations, like Zelda in *Pet Sematary*, with little in between.

Disabled women in movies have "pretty disabilities." If you're a *Wicked* fan, you know this as the "beautifully tragic and tragically beautiful" principle. A character with pretty disabilities is a woman whose disability doesn't conflict with her good looks. Her disability goes hand in hand with her attractiveness and how she is perceived and desired (if at all) by the opposite sex. Pretty disabled women are always heterosexual or in heterosexual relationships, because you can't have a disabled woman also be a queer character. Most of the pretty disabilities these women deal with are facial disfigurements, elevated to the same level as a physical disability because they limit the character's opportunities to interact with the outside world and are determined by the screenwriters making them not conventionally beautiful. Examples like this include Olivia Cooke's Art3mis in *Ready Player One*, Piper Laurie's Sarah in *The Hustler*, and Ingrid Bergman and Joan Crawford in the 1938 and 1941 interpretations of *A Woman's Face*. Those with invisible disabilities like deafness or blindness are tragic beauties who are missing a sense to interact with others while retaining their attractiveness so the non-disabled actress can keep her looks the same. This includes Jane Wyman's performance as a Deaf girl in 1948's *Johnny Belinda* and her role as a blind woman in 1954's *Magnificent Obsession*, and don't forget Stacy, the New York diabetic in Ann M. Martin's *Baby-Sitters Club* books and its subsequent 1995 feature film.

Like the outdated stereotype of a woman being attractive to a man once her glasses are removed, the presumption is that a simple thing like having their beauty validated by an abled man will change the disabled woman's life. Virginia Cherrill's blind flower girl in Charlie Chaplin's *City Lights* establishes the pattern of how disabled women are shown in movies, and in order to discuss it, we need to go back to some old friends: the Victorians. The Victorians' conception of beauty is still found in the beauty standards that remain today. As long as a disabled woman is beautiful, the audience shouldn't focus on any internalized pain associated with her health. In *City Lights*, the blind flower girl is sweet and innocent; her only flaw—outside of being a bad businesswoman—is her blindness, which Chaplin's Tramp is willing to look past because of her innate goodness. This manifests later in *Children of a Lesser God*, when William Hurt's James calls Sarah "beautiful, mysterious, and angry." The brilliance she possesses compels James to look beyond her deafness. These disabilities are an enticement to the non-disabled opposite sex. George Hamilton's Fabrizio Naccarelli in *Light in the Piazza* (1962) falls in love with Yvette Mimieux's Clara because of her mental delays. He thinks of her as naive and innocent.

In all of these stories, the first person the audience meets is the abled paramour: the Tramp, James, and so on. These stories are romances through a male lens, even if the female character is more interesting. And in movies where the woman is the central focus, like *Wild Hearts Can't Be Broken*, *The Other Side of the Mountain*, and *Ice Castles* the heroine is able-bodied before she becomes disabled, to situate her normal life (and romantic interests) before she is struck down by disability.

It's important to remember that when it comes to disabled characters, film teaches us that disability and sexuality don't mix. With regard to disabled women, sexuality is connected with fertility and because eugenic principles focus on disability as a sign of unhealthiness, being disabled means you're unhealthy *and* genetically flawed. This is why most disabled women in movies aren't mothers. So if a disabled woman is asexual, she must be barren, although most women on-screen and off are still judged on whether they have kids or not. Homer Parrish is allowed to marry Wilma and, through the implication of that union, have children because she is not disabled and the patriotism of the movie certainly wants to inspire people to have kids (this is the baby boom after all). Leah in *The Sign of the Ram* says, "I've got what I want out of life," meaning her sense of contentment. But the St. Aubyns tell Leah's assistant Sherida that Leah can't have children and thus her codependent relationship with her stepchildren takes the place of that. As much as Susan Peters is fantastic in the role, it's important to remember she still passes for able bodied. So while Hollywood might not see her as a sexually enticing, fertile woman, to a disabled person watching, it's hard to relate to her champagne problems because she's beautiful, wealthy, and conventional in appearance, sitting in what looks to be a fancy living room chair with wheels.

As Naomi Wolf writes in *The Beauty Myth*, "Men are visually aroused by women's bodies and less sensitive to their arousal by women's personalities because they are trained early into that response, while women are less visually aroused and more emotionally aroused because that is their training." Essentially, a man looks at a woman's body and judges it while their own bodies are not meant to be looked at or judged. Men are required to judge them based *solely* on whether they want a disabled woman at all. This is contrasted with stories about disabled men wherein an abled woman continues to love the man, in spite of everything. This is because, as Wolf says, women are trained to hone in on a man's personality while men focus on a woman's looks. So in disabled relationship narratives, the woman's disability is hidden and doesn't affect her physical beauty keeping the man interested. On the flip side, the abled woman in a disabled narrative stays in love with a disabled man because she is drawn more to the man's kind heart and personality over his overt physical appearance.

Like all women in Hollywood, disabled women on-screen have to remain, for lack of a better word, hot and fuckable. Sure, she may have innate inner goodness, but her ability to pass for non-disabled is what leads the male character to think he can fix something related to her disability and everything will be okay. If you're a disabled woman who isn't pretty, you're erased or perpetually lonely. In the 1961 feature *The Hustler*, Piper Laurie's character Sarah has a limp due to an accident. Because of this, coupled with her issues with alcoholism, she thinks that Paul Newman's Fast Eddie Felson won't love her. This in spite of her looking utterly gorgeous because she's Piper Laurie! But since she's a woman, and a disabled woman at that, any flaw is exaggerated a hundredfold when trying to capture the love of an abled man on-screen. A great example is the 1957 remake of *An Affair to Remember*. At the end of that film, Cary Grant's Nick realizes his beloved Terry (Deborah Kerr) is now a wheelchair user after she's hit by a car. Because she's pretty and therefore full of life, Nick considers it the greatest tragedy of all time. He melodramatically declares, "If it had to happen to one of us, why did it have to be you?" No matter that Kerr is still beautiful and seemingly healthy. She's alive after being hit by a car for crying out loud! The viewer must question whether the two can resume their delayed relationship because she can no longer walk. She now has a flaw that cannot be ignored. The movie ends with Grant and Kerr committed to staying together, but it comes with a caveat Kerr verbalizes: "If you can paint, I can walk. Anything can happen." The movie ends on a wish that her disability will be cured. That it's part of their happily ever after.

Disabled men struggle with questions of physical attractiveness in the movies, but they're seen as tragic romantics. Remember *Edward Scissorhands* in the previous chapter. The movie ends with Edward presumed dead after being forced to return to isolation in his castle on the mountain. The movie situates this as bittersweet because of the enduring love that exists between him and Winona Ryder's Kim. Movies with physically disabled men make the audience ask, "What person *wouldn't* want to date them?" because the man is positioned as having some type of charm, power, or other appealing masculine quality. Look at the dueling versions of *The Phantom of the Opera*: the 1924 horror feature and the 2004 adaptation of the Broadway show. Lon Chaney's Phantom in 1924 is a villain, and while he holds power over the narrative because of his dastardly deeds, it's the love of the opera ingenue Christine Daaé that causes him to kickstart his plan, believing her love will redeem his soul. Her rejection of him, and his eventual demise, is not a tragedy but the culmination of a horror movie. The 2004 interpretation, directed by Joel Schumacher and based on the Andrew Lloyd Webber musical, transforms the Phantom into a romantic antihero.

The Phantom, played by Gerard Butler with as little facial disfiguration as possible, is perceived as sexually attractive. And because of his allure, Christine (Emmy Rossum) fully reciprocates his advances while being scared of them. It's one of the funnier elements of the musical. If the Phantom sleeps on his right side you're totally able to ignore his facial issue. The Phantom's outward disfiguration is significantly minimized in comparison to Chaney's full face. The audience empathizes not just because he's a tragic romantic but also because his sexuality is retained. Another modernized take on a Chaney performance, the 1996 Disney version of *The Hunchback of Notre Dame*, presents Quasimodo as a character who doesn't end up with the love of a Demi Moore–voiced, pole-dancing Esmeralda, but he does save his French village from the evil of Judge Frollo and garners the respect of the community. Quasi doesn't need romantic love because he's got something greater: a sense of belonging. Hope that keeps him warm at night!

This is why Homer's relationship with Cathy O'Donnell's Wilma in *The Best Years of Our Lives* is so poignant. It illustrates how Homer is still desired by a woman. Homer's main issue is whether Cathy loves him, and the relationship with an able-bodied woman is a test of his masculinity. For things to go well, there is far more stress on Homer than on Wilma. Homer fears he isn't a "real man" and initially doesn't want to resume his relationship with Cathy because he thinks he can't offer her what an abled man can. He worries he will be a physical burden or another child for her. The bedroom scene between Homer and Wilma in *Best Years* is tenderhearted and requires both of them to be vulnerable. They let down their guards and mutually come to a decision to continue the relationship together. Homer has to trust that he won't be rejected; and when physical disabilities are shocking to normal people it's hard to believe that love will prevail. This is proven wrong when Homer shows Cathy his bedtime routine which she is more than willing to accept. Even then, the movie doesn't end on an interabled relationship. Homer and Cathy marry during the film's conclusion, but the final image isn't of him and his bride. It's of the psychologically, invisibly, disabled Fred and his beloved, Peggy (Teresa Wright).

There are exceptions to this rule, found mainly in the independent film community. In the 1992 feature *The Waterdance*, codirected by disabled director

Neal Jimenez, main character Joel (Eric Stoltz) dates a married colleague, a relationship that started prior to the rock-climbing accident that made him a paraplegic. Though both characters hope the relationship continues, it is Joel who makes the decision to end the affair and figure out his new way of life. In the 2004 indie comedy *Saved!*, set in a contemporary Christian high school, wheelchair user Roland (Macauley Culkin) enters an interabled relationship with classmate Cassandra (Eva Amurri). The relationship is presented positively, and while he and Cassandra break up briefly it is to allow Roland the opportunity to assert his own independence and resume the relationship with a more equal dynamic.

We've already looked at several depictions of "pretty disabilities" in previous chapters (including *Wait Until Dark* and *Hush*). But how do pretty disabilities work when removed from the horror genre? And how have they changed over the decades? Because of the Victorian tendency to show the disabled as sweet and innocent, pretty disabilities pop up in adaptations of classic literature of the era in characters who are children, like the wheelchair-using Clara in *Heidi* or Colin in *The Secret Garden*. The characters are wealthy kids who just need love to cure their disabilities, which are considered to be psychosomatic. The affection of an absent father helps them overcome their unspecified infirmities and restores their ability to walk in both of the above examples.

This idea of the beauty of love fixing aesthetically unpleasant disabilities is the entire crux of the 1945 wartime romantic drama *The Enchanted Cottage*, which illustrates the dueling distinctions in how disability and romance are different for disabled men versus women. Directed by John Cromwell, *The Enchanted Cottage* follows Oliver Bradford (Robert Young), who tries to come to terms with his facial disfigurement as well as having his arm disabled after being shot down during WWII. For a modern audience watching today, Oliver seems to have the most imperceptible disability. He's got a facial disfigurement that would make Gerard Butler's Phantom tell him to get over it. Robert Young wears a little makeup to create a slight eye droop and that's it. His arm he just holds against him. But you'd think Oliver's the Elephant Man as he dramatically says, "Do you think I want people to see the way I am? Don't I repulse you?" Ollie seems a little extra, but the people around him aren't any better. His fiancée, Beatrice (Hillary Brooke), acts as if he has a terminal illness. When she discovers he's disabled, she stammers out, "No one told me . . . I wasn't prepared . . . I'll try to be brave about it."

Dorothy McGuire and Robert Young are disabled lovers, alongside Herbert Marshall, in *The Enchanted Cottage* (1945). John Springer Collection / Corbis via Getty Images

Oliver soon meets the shy Laura Pennington (Dorothy McGuire), whose problem is that she's incredibly plain. It's placed on the same level as a physical disability, and that's not being facetious. That and her inherent goodness and belief in the magic of the titled enchanted cottage have the audience see her as coded to be Oliver's perfect romantic companion. The pair soon start a romance, which is apparently so salacious the tagline of the film's poster is that "the whole town whispered about these two." Why? It appears to have less to do with Oliver being betrothed to another woman while dating Laura, or even his deciding to marry Laura out of convenience. Maybe the whole town's talking as if to say, "Look at these two slightly disabled people in love! Scandalous! They could be fornicating and procreating!"

Oliver thinks Laura is the best option he'll find because he's so disabled and all. "No woman in the world would marry me unless out of compassion," he says. He doesn't want to be Laura's burden, albeit he's still ambulatory and rocking one good arm. So he can't open a pickle jar without getting creative but he's doing more than fine in life. The twist is that when the pair are in the enchanted cottage, their flaws and disabilities are erased. Oliver's face is fixed, as well as his arm, and Laura is transformed into Dorothy McGuire after a visit from the hair-and-makeup department. The movie's overall message is that the cottage lifts the veil from the eyes of these two. It shows them at their best and helps the pair's romance blossom by lifting their aesthetic impediments. But this only works when the couple is inside the cottage, because "a man and woman in love have a gift of sight no one else does." If one ascribes to the magic of the cottage, then they see Laura and Oliver's inner beauty manifest in the outside world, which is to say they are gorgeous and able. When Oliver reunites with his parents, who aren't convinced there is magic, they see their son and his lover as supposedly horrific-looking people. They refuse to see their son and daughter-in-law without their faults. It's similar to *Shazam!*'s "full potential" moment that makes Freddy Freeman a superhero and cures his disability. What's more ironic is that the film's narrator, their friend John (Herbert Marshall, one of the few physically disabled stars of the studio era), comes to the cottage multiple times. John, referred to in the on-screen credits as "The Blind Composer," despite being referred to by name multiple times, believes the magic to be true but the cottage apparently decides to tell him to piss off because his sight is never restored. Maybe John is just too disabled? Or is it because Oliver and Laura are so focused on their own looks that the cottage reminds them they don't have it *that* bad? Either way, John deserves something. Probably it's because *The Enchanted Cottage* sees the two characters mutually choose to buy into the house's magic and ignore their flaws, still loving each other in spite of them.

The love-conquers-all mentality doesn't always work in Old Hollywood. Take the 1935 romantic comedy *Hands Across the Table*. Manicurist Regi Allen (Carole Lombard) is determined to marry for money and doesn't care about anything else, just that her future husband is wealthy. One of her clients, Allen Macklyn is a rich wheelchair user who falls in love with Regi. Allen is a good man, and outside of him being a wheelchair user, there's no proper explanation for why he is still single. Yet Regi never entertains Allen as a romantic paramour, leaving the audience to assume it's because he uses a wheelchair. So she's just a straight-up ableist. Regi ends up falling for formerly wealthy, though now penniless, Theodore Drew III (Fred MacMurray). Regi learns to love Theodore for who he is, not for his money, which leaves poor Allen, played by perpetual also-ran Ralph Bellamy, to enjoy his money alone. The movie's message shows money cannot buy love, and it certainly can't buy you love if you're in a wheelchair.

In Mary Shelley's novel *Frankenstein* and the 1935 *Frankenstein* film sequel *Bride of Frankenstein*, there's a scene where the Creature encounters a lonely blind man living in a hut. The elderly gentleman doesn't shrink in fear from the hideousness of Frankenstein's creation, because he can't see the figure's face. Over the time they spend together, the blind man teaches the misunderstood monster about friendship and companionship. If you saw the Mel Brooks spoof *Young Frankenstein* you'll know he also taught Frankenstein's monster about the joys of smoking and drinking too. Much like the scene in *Freaks* with the microcephalics by the river, the intrusion of the able-bodied ruins any integration the Monster could have into society. Two hunters pop into the man's hut and discover the Creature, take the man away, and burn his home down. The Creature has lost his friend, and the blind man is now homeless.

This cinematic trope of a blind character understanding a person's inner soul is something I've dubbed "love is blind." As Naomi Wolf has already laid out, women are trained to focus on a man's personality, so in disabled movies where love-is-blind is employed, the audience sees a blind character, usually a woman, help a sighted or disabled and nonblind character (usually a man) find love and self-worth because the blind person can see something intangible in the other person. Think of this as a blind, manic pixie dream girl, or a reverse take on *Cyrano de Bergerac*. Since the blind woman is able to focus on her paramour's personality and presumed inner goodness, the suspense and conflict come from what happens when the sighted/disabled character is found out by his blind love and rejected or not. Blindness serves a dual purpose here, being both a literal disability and a metaphorical stand-in for a person's own inability to discover true love because of external factors in their lives.

The 1965 film *A Patch of Blue* takes the love-is-blind storyline to explore racism. *A Patch of Blue* was aimed at civil rights fence-sitters rather than an attempt to change the minds of those who were already racist. (It worked to more famous effect two years later, albeit with Poitier falling in love with a [sighted] white woman, in the excellent *Guess Who's Coming to Dinner*, released one year before what is generally agreed to be the end of the civil rights movement in 1968.) The story is about a blind white girl named Selina (Elizabeth Hartman) who falls in love with a Black man named Gordon (Sidney Poitier). Hartman's poor, blind, uneducated Selina is abused and treated like a servant by her mother Rose-Ann (Shelley Winters). Selina spends her days at home and is told to enjoy her "nice, quiet life." She convinces her grandfather,

Ole Pa (Wallace Ford, who was also Phroso in *Freaks*) to walk her to a nearby park during the day, and it's here that she meets Poitier's Gordon.

Elizabeth Hartman is the beautiful, blind Selina in love with Sidney Poitier's Gordon in 1965's *A Patch of Blue*. Metro-Goldwyn-Mayer/Moviepix / Getty Images

A Patch of Blue uses Selina's blindness to craft a somewhat trite but pointed critique at race and class, but what the film does so skillfully is create an interplay with race and disability. It's Selina's story, but she comes at things from a position of subservience. It is Gordon, the sighted Black man, who holds some power during his interactions with her because of her blindness and her lack of formal education. Selina is poor white trash, and Gordon wants her to learn how to live "properly," not as a blind woman but as an educated white woman. Selina doesn't know how to be a proper adult, nor does she understand how society makes it possible for blind people to live independently. She has no idea schools for the blind exist, and she doesn't know what Braille is. Gordon becomes her guide on how to be an independent blind woman. Like Professor Higgins in *My Fair Lady*, Gordon teaches her proper English and how to interact with others and buy groceries. Gordon turns into Selina's caretaker, which his brother Mark (Ivan Dixon) thinks will cause problems for him since Selina is white. He tells Gordon that he should "let white take care of their own." Because this is 1965 and a movie aimed at those neutral toward race relations, the film makes Selina a woman who quite literally doesn't "see" color. She mentions how she had a Black friend as a child, a "colored" girl named Pearl, which, to today's audience, is a crude attempt to downplay Selina's own white privilege. The script makes Selina a good example for white people and makes sure Selina is grateful, almost overly so. Part of this stems from her desperate need for love. She's regularly telling Gordon how much she loves everything and how happy she is just to exist in the shadow of his smile. I might have exaggerated that last part, but it's not too far off.

The only place Selina has any individual autonomy is in her burgeoning sexuality. Selina puts her hands over her own breasts while holding Rose-Ann's bra against her own body and connects the bra with maturation and sexual development. She says she's had "experiences" when Gordon calls her a baby. Unfortunately, Selina doesn't known about consent, as the "experience" came through a raped committed against her by one of her mother's boyfriends. "I don't think she [Rose-Ann] ever forgave me for that," Selina says about the encounter. It's because of this that the audience sees that part of Rose-Ann's hatred of Selina stems from seeing her daughter as competition for men. Selina's desire for Gordon becomes her first attempt at a consensual romantic relationship. However, because of the ongoing racism in 1965 and the Hollywood production code of the time, Gordon and Selina's romance is sanitized. Selina is the instigator of the relationship as well as any physical affection. When the two finally share a kiss it is Selina who kisses Gordon, not the two mutually kissing each other. (In the South, this scene was completely removed because it was considered "race mixing.") Gordon's feelings toward her are ambiguous. It's never clear whether he thinks of her as a girlfriend, a kid sister, or a random woman he's met.

A Patch of Blue's race relationships leave a lot to be desired by today's standards, but it's remarkably progressive in how it explores disability adaptations and what blind people experience living in major cities. It would be thirteen years before *Coming Home* detailed an authentic look at living independently with a disability. Take note, the next time you watch a movie about a disabled person, of whether it's situated in a small town or a large city. Some limit their disabled characters to just their own small neighborhood.

Because the traffic signals aren't crafted for the hearing impaired, Gordon shows Selina how to cross the street by listening for when the cars slow down. It's still sporadic to find Deaf-friendly crossing signals today outside of major cities. Selina learns where the deli is by smelling for fresh bread. (She does toe the line between being disabled and a bloodhound.) And when she wants to call Gordon on the telephone we watch her call the operator and have them connect the call for her.

Peter Bogdanovich's 1985 feature *Mask* is the gender-swapped example of the love-is-blind story. Based on the true story of Rocky Dennis, the film follows Rocky (Eric Stoltz) as he goes to a new school, attempts to corral his wayward mother, Rusty (Cher), and finds his own sense of identity while dealing with a severe craniofacial deformity that eventually leads to his death at a young age. In the film's third act, Rocky becomes a camp counselor at a summer camp for the blind which is where he meets Diana (Laura Dern), a blind camper.

Rocky and Diana have equal weight in their burgeoning relationship with both finding a level of trust in the other. The fact that Diana can't see Rocky's face takes the pressure off for him to overcompensate. At one point Rocky lies about his looks and Diana is aware he's lying. He eventually comes clean to her and feels comfortable enough to let her touch his face—which most blind people will tell you is not a thing they do—and realize how he truly looks. Their relationship ends abruptly once the summer is over and Diana's parents come to pick her up. Like the hunters interrupting the blind man and Frankenstein's monster, once Diana's parents meet Rocky and see his face, they prevent her from seeing him. When Rocky and Diana briefly reunite she tells him she's going to a different school and is unable to see him anymore. Rather than make an effort to find out why she never heard from Rocky, something she says she was concerned about when they meet again, Diana just moves on with her life. Diana and the camp provide a temporary respite for Rocky. He is worthy of a romantic partnership, but it's fleeting, and because he's already living on borrowed time—his condition is fatal—the audience sees this as his one shot at true love.

Mask is ultimately the story of how a disabled person's true love really is their mother. The film's main focus is on the close relationship between Rocky and Rusty, a free-spirited biker babe dealing with drug addiction and juggling various men in her life. In a lot of ways, *Mask* is evocative of the "caretaker cinema" genre of disabled narrative. Rusty advocates for her son to be treated like everyone else and shows her personal growth independent from him, despite there being several instances where Rocky acts more like a parent to his mother than his mother is to him. Even his fate at the end is meant to highlight

Rusty's strength as a mom as she copes with her grief. (Thankfully, the movie never portrays Rocky's disability as a punishment for his mother's past.) I can't fault Cher's performance, however, which is pretty fabulous. This is Cher's movie and is a celebration of parents standing by their disabled children.

The film tells us from the beginning that, at sixteen years old, Rocky has beaten the odds with regard to his life expectancy. So the audience spends the runtime prepared for Rocky's eventual death. The way the scenes are edited within the film, and the narrative trajectory, is that Diana leaving him, coupled with the realization that his best friend is not going on a preplanned trip with him, makes Rocky depressed and lonely. Rocky's death two scenes later plays out as if he's given up on life. His death becomes a form of suicide. It's akin to the beautifully tragic demise of Victorian heroines, whether that be from wasting away or just using too many pillows. Unless audience members do additional research, most take the concept of "based on a true story" literally. This is why true stories are the fulcrum of movies about disability. The audience can't criticize the content, because these things allegedly happened. If the audience isn't willing to look into the facts, fiction becomes truth. It's why you're reading an entire book about how movies romanticize disability, after all.

If there is a romantic plotline in love-is-blind narratives, it's in the non-disabled man who seeks personal redemption through the love of a blind woman. Much like the Phantom and Christine in 1924, stories like this don't focus on the blind woman but on how the man tries to make himself a worthy person in society with the help of her disabled validation. You know that old chestnut about a woman being able to change a man? Disabled women do it all the time in movies!

That's what happens in the 1954 Douglas Sirk melodrama *Magnificent Obsession*. Sirk's films are explorations into the roles women played in the changing 1950s landscape. His 1955 feature *All That Heaven Allows* looks at the interior life of a widow whom everyone in town, including her own children, expects to live in widow's weeds her whole life. With *Magnificent Obsession*, Jane Wyman's character, Helen Phillips, loses her husband, a prominent local doctor, after the town's sole defibrillator is used to save the life of wanton playboy Bob Merrick (Rock Hudson). Helen is understandably upset, and Bob can't deal with his guilt over what happened. Forty minutes into the movie Helen is blinded after stepping in front of a car. Apparently being hit by a Buick only boggles the retinas, as that's Helen's sole injury. Bob Merrick is the film's able-bodied buffer who, through his relationship with Helen, learns how to be a productive man in society. His "magnificent obsession," as the title implies, is his desire to find a cure for Helen's blindness. In Bob's attempt to fix things, he decides to pass himself off to Helen as Robby, a poor medical student who in no way sounds like the same man she was interacting with in the first half of the film. Love, of course, blossoms between the two. Helen is a beautiful, blind cipher who spends her days sitting on the beach with a neighborhood child while rocking some sweet cat's-eye glasses. The neighbor girl appears to be Helen's sole friend; another example of disabled women and actual children placed on the same level. The girl follows Helen everywhere like a bodyguard, commenting on how she finds Helen "remarkable" for wanting to spend time by herself.

How brave this blind woman is for wanting to sit, alone, in the quiet and not hear constant yammering. Bob catfishes Helen because he knows she hates him and presumes she won't understand he's changed. Can you blame her? Her husband died in order to save him! He's not the reason the town only had a single defibrillator, but he didn't help. When they fall in love it's hard to sympathize with Bob because he continues to keep up the charade when he doesn't need to. What's even harder to parse is the fact that Helen never seems to recognize the voices of her friends and loved ones. We've already seen this in *Pride of the Marines* when Al Schmid's friend, someone he's known for months, comes and introduces himself. Al points out that he's aware of whom he's talking to. Helen doesn't have any spark of recognition hearing Bob's voice.

When Bob discovers the top doctors in Switzerland can cure Helen's blindness he spends his own money to send her there, attributing his actions to a secret admirer. (This isn't the first time Hollywood takes a disability-focused trip to Switzerland, by the way. It's the Amsterdam of the disabled with all manner of high-end medical experimentation and euthanasia chalets you might need.) He's like Chaplin getting the money for the blind flower girl in *City Lights*. Helen decides to go, and Bob buys her house so she'll have a place to live once she's back. Nothing weird about it at all. Helen doesn't investigate any of this, because she is the beautiful blind creature being moved like a chess piece from A to B. Helen is morose about the trip, saying, "I'm going to visit Europe and I want to be able to *see* it." Helen got an all-expenses-paid trip to Switzerland and has the ultimate safety net—this is a moment when you *should* be grateful, girl.

As if there couldn't be anything worse the doctors discover Helen has a brain tumor and needs surgery to save her life. Now not only does she need surgery to cure her eyesight but she also has a brain tumor and needs even more surgery to live? This sounds like a scam. One of Helen's friends says, "What has she done that all this has happened to her?" It's probably because, like most disabled characters going back to the Victorian times, Helen is a Christlike, martyred disabled character so everything bad has to happen to her. The disabled are sin eaters, dontcha know? Helen exists to be buried underneath trauma for Bob to fix. Bob becomes a doctor in the wake of hearing about Helen's diagnosis and opens up a whole hospital wing in her honor. He calls the medical team and discovers the only doctor that can save her . . . is Bob! With a literal heavenly choir playing over him, Bob performs Helen's brain surgery and saves her life. Helen, in the final scene, says, "I think I see some light. . . . I think I'm going to see." Helen is the living embodiment of Bob's success as a doctor and a man. Saving her implies to the audience that he can also save humankind. Disabled women standing by their man and making them better for humanity.

We mentioned it while talking about the Tramp and the blind flower girl in *City Lights*, as well as Duchess Josiana's interest in Gwynplaine in *The Man Who Laughs*, but alongside Hollywood sexism, there's a history of fetishization regarding disability, especially disabled women. As Wolf says in *The Beauty Myth*, sexual harassment is tied into perceptions of female looks: "Beauty provokes harassment, the law says, but it looks through men's eyes when deciding what provokes it."

The one unifying element for all women, regardless of age, race, sexual orientation, or ability is the collective fear of sexual assault. Being a woman is already dangerous in our society, but movies show that being a disabled woman makes you a victim from the minute you're born. During and after the #MeToo movement, debate about the role of sexual assault and rape in film became a topic of conversation, but disabled women are often forgotten or excluded from these conversations. If you were to watch movies exclusively about disabled women, you'd assume rape is lurking around the corner with how frequently it is employed or alluded to. Male sexual enticement in movies emphasizes a disabled female character's vulnerability, making her ripe for sexual harassment and assault. Their beauty, coupled with their disability and the helplessness predators think it comes with, provokes male harassment. Fetishization can turn into outright sexual violence. According to Disability Justice, 83 percent of disabled women will experience sexual assault in their lives, and "women with a disability are far more likely to have a history of undesired sex with an intimate partner."

Before she played the blind Helen in *Magnificent Obsession*, actress Jane Wyman won an Oscar as deaf farm girl Belinda McDonald in *Johnny Belinda*. Outside of Wyman playing both, the two characters do have commonalities. Tragedy and bad luck have followed Belinda since the day she was born, as with Helen. What's different is that Belinda's mother died in childbirth, and at a year old Belinda became sick and was left deafened. None of Belinda's family members is educated enough to teach her ASL or any other form of communication, leaving Belinda in a world of silence. Since Belinda can't talk the town refers to her as "the dummy." Dr. Robert Richardson (Lew Ayres) takes a shine to Belinda and becomes her hearing guide through the valley of deafness. He commits to teaching her sign language, similar to how Gordon helps educate Selina on her blindness in *A Patch of Blue*. Robert's approach to teaching Belinda is a tad unorthodox, though; he introduces himself by grabbing her by the shoulders and saying, "Don't be afraid," while simultaneously signing and pointing. She'll definitely understand you, doc!

When Belinda isn't having strange men gesturing at her, she's being sexually harassed by Locky (Stephen McNally), one of the men in town. Actually, nope, all the men in this movie are questionable after all. But unlike the good doctor, Locky gives attention to Belinda that she doesn't reciprocate, and he isn't interested in helping her either. When Locky discovers that his girlfriend has an unrequited crush on Robert he gets incredibly angry, goes after Belinda, and sexually assaults her. Considering how many of Locky's motivations are fueled by Robert, the rape comes off more like a man marking his territory than anything else. Belinda becomes pregnant and has a baby boy but refuses to disclose who the father is. The town starts gossiping that Robert is the father of Belinda's baby. What's weird is how the townsfolk turn Robert into a social outcast because Belinda "can't defend herself [and] can't even talk." It's unclear whether they're upset that Robert could be a rapist or because he decided to attack a Deaf girl in general. Robert wants to make an honest woman out of Belinda and marry her, but instead of discussing this with her he goes to her father. He doesn't consult Belinda at all. Now that her body's been violated, it's tough to watch hearing people continue to take away Belinda's autonomy, no matter how good their intentions. Belinda rejects Robert's proposal. She doesn't want him to marry her out of pity. Instead, she bears what the townspeople think and say about her with grace and dignity, content to raise her son, Johnny, on her own.

Jane Wyman won an Oscar for her performance as the Deaf Belinda in *Johnny Belinda* (1948). Archive Photos / Stringer / Getty Images

The townspeople have their ire stoked by Locky, unaware that he is Johnny's father and Belinda's attacker. Because of Locky's influence, they collectively presume she's an unfit mother and the court should take Johnny away. You might be surprised to hear how common removing children from disabled parents is, irrespective of circumstances. One in ten children of disabled parents is at risk for removal from the home by child welfare officials purely because the parent has a disability. As of 2020, those removal rates sat at 80 percent, particularly if the parent has any form of intellectual disability. The viewer knows there's no doubt that Belinda is intelligent, merely that she doesn't have the tools to communicate. But because she is Deaf, the implication by the townsfolk is she has diminished mental capacity. They think they're doing Belinda a kindness. One person says, "I almost feel sorry for her. It's good she can't think or feel." Another says, "If the girl had normal intelligence she would be grateful." Sure, they refer to her as a "creature" and cling to the idea that because she's lacking an essential sense like hearing that she has no maternal instinct or capacity for love.

PRETTY DISABILITIES   **147**

Disability can be a vulnerability, and movies focused on the trauma of disabled female bodies are all too relatable. I experienced sexual harassment firsthand, motivated, in large part, because I was disabled. My sophomore year of high school I was routinely harassed by a male classmate who spent his days asking me how I had sex. He was so curious about this that he submitted it as a question in an anonymous Q&A box passed around during Sex Ed week. During school dances he'd grind on the back of my wheelchair despite my continued pleas that he go away. I was told it was all in good fun and nonthreatening by his male friends. When I complained about it to teachers and the principal I was told, "Don't mind him. He's just doing it because he likes you. He's doing it because he can't express his feelings properly." These all acted to convince me I was overreacting. Maybe I was being too harsh. I should be flattered, according to everyone. I internalized the idea that he was trying to prove to me that he didn't mind that I was disabled. My wheelchair would be an impediment to any future relationship so I should take what I could get. This guy chose to see me as just a girl he wanted to date, not a disabled girl. Then again, I wonder: If this was how he acted around a disabled girl, did I even want to know how he was around abled ones? This stuck with me for a long time and, with the benefit of hindsight, I'm relieved things never progressed beyond him just being gross. When I watched Guillermo del Toro's *The Shape of Water* in 2017 I unexpectedly found myself triggered because I saw my high school experience writ large. For the first time, a movie took a sobering look at sexual harassment against disabled women and how a simple phrase like "I don't mind" becomes a loaded, terrifying expression.

The Shape of Water follows Elisa (Sally Hawkins), a Deaf and nonverbal janitor at a mysterious government facility in the 1960s who falls in love with a half man/half fish creature being held at the facility and referred to only as Amphibian Man (Doug Jones). Del Toro's movie wonderfully deconstructs what disabled women experience far too often in reality: sexual harassment gussied up as kindness. As Elisa starts to develop feelings for the Amphibian Man it brings her into closer contact with government operative Richard Strickland (Michael Shannon), the man holding and controlling the Amphibian Man at the facility. Strickland is sexually attracted to Elisa, turned on by her inability to speak and her presumed helplessness. According to a 2022 survey by Disability Justice, 50 percent of girls who are Deaf have been sexually abused compared to 25 percent of girls who are hearing.

Strickland becomes full-on obsessed with her. The script critiques the entire love-is-blind principle because Strickland's desire to see past Elisa's deafness is motivated by a need for control. Much like the unnamed killer in *Hush*, Agent Strickland is another man who tries to hold power over a Deaf woman. Strickland corners Elisa and tells her he "doesn't mind" that she can't hear or speak. Because disabled people, regardless of gender, are expected to show gratitude, there isn't nearly enough said about how the phrase "I don't mind" is a way to weaponize and leverage this. Strickland is a misogynist who believes he is a physically superior man. He says God looks "more like me," implying he and God are white, verbal, hearing men. She should be lucky to have his interest, in his eyes, and he won't stop at committing violence against her just because she's Deaf.

There are certainly critiques to lob against *Shape of Water* regarding Elisa's relationship with the Amphibian Man. It reiterates the idea that disabled people find love and acceptance exclusively in monstrous, or similarly disabled, relationships. Not to mention Elisa is a conventionally attractive, ambulatory white woman played by a non-Deaf performer. But her relationship with the Amphibian Man is satisfying, both sexually and psychologically.

They are true partners, and that is a good balance in a movie where the villain is the good-looking, hearing man that, in any other movie, would be played up as the right man for Elisa. Imagine if Lew Ayres's doctor was the villain in *Johnny Belinda*. Then again, that introduction between the pair felt that way. With the Amphibian Man, Elisa has a relationship not based on incompleteness—nor is it founded on misogyny or gratitude—but mutual love and respect. She says, "The way he [Amphibian Man] looks at me, he doesn't know what I lack or how I'm incomplete. He sees me for what I am, as I am." It's the reverse of the love-is-blind concept. The Amphibian Man *sees* Elisa. He doesn't look past her deafness but takes everything in and loves her for it. (Just remember that next time you refer to it as the "fish-fucking movie.")

M. Night Shyamalan's 2004 film *The Village* twists the narrative by having a disabled man harass a disabled woman. The beautiful and blind Ivy (Bryce Dallas Howard) lives in an idyllic 1800s-era village where she is friends with the mentally disabled Noah (Adrien Brody). It's clear Noah and Ivy are friendly, but she is not attracted to him as a romantic prospect. When she announces her marriage to another town member, Lucius (Joaquin Phoenix), Noah shows up at Lucius's house and stabs him multiple times. Noah is motivated to violence because he thinks he has ownership over Ivy and clearly understands he's done something wrong. Remember, disabled people aren't immune from being terrible. Ivy decides she is the only one who can save Lucius and goes on a mission to get medicine for him. Ivy is a badass character. She doesn't have any sixth sense, as some blind characters do. She treks through the woods and relies on her ingenuity and own ability. The townspeople have zero faith in her ability to succeed, with one woman telling her father, "How could you send her? She's blind." Noah, though, can't let Ivy go and starts to stalk her through the woods, masquerading as one of the creatures the town is told to fear. Ivy outsmarts and kills the monster, never realizing it is Noah—a pointed metaphor, to be sure—and returns home with the medicine to save Lucius.

A final subset of pretty disability movies consists of something I call "hurting to help/helping to hurt." Movies in this category have highly accomplished, formerly able-bodied women who become disabled and search for a new sense of purpose. These movies position their female character as someone at the top of their field, typically the world of sports. The moral of these movies is that the women were once at the peak of physical perfection and found a new, metaphorical, mountain to climb and conquer. Once the woman is disabled, her able-bodied partner must implement tough love to get her back on top again, acting as makeshift lover and coach. There has to be some reason for a man to stay with them!

A spate of these movies came as the result of the massive success of 1970's *Love Story*, a romantic drama that follows a couple with vastly different backgrounds. Trying to overcome their individual differences, they are struck by tragedy when heroine Jenny (Ali MacGraw) dies at the age of twenty-five. It's beautiful, it's sad, it's romantic, and it inspired a lot of other movies to find different ways to tell the same story. One is the 1975 film *The Other Side of the Mountain* and its 1978 sequel.

Based on the true story of skier Jill Kinmont (Marilyn Hassett), *The Other Side of the Mountain* shows what happens after Jill is paralyzed in an accident and can no longer ski. Where the characters in *Love Story* deal with class issues and cancer, *The Other Side of the Mountain* deals with paralysis . . . and never trusting airplanes. Jill opens the movie bemoaning her lot in life. She talks about how every morning, she wakes up and experiences "those first moments where I forget who I am and remember who I was." Who isn't excited to spend the next 103 minutes with her! She's highly dependent on her mother to do everything for her. (In the sequel, that codependency puts a strain on Jill's life and relationships.) When Jill is paralyzed, the doctors tell her how lucky she is. If the fracture had been lower, she'd have the use of her hands; but if it was higher, she'd be on a breathing machine. Dialogue between her, the doctors, and her family revolves around one thing: Will Jill ever walk again? One conversation sums things up perfectly:

Doctor: All we can do is hope.
Family: Hope that she'll walk?
Doctor: Hope that she'll live!

Cue the orchestra and commercial break! Everything in her life revolves around Jill becoming ambulatory. People are counting on Jill to walk, dammit. It ends up drowning out her pity party and gives her something to do besides whine. The boyfriend she has prior to her accident, also a skier, comes to visit Jill and anticipates her taking her first steps toward him. The camera closes in on his face as he realizes she can't even pick up a potato chip. "Jill, aren't you gonna walk?" he asks. (He says this like she's a dog, and he expects her to do a trick.) Cue that orchestra again.

Jill's sad confession that she's never going to walk again is accompanied by the sappiest, saddest *Love Story* theme–level song you can imagine. As Jill narrates in the aftermath of this conversation, "Buddy [douchey boyfriend] called me a week later and I never heard from him again." It's laughable, really, considering when Jill's life is contrasted against that of her friend Audra Jo (Belinda Montgomery), who gets sudden-onset polio in the middle of the night, while sleeping next to Jill no less, and becomes a full-time wheelchair user. I'm starting to wonder if Jill is the angel of death. AJ takes to disability like a duck to water. We see her drive, gather a community of disabled friends, and live her best life. Her story is way more interesting than the one we're watching.

Because this is a romantic drama, Jill needs to find the right kind of man to put up with her and get her life back in order. Enter Dick Buek (Beau Bridges), a pilot and all-around nice guy who knew Jill prior to her accident. He knows the real Jill hiding in that wheelchair. Dick is the savior Jill needs to put everything back on track. He's so determined to get her out of that chair that he scoops her up like a sack of potatoes and carts her places, whether she likes it or not. The line between consent and kidnapping was blurry in 1975.

Dick isn't a regular boyfriend, he's a cool boyfriend! He tells Jill straight up, "You're gonna have a hard time attracting a man . . . you're not getting any sympathy from me." He teaches her to swim and stops holding her upright, only to be surprised when she starts drowning. The line between swim lessons and attempted murder was blurry in 1975. He also spends an inordinate amount of time shouting at Jill. In one scene the pair argues in the street as Jill sits in her wheelchair . . . in the street . . . unable to move, while Dick loudly "discusses" things with her. The cherry on the cake of their toxic relationship is a dinner scene between Dick, Jill, and her family. Jill only has partial use of one hand so she asks Dick to help her cut her food. Dick refuses, smiling at her parents as he says, "You can't spoil her." Love the energy, Dick, but Jill is better off using that partial hand strength to stab you with a fork. Is she seriously supposed to pick up the meat with her mouth and gnaw it like a dog? This method apparently yields results as Jill finds a new career as a teacher. Dick, thankfully, ends up dying in a plane crash and leaves Jill committed to living life for him, setting up the sequel three years later. I don't know, Dick, spoiling her might have prolonged your life.

Another *Love Story*–esque melodrama that uses the same formulaic beats as *The Other Side of the Mountain* is 1978's *Ice Castles*, a movie that sells the premise that any problem is solved by a guy yelling at a disabled girl to stop crying about her life. *Ice Castles* is inspiration porn to the extreme. Lexie Winston (Lynn-Holly Johnson) is a figure skater praised for her natural talent. Considered geriatric in the figure-skating world at the ripe old age of sixteen(!), Lexie gets an opportunity to enter the sport professionally. She starts gaining acclaim in the figure skating world only to be blinded in an accident. Her boyfriend, Nick (Robby Benson) vows that he'll get her back on the ice.

Ice Castles is on the edge of being a disabled feature because it spends over an hour of its screen time looking at Lexie's abled life before fate cruelly hobbles her with that torturous thing called disability. The narrative is more about how fame and power corrupt as Lexie claws her way to the top of the figure skating world's Midwest Regional Championship! Just below the Olympics, ladies and gents. Lexie's meteoric success causes her to turn her back on hometown honey, Nick, and start dating older men. Her blinding comes after a freak run-in with patio furniture someone left on the ice rink, the ultimate cruel twist of fate and payment for her hubris. The doctor immediately gives up on Lexie having any reason to live outside of figure skating. "I'm sorry we couldn't do more," he says. "We understand she was very promising." Might as well skate your way into the middle of a pond, Lex.

After the blinding, Lexie spends her days turning waxy and pale. Her isolation is so extreme that her friends have little patience for her "sit[ting] in her attic wearing her dead mother's clothes." Mental breakdown doesn't factor into anyone's thoughts, does it? Honestly, Dick in *Other Side of the Mountain* is bad, but everyone in Lexie's orbit acts less like she's suffered a traumatic injury that's changed her life and more like she got a bad dye job. I'm not sure if that's progressive or not, all things considered. Lexie's dad and Nick teach Lexie how to skate again, with Nick telling Lexie to "feel the ice." He sees no reason why she can't do a triple axel, like a blind Tonya Harding. "If nobody made her do anything she didn't want to do, she'd be up in that room staring at the goddamn walls," says Nick. There're some real "let me save you" vibes coming out. Lexie competes again but hides her blindness from the audience at the rink. She does well at the competition and lands that triple, with the movie selling it as a victory for Lexie *and* Nick, because nothing says feminism like a guy getting equal credit for a woman's accomplishment. *Ice Castles* tells its disabled viewers nothing is stopping you from becoming champion figure skaters! Hit that ice and land that triple. Have you even tried?

I know you're probably demoralized by this point, but let's go out on a high note looking at a movie that uses its disability politics for good. The 1991 Disney movie *Wild Hearts Can't Be Broken* is the story of Sonora Webster (Gabrielle Anwar), a teenage girl who wants to be a professional diving girl. What's a diving girl, you ask? It was a carnival stunt wherein a female rider rides horses off a diving board into a pool of water. (This was a real thing!) Sonora starts gaining success in her profession but becomes blind after her retinas detach in a freak diving accident. But Sonora, undaunted, is determined to ride again with the help of her love, Al (a post–*Sixteen Candles* Michael Schoeffling).

It takes over an hour for Sonora to become blind in a similar "cruel twist of fate" model as the other movies discussed in this chapter. What's different is how much agency Sonora has in how she handles her blindness. She initially hides the fuzzy vision she has in order to keep working, which results in her blindness transitioning from temporary to permanent. But unlike the other "hurting to help" movies discussed, Al doesn't yell at Sonora to get her back to doing what she loves. Their interactions are motivated by love for each other and are relatable adult conversations any couple would have after an accident like this has changed their lives forever. He actually retreats inward and is hellbent on protecting her. Al tells Sonora she can't run away or hide from her blindness but that she has to adapt to it. That being said, he doesn't ever want her to dive again. He offers genuine support, and if he's frustrated at anything it's that what he thinks Sonora is doing is reckless. She, on the other hand, genuinely wants to dive again and refuses to live her life in fear.

When Al refuses to help Sonora get back into diving she takes the initiative to relearn by herself. Her horse Lightning has a special bond with her that helps her to sense him and perform the dives. When it's time for the big finale, the person funding the entire circus refuses to let Sonora perform the stunt because "these people didn't pay good money to see a blind girl kill herself." Considering our discussion on *Freaks*, this carnival in the 1930s would absolutely have people pay good money to watch a blind girl kill herself.

This is, however, a Disney movie. Everything turns out all right, and Sonora accomplishes the dive. She says in voiceover it was the first of several dives she did while blind, and the audience never knew she couldn't see. *Wild Hearts Can't Be Broken* is great, but between this and *Ice Castles*, it's a bit insulting that the true miracle is an audience is fooled into believing someone is sighted, especially in a carnival movie like this. It's like a magician doing a trick while blindfolded; you'd think the bigger selling point would be seeing a dive like this performed by a blind girl or a triple axel landed by a person who can't see. There's no desire to normalize Sonora's blindness and say she did it in spite of her disability. Am I saying *Ice Castles* is good, then, because Lexie does the jump and the audience finds out she's blind? Eh, kinda, but we don't know if Lexie goes on to skate beyond the finale. *Wild Hearts* ends with an even better story of how Sonora found success as a blind diving girl. Then again, if it was true to life, Sonora would get a short but lucrative endorsement deal, make a spectacle of herself and be lost to obscurity, poverty, and the brief glimmer of remembrance in the form of the occasional answer in a bar trivia night. I do love the movie, though, and forgive its faults.

9 CARETAKER CINEMA

We've spent a lot of time talking about the characters and people who play disabled characters on-screen, but we haven't looked deeply at those behind the camera who make the movies these disabled characters inhabit: primarily able-bodied screenwriters and directors. You have no idea the number of well-intentioned creatives who have talked to me about knowing a disabled person who inspired them and compelled them to utilize said disabled person's story for a project. The Sebastian Stan–starring film, *A Different Man*, which we'll discuss later, does a great job illustrating the co-opting of disabled stories by able-bodied creatives in a plotline involving a playwright who uses (or hijacks, depending on your thoughts) her disabled neighbor for an off-Broadway show. These creatives have their heart in the right place, and as three in four people in the US don't have a disability, we need their allyship. But they often have little experience living with a disability and are reliant solely on these associations with disabled people—they're disabled by proxy. So when they get things wrong or have disabled people (like me) critique them, they respond, "But I know someone" or "This is based on a real person I've met." It's a big reason why true disabled stories are translated into film projects, to head off criticisms.

You've heard about the able-bodied buffer numerous times already and how its insertion in movies is an attempt by an abled creative team to bond the presumably able-bodied audience to a disabled character, either through a character who was once "like them" or by someone who enters into the disabled person's life and now is in some form of dual role. This latter element is a subgenre of disabled narrative I call "caretaker cinema," and it's the co-opting of disabled narratives to focus on the real person the audience should support and be inspired by: an abled caretaker.

There's also an assumption that every disabled person automatically comes with a caregiver so a caretaker cinema performance manifests in a few ways. It can overlap or involve multiple characters in the same story. Really, anyone with a tangential connection to disability counts in these narratives. Audiences gravitate to preconceived formulas, so they look for characters like them—that is, abled. You have stories focused on parental/child relationships, wherein the parent and disabled child navigate the changing power dynamic in their relationship. This technique is popular because the first caregiver anyone has in life is their mother. Films like *Mask* and the 1978 sequel to *The Other Side of the Mountain* look at codependent parental relationships. Siblings are also fodder, with the best-remembered example being 1962's *What Ever Happened to Baby Jane?* Bette Davis plays abled sister, Jane, to Joan Crawford's wheelchair user, Blanche. If you look at the movie through a disabled lens it posits abled siblings resentful of their disabled brothers and sisters. In interabled sibling relationships on-screen, the able-bodied child sublimates their own desires in order to care for a disabled sibling. Other examples include *What's Eating Gilbert Grape*, *Rain Man*, and the 2003 Christmas film *Love, Actually*. You probably forgot the *Love, Actually* plotline where Laura Linney's character has a mentally disabled brother who becomes the ultimate cockblocker. Disabled people: ruining abled lives since time began. No doubt it gets lost amid the Mariah Carey songs and the fat-shaming of a perfectly healthy looking woman because it was the 2000s.

More common are interabled relationships that involve a disabled person and a non-disabled paramour. The able-bodied person can be medical personnel, like a doctor, therapist, or in-home health aide. Or it can be a spouse, usually a wife, tasked with medical caregiving. The abled person's story focuses on how they manage their own life and autonomy while trying to remain the point of stability for the disabled lead and the able-bodied audience. The central conflict of films like this is that a relationship, whether that be friendship or romantic, with a disabled person is emotionally and physically taxing. It's as if to say that dating a disabled person is so medically complex that it consumes all your own hopes and dreams. Think of that next time you're swiping on Tinder, ladies! Because of this, the sexual and romantic dynamics between disabled and abled people are confused. The line between professional and personal is blurred, and too often the emphasis is that disabled people only find romance or fall in love with a caretaker or someone who otherwise understands their complex and myriad health concerns. Rarely do movies look at the real-world consequences of this lack of boundaries. Per a 2018 study, 95 percent of individuals with a disability who are victims of violent crime can identify their perpetrator, and 40 percent of disabled people experience crime by a casual acquaintance like a caregiver or another person they see on a semiregular basis.

But Caretaker Cinema 101, and one of the oft-cited examples of disability in the movies, is best exemplified by Arthur Penn's iconic 1962 adaptation of William Gibson's stage play *The Miracle Worker*. The story of Helen Keller (Patty

Duke) and her teacher, Annie Sullivan (Anne Bancroft), is a sensationalistic, showy movie that garnered Oscars for its leads and became the gold standard for the myth that the quickest way to earn an Oscar is by playing disabled. It's also 106 minutes of watching Duke and Bancroft slap each other, run around, and generally be unpleasant to hang out with. (One of the most controversial takes I present to you in this book: *The Miracle Worker* is a bad movie.) What's frustrating about *The Miracle Worker* is that, in spite of it being made while the real Keller was still alive, it gives us an overwrought origin story that revels in domesticating the wayward Helen by bringing her to heel through violent control.

Anne Bancroft is the Annie Sullivan to Patty Duke's Helen Keller in *The Miracle Worker* (1962). Bettmann / Getty Images

The Miracle Worker is caretaker cinema in two ways: in Anne's interactions with Helen, and Helen's interactions with her parents, specifically her mother Kate (Inga Swenson). We meet Helen as a baby in her crib as her parents scream bloody murder after discovering she is blind and deaf. Kate yells, "Look at her eyes" with all the terror in her voice as when Rosemary Woodhouse meets the infant Antichrist for the first time. Helen's father, Arthur (Victor Jory), just takes to yelling incoherently in the infant's face. (Let's hope there's a baby doll in that crib as a stand-in for baby Helen.) It's an aggressive way to open a movie, to say the least. After that inauspicious beginning, Helen grows into a child who aimlessly wanders, gets caught in things, and turns into an otherwise dirty ragamuffin with no help from her parents or brother. It's fascinating how many disability-centric movies have the disabled character turn gross and unclean (Arnie in *Gilbert Grape* is another example). Everyone in Helen's family is happy to complain about her inability to clean and take care of herself, but no one wants to actually clean or take care of Helen. The real Helen Keller was six years old when she first met Anne Sullivan, but because Patty Duke played the character as a fifteen-year-old the movie asks, "Why can't Helen wash herself? Own a home?! Be an adult?! What's taking her so long?" Enter Anne Sullivan, a legally blind teacher at the Perkins School for the Blind tasked with teaching Helen how to communicate and become a productive member of society. Aside from her blindness, Anne suffers from her own personal trauma. She has a bum hip and, as a child, raised her little brother who was eventually removed from her care. Helen acts as a stand-in for Anne's brother, their friendship giving Anne the closure she needs.

Since dealing with two disabled people is a bridge too far, *The Miracle Worker* chooses to ignore, or at least push to the side, Anne's own disability. It's not outright ignored, but since Anne is an example of a blind person who has adapted to her blindness, it's not the focus so much as Helen learning to speak. You can see where this underplaying manifests in real world misinformation. I've had friends be surprised when they find out Sullivan was also blind. Then again, Helen Keller and Anne Sullivan have retreated into disabled legend. There are even misinformed claims proliferating on the internet that Keller's disabilities were faked. Back in 2021, TikTok was ablaze with people claiming Keller wasn't even a real person, a stark reminder of how so many people know of this movie but haven't watched it.

Helen's father is an equal opportunity ableist. He admits he doesn't enjoy talking to Anne when she's wearing sunglasses, needed to protect her sensitive eyes. And Helen's brother James (Andrew Prine) jokes that, with Anne, "Now we have two of them to look after."

Anne is the able-bodied caretaker by default because she is less disabled than Helen—Anne can speak and hear—and she's a guide for Helen on how to get along with others in society. Anne's teaching methods are unorthodox, to put it mildly, and involve a lot of violence. Anne slaps Helen, puts her in a headlock, denies Helen food, all the things you see during a six o'clock news segment about abusing the disabled. Is Anne also being disabled meant to negate her violent responses? If anyone's gonna slap her, it should be one of their own, right? Then again, Anne thinks Helen is a spoiled child, coddled by her parents, who just want her to learn some manners. They can't have it both ways, though, according to Anne. If they want their daughter to learn how to fold her napkin, then Anne has to go WWE on her! Anne Sullivan walked so Beau Bridges's Dick Buek could run. ("We don't want to spoil her" plays constantly when I watch *The Miracle Worker*.)

Helen's parents can't connect with their daughter, so when Anne tells the Kellers she needs to take Helen and move her out of their house, they don't put up much of a fight. Not even when they hear Anne say Helen "has to be dependent on me" for everything, including "the air she breathes." Kate and Arthur aren't even allowed to visit. Kate waffles a little at being away from her child, but the movie reminds us that the separation is for Helen's own good and her parents will thank Anne when Helen talks to them. What's the point of having children if you can't talk to them? In reality, the move was motivated more so that Helen and Anne could travel to different schools for the deaf before Keller graduated and attended Radcliffe College at Harvard University, none of which is depicted in the film. Cue more wacky adventures with Anne and Helen living in a house and slapping each other.

We know nothing about Helen as a person or her interior life. Patty Duke doesn't narrate to give audiences an able verbalization of her inner thoughts, which makes sense, but one is hard pressed to know if Helen has any joy in her life at all. Anne talks out loud to let people in on what Helen is thinking, but this is *Anne's perception* of what Helen thinks, not *what* she thinks. She certainly doesn't lie when she says she controls every aspect of Helen's life. As with other movies about Deaf people, including *Children of a Lesser God*, the emphasis is on Helen to speak to prove that Anne's methods work. So with six minutes left in the movie Helen finally speaks, with no rhyme or reason short of it finally clicking in her head. When Helen speaks, it's a moment of joy for her, but the camera looks at Anne, who wisely says, "She knows," as if she's Muldoon in Jurassic Park and Helen is the raptor who has just had her own "clever girl" moment. We don't get Helen and her parents reconnecting, which is the entire reason why Anne was hired. Anne Sullivan, Deaf whisperer.

When you think of this movie it's often with the scene of Anne teaching Helen how to say "water" while cranking a water pump in mind. This is such a pop culture and historical touchstone that the US Capitol has a bronze statue re-creating it. Keller and Sullivan continued as companions until the latter's death in 1936, with several books written regarding the intricacies of their relationship. What people don't know are Helen's solo accomplishments, like becoming the first Deaf and blind graduate of Radcliffe to garner a bachelor's degree. She worked for the American Foundation for the Blind and advocated for schools to carry Braille and other blind reading materials. She also cofounded the American Civil Liberties Union and was an early supporter of the NAACP, birth control, and anti-lynching laws. She also was a Socialist who read Marx and was investigated by the FBI as a potential Communist. That childhood of slapping certainly radicalized her! By limiting the scope of Helen's life to learning to speak, the need to look at the woman's mixed reception to disability discourse is unnecessary. Citing Kim Nielsen, Joy Davis points out that Helen supported eugenic policies until 1938, and while she publicly supported legislative policies and funding for disabled programs, support was fueled more by the American Foundation for the Blind, which was funding Keller and Sullivan's lifestyle. Either way, it'd be great to see a movie look at Keller's flaws. Keller herself died in 1968.

What caretaker cinema looks like: a medical professional who comes in like a cool teacher entering the inner city to turn a disabled person's life around. History has told us Anne Sullivan might have benefited (or exploited, depending on your view) Helen Keller, but we don't see it in the movie. However, caretaker cinema places disabled characters in a position where they help an able-bodied lead grow . . . and if that able-bodied lead gets some form of financial windfall, all the better. Remember, a disabled character is always of use to the abled, so there needs to be some type of incentive for the abled person to invest their time, energy, and love into them. The average (able-bodied) person's own journey is the highlight, and the disabled person is happy to have a purpose in helping the abled person find themselves. Placing an average, unskilled person in a medically adjacent caretaker role turns the narrative away from drama to something like a comedy or romance. The 2017 film *The Upside*, an English-language remake of the 2011 French comedy *The Intouchables*, sets this up.

Kevin Hart plays Dell Scott, a down-on-his-luck parolee and "life auxiliary" for the wealthy, paralyzed Philip Lacasse (Bryan Cranston). No matter what Google says, I'm still convinced the phrase "life auxiliary" is a fancy, made-up, ableist retconning of the term "in-home healthcare aide." This is Dell's story. The first scene shows him in the literal driver's seat of a very expensive car. A hint of the riches to come for him! Dell is trying to make ends meet and restore the fractious relationship he has with his ex-wife and son. Philip, a man who describes himself as richer than Jay-Z, was disabled in a paragliding accident.

He has a dual use in *The Upside*. Philip isn't just changing Dell's life by showing him the resilience of disability. He's changing Dell's circumstances by opening doors historically shut to Black people, both monetarily and professionally. He gives Dell a job that boasts a significant salary and also lets him live in Philip's penthouse rent free. Thanks to Philip's prestigious professional connections, Dell is put in situations where he can take advantage of the wealthy. Philip sells one of Dell's tacky paintings to his racist neighbor under the guise of the "unknown painter" (really Dell) being a hot new artist in the making.

Philip fixes Dell's life with no overwrought discussion or awareness of how white privilege works. Dell doesn't seem concerned either, blithely acting like "if you can't beat 'em, join 'em." Chapter 4 already laid out the fallacy of showing financially independent and highly wealthy disabled people. It makes the average audience member think disabled people are made of money or otherwise don't need it. But in *The Upside* the relationship between the caretaker (Dell) and the employee (Philip) is financially advantageous to one person only: the able-bodied caretaker. Philip, with his extreme wealth, is a piggy bank in a wheelchair. He says, "Money can't buy everything" but it feels so hollow when he's wheeling around in his extremely expensive, tricked-out electric wheelchair through a massive apartment in New York City with small portable ramps discreetly placed in the frame, plus an elevator. He has every accommodation known to humankind, so I'd say money can damn well buy most everything, Phil. Tell me more about your challenges as I convince my insurance company to replace the wheels on my manual wheelchair.

The Upside is littered with teachable moments for the carer acting as the audience surrogate. When Philip and Dell go to a diner, Philip is surprised when the waiter talks to him. He points out disabled invisibility, which is relatable. But then there are other moments that are eye-roll inducing, like the movie's reliance on gay panic. Dell is terrified of helping Philip with his disabled bathroom problems because, gasp, it involves male genitalia and Dell, double gasp, is also a man! Dell gets grossed out about having to see Philip's penis while helping him with his catheter, and later gets indignant when Philip gets an involuntary erection. But since Dell and Philip have a mutually beneficial relationship Dell focuses less on the fact that he's got a pretty damn good job that is shockingly low maintenance and more about how he's giving a disabled man an opportunity to live.

As far as Dell sees it, he puts up with a lot and should get a thank-you from Philip for everything. Dell opened up Philip's world, taking the disabled man out of his swanky townhouse and helping him interact with the outside. Never mind that Philip could have gone out without Dell's help, but since Philip falls into the trope that disabled people suffer from year-round depression it takes Dell's quirkiness to bring him out of his wealthy shell. Dell tells Philip he is ungrateful because Philip's friends buy him expensive gifts that the disabled man doesn't appreciate. Dell reminds Philip that he can have fancy parties. Dell then proceeds to start breaking Philip's expensive things. (If I had a nickel for every movie that saw an abled person trashing a disabled person's house to prove a point, I'd be as wealthy as Philip Lacasse) Dell gets a far grander (financial) reward for deigning to be Philip's friend, which crosses out Phil as the white savior. Dell leaves Philip's employment with enough money to buy his ex-wife a house in a safe neighborhood. He also gets a new job at a high-tech wheelchair supplier, which ... durable medical equipment is the biggest racket in the healthcare industry so thanks for being part of the problem. What happens to Philip? He's grateful for what he has, potentially engaging in a relationship with his put-upon vice president, played by a wasted Nicole Kidman, and learns how to be a real boy, thanks to Dell.

Caretaker cinema blends a person who takes care of a disabled person's physical needs with their own emotional needs. A caretaker becomes a partner, and sometimes that partnership is a sexual one. A disabled movie that employs the caretaker cinema trope in a romantic context shockingly erases the line between employee and sex worker. "Are you a caretaker who wants to have sex with your disabled client?" is a question brought up, albeit in the meanings, of several disabled films. Sexual harassment laws say what? Outside of the multiple levels of questionable power dynamics at play—employer versus employee, financial status/need, abled versus disabled—films that equate a paid caretaker with a sexual partner emphasize that a disabled person's world is crafted and defined by those actively taking care of them and that their dating options are exclusively restricted to this pool. There's an added dichotomy with how it plays with gender. Men retain some semblance of power that is never diminished by their disability. The majority of disabled men on-screen are physically disabled and have a romantic partner able to see past their aesthetic imperfections, though there are outliers. Disabled women are beautiful and determined to convince a man to see past their physical imperfections, visible or otherwise.

The Upside makes a pretty good case to disabled viewers about why they should limit their dating pool to people who know them in a caretaking capacity. Philip has two romantic prospects: his business associate Yvonne (the aforementioned Kidman), whom he actively employs and pays a salary to, and Lily (Julianna Margulies), a woman he corresponds with via letters. Lily is a normie and the "epistolary relationship" she has with Philip is maintained because he thinks she has zero idea he's in a wheelchair. If she did find out, says Philip, she'd reject him. Dell rightly assumes Lily has already Googled Philip and forces, or, as he says, gives Philip "a little push" into calling her and arranging a date.

The couple meet, and it starts out as a positive depiction of an interabled relationship. Lily tells Dell to leave and comes off as totally prepared for her date with the wheelchair-using Philip, helping him eat while she maintains a conversation with him. So far, so good! Things take a turn as the camera, as Lily's POV, zooms in on a very small sauce stain on Philip's lapel. Then she notices his hands don't move. She knew he was paralyzed going in, so not sure why this is something she focuses on after thirty minutes of talking to him. Lily eventually says she thought she could "handle" Philip's disability but that "it's not what I expected." Lily doesn't go into what her specific expectations were, mind you, so she comes off as a fickle bitch. After unburdening herself to Philip, she asks if they can remain friends and when he, understandably, gets indignant, she responds with "I shouldn't have been so honest." Taylor Swift must have written the line "so casually cruel in the name of being honest" in "All Too Well" about Lily. Prove me wrong. The scene is a cruel reminder that Philip expects too much from abled women. His personality and his money (let's not forget the money) just aren't enough for a woman to ignore his extreme disabledness. Maybe that's what he meant money can't buy! The only one built to look at his disabled penis is Dell, like it or not. Okay, maybe Yvonne, but we don't see any overt affection between the two so who knows. She's also still an employee, reiterating the concept that able-bodied people who know the "real" (i.e., abled) version of the disabled person understand and accept their unique challenges and see past their disability enough to date them.

Dell brings in sex workers to give Philip and him massages in *The Upside*, but there's no reason to believe sex took place. In *Mask*, Rusty brings home a sex worker for Rocky, with the humor derived from the teenage boy and the prostitute chatting about life and having an innocuous breakfast the next morning. Sex is a tricky topic with regard to the disabled. There's still an assumption that disabled people don't have sex or aren't sexually desirous. Interabled relationships exist, but there aren't enough stats to showcase how frequent they are. Too often it's situations of like attracting like. *The Shape of Water* has Elisa's romantic prospect being the Gill Man. He respects and loves her, but it plays on the stereotype that disabled people can connect solely with similar outsiders. Some movies go so far as to have the caretaker associated outright with sex work. In the 2016 adaptation of Jojo Moyes's best-selling book, *Me Before You*, the caretaker-as-partner trope goes down some of the weirdest, and most disturbing, roads you've ever seen, ushering in all the complicated power dynamics you'd think of between an abled hired carer and their disabled employee while adding in a heavy layer of suicide porn.

Me Before You follows wealthy white man Will Traynor (Sam Claflin), a bitter quadriplegic living in a massive English castle. That's right, he lives in a literal English castle. He's committed to killing himself, not because of the castle but because of his disability so his family hires a quirky, inexperienced caregiver named Lou (Emilia Clarke) to help him with his daily needs and, hopefully, rev his inner engine enough to convince him to keep living.

I read Moyes's book in preparation to see the movie when it dropped in 2016. I subscribe to the principle of knowing thy enemy, so I went in prepared for what was to come. The studio reps at my screening handed everyone branded *Me Before You* tissues prior to start and while I did cry, dear reader, it had more to do with what I (and other disabled viewers) were forced to endure than with anything passing for sadness at the plot.

Me Before You shows being a disabled caregiver as a job literally anyone can do. It's the only job where one's inexperience is what makes them shine. When Yvonne introduces life auxiliaries in *The Upside*, those with experience are played up as phony and remarkably ableist. Sure, the guy who answers his interview question with "I don't hear 'disability.' I hear 'this ability'" is problematic AF. It's a pandering, ableist answer on par with someone trying to cast aside white privilege by saying they don't see color. But it's not wrong to expect a stranger who is going to care for my health and person to have some modicum of knowledge about disability, not a guy like Dell who comes in off the street and asks why Philip's arms don't work. Where you might see charm, I see a potential negligence case. The same is true for Lou in *Me Before You*, who takes umbrage with the fact that Will ignores her and leaves her to do nothing more than hang out in a castle all day reading books. Then again, Lou doesn't appear to have the ability to smell out a bad scene. The ad she reads mentions the Traynors are seeking "care and companion[ship] for a disabled man," yet when she arrives to meet Will's mother, who is also the house manager, the woman says, "Think of yourself as a friend rather than a paid professional." Lou is told her role is to "cheer him [Will] up." Will's mom also makes a stray comment about what Lou is wearing, starting the strange interplay between employee and sex worker that, by the end, is nonexistent. Lou isn't fazed by any of this.

Will Traynor, like Philip Lacasse, is so privileged it's ridiculous. He's got a castle; I can't get over that! Even Will's accident stems from him being kind of an entitled shit. Just as with Christopher Reeve's *Rear Window*, Will's accident is an advertisement for why cell phones are dangerous. He's distracted by a phone call while crossing the street and is hit by a car. Will is perpetually angry, like any good bitter cripple, as well as suicidal. Everyone in Will's life, including his own parents, talk about his "choice to die" as if his desire to commit suicide is analogous to a cancer patient stopping chemotherapy. *He wants to kill himself, so his decision should be respected!* Hard to believe that anyone would feel the same way about an able-bodied, healthy person making a "choice" to kill themselves. Will says, "I get that this could be a good life, but it's not *my* life" (emphasis mine). Where is the line drawn between a good and bad life?

Moyes wrote the script for the film version of her book, itself inspired by two people she knew who required twenty-four-hour care for unknown reasons, coupled with a story she read about a young man who became a quadriplegic. "I was so shocked by his story because, as a parent, I couldn't understand how you would ever agree to take your own child to end their life," she said in a 2016 interview. "I was probably quite judgmental as well."

She utilizes caretaker language by looking at the situation through the lens of a parent to discuss her shock and surprise about what she is writing about. She goes on to place herself in the disabled person's situation but emphasizes she understands little about the realities of it, short of her own, able-bodied thinking. "I didn't know much about quadriplegia. I didn't know about the health aspects," she said. "It's not just a matter of being in a chair, it's a constant state of interventions and indignities and health problems. I started to think, 'What would it be like if someone you loved made that decision? What would it be like if you were that person?' . . . I think I would be bitter and angry and envious of people who still got to use their bodies." What's funny is that, while she acknowledges her lack of awareness of quadriplegia, instead of advocating for disabled people to tell these stories she co-opts it. Caretaker cinema is about closing the door on the disabled and talking over them. Beware of Greeks bearing gifts or, in this case, an able-bodied person saying, "I understand your story because I read about it. . . ."

Lou, hoping to change Will's mind, takes him on expensive vacations (with his money), where she subsequently falls in love with him. Because the true protagonist is Lou, the viewer watches her learn about disability through knowing Will, discovering several teachable moments, and growing into her own person. Lou plants herself firmly in the role of Will's advocate, no different from a mom like Rusty in *Mask*. Unfortunately, Lou's desire to help Will is at the expense of what he wants. Lou takes Will to a racetrack and doesn't listen when she's told the ramp to his car will sink in the mud. When it does exactly what she was warned it would do, she forgoes Will's dignity and solicits strangers to help lift him and his chair. When Lou and Will are denied entry into a restaurant at the track, it is Lou who starts yelling and embarrassing Will. Even Lou's love for Will is on her terms. She declares she loves him and expects him to immediately change his plans. He should be grateful and reciprocate her love. When he doesn't, she takes it as outright rejection of her and gets upset. Imagine if this situation played out in a real caregiver/caretaker relationship. Will could just be uninterested in dating her. Yes, Will shouldn't want to kill himself and the fact that he has people who care about him—not just Lou but his parents as well—should be an enticement. But Lou is kind of making it about her.

Will decides to go through with the suicide and travels to a beautiful death chalet in Switzerland to do the deed. His death isn't depicted on-screen but is punctuated with a feather wafting on a breeze, à la *Forrest Gump*. But Will's death isn't in vain, oh no. Will's death makes Lou realize how precious life is and also what can be accomplished with someone else's money. He leaves Lou a significant sum of money to "buy [her] freedom" from the small town she appears happy living in. "Knowing you still have possibilities is a luxury," says Will's disembodied voice to Lou in a letter he pens before his death. Disability is, per Will, a one-way street with absolutely no room for choice. This said by a man with no financial issues and limitless possibilities, regardless of ability. He closes out the letter by telling Lou, "I'll be walking beside you." Lou can be happy spending Will's money and believing, like Lieutenant Dan's priest talking about the kingdom of heaven, that his death cured him of his disability.

A movie where a sex worker is a caretaker, or at least presented in a therapeutic capacity, is found in the 2012 film *The Sessions*, a frank and funny exploration of sex through the eyes of a severely disabled character. Based on Mark O'Brien's 1990 article "On Seeing a Sex Surrogate," the movie follows O'Brien (John Hawkes), a polio sufferer who spends his days in an iron lung, as he engages in a relationship with a professional sex surrogate named Cheryl (Helen Hunt). *The Sessions* is underrated. It never shies away from showing the hilarious and cringey interactions between Mark and Cheryl and tries to explicate why blending sex work and healthcare work is problematic. After watching so many disabled characters bemoan their lack of love, or who go off and kill themselves because they think they're doomed to eternal loneliness, it's nice to watch one just try to get laid. It's one of the few times I'll forgive an able actor like Hawkes in the role, especially considering that polio is fairly eliminated in the West. Mark is a journalist and spends time interviewing various disabled people for an article he's writing on disabled sexuality. His interviews are with actual disabled performers, including scene-stealer and wheelchair user Jennifer Kumiyama, who recounts some wild sexual experiences, and their stories are fun, kinky tales that are weird and varied for everyone to hear, not just disabled people. It's a very sex-positive movie.

Cheryl is a sex therapist of sorts, rooting out Mark's hangups about his life and sex. The script highlights the shame and embarrassment disabled people face for wanting to have sex, much of it motivated by the stereotypes that situate us as too difficult to deal with sexually. Mark is also deeply religious, so alongside his disability he is also mired in Catholic guilt. Outside of Cheryl, Mark's female interactions include Amanda (Annika Marks), a sweet young woman who, like *Me Before You*'s Lou, has no caretaking experience prior to meeting Mark. She's just pretty and willing to learn. She brings Mark out of his shell, and while their relationship is platonic, Amanda's boyfriend finds her intimacy with Mark alarming. When Mark proposes to Amanda she says no, thinking he's motivated by her beauty and kindness to him, which isn't untrue. Mark's world is bound by caretakers and his relationships with medicalized personnel, so his confusion about what a real relationship looks like makes sense. Mark thinks that by having sex and meeting Cheryl, *she* will change *his* life. That sex and a relationship are all that're needed to create a sense of fullness for him. Mark thinks having sex, especially with an abled woman, will negate the feelings he's had about being disabled.

It's hard to say people are ableist all over if you aren't putting yourself out there, yet the fact that there are few disabled relationships on-screen and in popular culture does a lot to reiterate that disabled people don't have them. If they did, wouldn't we see them everywhere? Cheryl develops feelings for Mark as they start their sex therapy, though it's unclear why out of all Cheryl's patients, Mark is the one she has such deep feelings for. After completing his therapy with Cheryl, Mark ends up meeting Susan (Robin Weigert), another woman with medical connections whom he eventually marries, but the script says she is not his only option; rather, she's the woman he genuinely fell in love with. Mark O'Brien passed away in 1999 at the age of forty-nine, and though the movie ends with him discussing his death, it's presented as a life well lived and, I'm assuming, well laid.

Movies where disabled characters have relationships with noncaretakers—and, though disabled, are in charge of their sexual autonomy—are outliers.

There are other rare examples of authentic sexual interactions between disabled characters that aren't reliant on caretakers but are regular ol' sexual situations. The gold standard of disabled sex scenes in a noncaretaker situation is 1978's *Coming Home*. When Jon Voight's Luke and Jane Fonda's Sally finally jump into bed, it's an amazing sequence, sex aside, as the audience watches the interrelationship between intimacy and communication. It's hot regardless of ability. Luke tells Sally exactly what he needs to be comfortable, free of any medical language or awkwardness. Sally asks Luke if he can feel anything while they have sex, to which he responds, "I can't feel it, but I can see it." With a single line of dialogue, you understand exactly how Luke sees and responds to sexual stimulation.

Jon Voight is the self-sufficent Luke Martin in *Coming Home* (1978) opposite Jane Fonda. Michael Ochs Archives / Stringer / Getty Images

Luke in *Coming Home* is concerned with Sally's sexual satisfaction during the sequence detailed above. Compare that to *Me Before You* when Will tells Lou he can't give her what she wants and turns down the opportunity to have sex with her. Hard not to think it's because he doesn't want to engage in any sex that would not give him pleasure or mimic abled sex 100 percent. In *The Other Side of the Mountain: Part II*, Marilyn Hassett's character Jill starts a relationship with her landlord, John Boothe (Timothy Bottoms), that eventually turns sexual. Jill's accident happened when she was a teenager so she mentions to John she is a virgin. (Remember, Ron Kovic in *Born on the Four of July* is another disabled virgin who eventually gets laid.) The sex act itself isn't on-screen, but Jill's character expresses what she wants and, more importantly, has it reciprocated by her partner without any sense of judgment. *The Waterdance*, codirected by disabled filmmaker Neal Jimenez, makes a point of having its lead character engage in sex, emphasizing the logistics of quad sex in a way that can be cringe-inducing, due to its awkwardness, but always authentic.

There's one relationship that is the backbone of caretaker cinema narratives, that blends the work of a caretaker with the fun of someone you can have sex with free of any troubling questions: wives. It's always wives in these movies. You might get an *Other Side of the Mountain* here and there, where an abled man has a relationship with a disabled woman but you never see an abled husband deal with a disabled wife in a film. Women see past physical aesthetics, after all. They can date a disabled man and take care of them, but men don't put up with that. Stats bear this out. Studies conducted in both 2009 and 2016 illustrate that married women who come down with a severe or terminal illness are at a higher risk for divorce compared to married men in the same situation. If you want a film example, there's always *Home of the Brave*.

Movies in this vein crib a lot from Ron Howard's 2001 film *A Beautiful Mind*, with its love-conquers-all narrative and a committed wife able to fix everything through her own determination and awareness of her disabled husband's unique disabled challenges. The Oscar-bait-y films *The Theory of Everything* (2014) and *Breathe* (2017) tell similar stories of a brilliant (and British) man struck by disability who continues being brilliant through the help of his wife. Said wife sublimates and struggles to balance her needs, and the needs of their family, alongside his. And don't forget the significance of these movies being based on real people. Able-bodied family members in charge of these narratives bring in an extra layer of caretaking while limiting criticism. "The family is cool with it, so screw your ableist claims." These movies become about the stewards of the disabled person's life and emphasize the legacy the steward places on the disabled person.

The Theory of Everything is supposed to be a biopic on the life of famed physicist and cosmologist Stephen Hawking, yet screenwriter Anthony McCarten specifically adapted the memoir of Hawking's wife, Jane. McCarten also spent time interacting with the real Jane, not Hawking himself, though the physicist gave the movie his blessing; the film was made four years prior to his death. With Jane Hawking established as the able-bodied buffer, the audience meets Stephen (Eddie Redmayne) first, prior to his disability. It takes twenty-four minutes for him to receive a diagnosis of motor neuron disease, which is pretty early for movies like this. He's told his life expectancy is two years, but since this is a two-hour feature and Hawking was alive at the time we already know he'll defy the odds. Stephen goes into a depression after his diagnosis and pushes aside his friends and Jane (Felicity Jones). When Jane refuses to go away, Stephen tells her, "You don't know what's coming. It'll affect everything." He's not wrong, but with her being an abled wife and based on those divorce stats, she implies she ain't going anywhere. Jane is a Good Woman and says, "We're going to fight this illness together." As Michelle Dean wrote for *The Guardian* upon the release of *The Theory of Everything*, "If that [above quote] sounds a little pat to you, it does to me, too. This scene never appears in the memoir."

The pair marry, and the movie vacillates between Stephen adapting to his increasingly deteriorating condition and Jane caring for him and their kids. We're treated to *totally* nonexploitative scenes of him trying to walk, sliding down stairs (why buy a home with stairs at all?), and struggling to eat at the family dinner table. Thankfully, there's no scene of Jane telling Stephen, "We don't want to spoil him." (I'm starting to think Dick Buek wasn't a good boyfriend.) It's weird how movies love finding humor in situations where wheelchairs can't fit through doors or characters navigate inaccessible locations. Kudos to this movie, alongside *Breathe* and *Me Before You* for showing bulky, supportive customized wheelchairs, at least. Stephen also gets carried by his friends and just plopped in places like a sack of potatoes. There are also several scenes of Jane pulling a bulky hospital wheelchair around because she isn't gonna call anyone for help. She's a strong wife.

Jane runs between the various people who rely on her. She goes from putting a sweater on Stephen to caring for a crying baby, the scene saying both need her in the same way. When Stephen gets a motorized wheelchair he and the kids use it to fly around the living room, breaking stuff in their wake. Jane is a mother to her husband as much as she is to her children. When Stephen starts choking, Jane saves him and, afterward, goes to secretly cry in another room. It's unclear whether she's crying out of frustration or helplessness, though why not both? When Jane finally tells Stephen she does need help, it's not because of her but because their son is "missing out on a childhood." Jane finds help in the kindhearted choir director Jonathan (Charlie Cox), and the two abled people eventually fall in love. It's okay, though, because Stephen himself is in love with his nurse, who enjoys looking at nudie mags with him. The boundaries here. It is nice seeing Hawking presented as kind of a shit, all things considered, which is based on truth. Hawking was known to belittle Jane's work and her own ambitions, which isn't focused on in the movie because we can't have him turn against the one woman willing to put up with him. The two do split but remain close companions, with the understanding being that Hawking probably wouldn't have survived without Jane.

It's doubtful *Breathe* would have existed if not for the success (and awards significance) of *The Theory of Everything*. *Breathe* is the "inspiring true love story" of Robin and Diana Cavendish (Andrew Garfield and Claire Foy, respectively) who maintain their love for each other as they grapple with Robin coming down with polio. Diana learns to care for Robin and the pair become involved in the creation of a portable ventilator that helps them travel the world. Unlike Hawking, Robin Cavendish was a guy who loved traveling and spent a lot of time in Kenya in the 1950s, but don't worry, there's no white colonizing here if you're curious. It's a story that, short of playing to those who love inspiring disabled stories, seems like it was greenlit for a party of one, specifically the Cavendish family. Jonathan Cavendish, the real-life son of Robin and Diana, and his production company made the movie. Robin and Diana have a picture-perfect life (baby, happy marriage, hanging out in Kenya like it's *Out of Africa*) before—boom!—polio. Robin's illness plays similarly to Hawking's, including his family members and doctors writing Robin off for dead. The doctor tells Diana, "The mercy of [polio] is they don't last long." Robin becomes depressed and pushes Diana and their infant son away. Notice the pattern? Frustrated, Diana tells the doctors she'll care for Robin and give him a happy life.

Where Jane Hawking was a nursemaid and mother to her grown husband and children, Diana is this close to earning a medical degree herself with how quickly she takes up everything associated with Robin's illness. She learns how to work with a tracheostomy tube and finds a way to get Robin physically out of the polio ward and back home. Said home is inaccessible with stairs but baby steps. "No nurse. Just Diana" isn't just a line of dialogue but *Breathe*'s *entire* theme. Jane Hawking admits when she's overwhelmed and needs help. Not Diana Cavendish. Diana's friends and family tell her she needs to go out and have an identity away from her husband but she says hell no. Her life is consumed by making Robin's life accessible. Screw Audrey Hepburn's "world's champion blind lady." Diana Cavendish is going for disabled caretaker sainthood here. The film ends with Robin dying in 1984—similar to *Me Before You*, he goes the privately triumphant euthanasia route—but before he does he tells Diana "you can be free at last," as if he's God granting Diana a miracle. The disabled Robin makes his death the greatest grand gesture for his partner: releasing her from the burden of being with him. Diana responds with "my life is your life." The audience wonders what Diana will do now, since she seemingly has nothing outside of her husband. The final image of the movie is Robin standing with Diana despite the fact he spent more time with her as a disabled man than he ever did as an abled one.

We need disabled allies, so I don't want to end this chapter with people assuming the moral of this chapter is: Don't help disabled people. The issue is how twisted in knots stories become about blending allyship with caretaking and romance. While disabled people are only one thing, caretaker cinema makes the abled protagonist do everything. It also fails to explore the murky boundaries that come from having relationships with caretakers. Really, let's just expand the world for disabled heroes. They don't always need to date their caretakers, nor do their caretakers have to be doctors. Screenwriters, let's challenge ourselves to broaden the scope for both sides.

10 CRIPPING UP AND THE OSCAR MYTH

It's said the greatest lie the devil ever told was convincing people he didn't exist. I'd say it's actually that if you play a disabled character you're automatically guaranteed an Oscar. As *Tropic Thunder* laid out, and as discussed back in chapter 5, disability narratives can be showy Oscar-bait. An actor plays someone with cognitive disabilities, emphasizes their extensive research on their press tour, and, if they play the disability card *just* right, goes on to win an Oscar. You aren't always walking away with the little gold man, but it certainly is a quick way to get on the ballot.

The practice of able-bodied actors playing disabled people, otherwise referred to as "cripping up," has been around forever. Never forget early shorts like *The Legless Runner* and *The Cripple's Marriage*, along with Golden's *The Deaf Mute's Ball* (1907) from chapter 1. Nearly every movie we've discussed has involved an able-bodied actor putting on a disability as if it were a costume, "wearing" their wheelchair or mobility aids like a coat, and taking them off when the cameras stop rolling. Some of the justifications made today about the decision to crip up are that acting is the art of performance and movies are fantasy, which are true. The problem is that this is perceived as acceptable. If one were to say this about playing another minority, like Kirk Lazarus and his usage of blackface, there'd be more backlash. Not to mention, this implies that the playing field is level and that disabled actors are being auditioned alongside, and in the same numbers, as abled actors. Which isn't true. Bryan Cranston, while doing press for *The Upside*, acknowledged that "you can understand, but you cannot really know what it feels like to live in that skin" when asked about playing a wheelchair user himself. Two years later, when asked about the film again, Cranston seemed to about-face. "If I, as a straight, older person, and I'm wealthy, I'm very fortunate, does that mean I can't play a person who is not wealthy, does that mean I can't play a homosexual?" He later said in another interview with Sky News that, while opportunities for disabled people should certainly be expanded, "Where does the restriction apply? Where is the line for that?" People should be able to play whoever and whatever in movies, but that works only if disabled talent are on the same level as their abled counterparts. Until that day comes, Cranston is gonna get a "Sure, Jan" from me.

Cripping up yielding prestige is a newer phenomenon. According to a 2020 article from the USC Annenberg Center for Health Journalism, "In 93 years of Oscar nominations, 63 [nominations] are for actors portraying characters with disabilities. 27 actors are winners and only two of those are actual performers with disabilities." If you're curious, those two mentioned are our old pals Harold Russell, for *Best Years of Our Lives*, and Marlee Matlin, for *Children of a Lesser God*. Troy Kotsur's Best Supporting actor win in 2021 for *CODA* now makes it three. "But Kristen," you say. "How does one win an Oscar for playing a disabled person? What's the secret ingredient?" Part of it, as already mentioned, is playing a disabled person who's charming and has a special talent, like RDJ mentions in *Tropic Thunder*. The old "of use" principle. One thing a movie hoping to leverage disability for an Oscar does is find a true story to crib from. My family and I joke constantly about who will play me in the movie of my life. (Anna Kendrick, whenever you're ready, call me.) Any good Oscar-bait movie that involves disability includes a real person to bring in an established framework for the story, and a mien of authenticity. Either the central character has done something remarkable that developed after their disability, or their ability to survive and thrive while disabled *is* the narrative. The "based on a true story" factor also discourages any criticisms that comes as the result of artistic license and/or ableism. Have a problem with this abled actor playing a disabled character? They were selected by the real person, or the real person gave their blessing. Don't like a narrative tweak to the story? It's not a documentary. Plus, the actor did a ton of research and work to get the performance just right. These are the facts, people! They're unimpeachable.

When Disney produced the movie *Christopher Robin* in 2018, most saw the title character (played by Ewan McGregor) as a stand-in for *Winnie the Pooh* author A. A. Milne. This isn't an A. A. Milne biopic, but it takes selective elements to create a Christopher Robin who wants to connect with his daughter and revisits the fictional characters that lived in his mind. It's certainly a movie heavily *inspired* by Milne's life. The problem is Milne really did have a daughter, named Clare, who lived with cerebral palsy. But if you watch *Christopher Robin*, you believe the fictional interpretation of that character is an able-bodied, bright-eyed tween. *It's not a biopic! This is a movie where Ewan McGregor talks to CGI versions of a teddy bear and a pig, Kristen!* The problem is that, unless disability is the central narrative, it's easy for screenwriters to erase actual disabled people from the cinematic historical record. History becomes fiction and if disability isn't necessary to the fiction we get outright erasure. Don't forget 2017's *The Greatest Showman*, the story of a kindhearted, lovable P. T. Barnum (Hugh Jackman) and his desire to make everyone see disabled circus oddities the way he did: as people! I can't lie, the movie's earworm songs and earnestness make me forget the real P. T. Barnum was a schmuck who exploited disabled and Black people for decades. Hell, the movie has you think Barnum paid everyone who worked for him (and that they all live in the museum he runs, but that's another story). The movie views the circus world through the rosiest of rose-colored glasses, with the oddities having minor aesthetic issues—there's one little person and a host of able-bodied people in makeup and prosthetics—as everyone sings about acceptance. The irony shouldn't be lost on anyone that the film's Oscar-nominated song "This Is Me," a song about body acceptance, is now used to hawk a medication people use for weight loss. Don't worry, just enjoy those songs! We know movies are fictional, no matter if they're biopics or not, but movies like *The Greatest Showman* and *Christopher Robin* illustrate the ways able-bodied screenwriters and directors trick the audience into not asking about how disability is portrayed, or erased, to tell a story.

In the case of Oscar-bait films, biopics are recognized by awards bodies for their pomposity and seriousness, the way they demonstrate the triumph of the human spirit. Like it or not, true stories and real people are the surest (some might say laziest) way to get into the Oscar race, especially if their focus is on the audience's dazzlement and amazement by the perseverance of transcending a disability. Patty Duke's portrayal of Helen Keller in *The Miracle Worker*, and her learning how to say and identify water, is a prime example that yielded five Academy Award nominations, including wins for Duke and Anne Bancroft. They show how certain people are celebrated and revered through the leveraging of disability and the power of inspiration. Even a deserved win, like Harold Russell's two Oscars for *Best Years of our Lives* falls into this category. Russell rightly won two awards, but the movie existed because Major General Norman T. Kirk used Russell to show vets "the inspiration they needed." And after winning those two Oscars we know Hollywood was unwilling to let Russell continue acting. Once the inspiration wanes and awards season ends disabled winners find themselves out in the cold.

The prototype for the cripping up Oscar is found in David Lynch's 1980 feature *The Elephant Man*. As with later Oscar darlings like *Forrest Gump*, *Rain Man*, and *Sling Blade*, this one had everyone in 1980 yelling, "I am not an animal. I am a human being" like it was *Network*'s "I'm mad as hell."

It's hard to dislike *Elephant Man* entirely because of how Lynch (who also cowrote the script) tells the story, coupled with John Hurt's fantastic, Oscar-nominated performance. But the movie employs formulas of the past to tell a sensationalized and tragic story. The film lays out the story of John Merrick (Hurt), a man living with severe physical deformities. Merrick is routinely abused and exploited by a man named Bytes (Freddie Jones), who puts him in exploitative traveling circus acts when he isn't beating him to a pulp. Merrick, sickly and weak, is saved by Dr. Frederick Treves (Anthony Hopkins), who teaches Merrick how to communicate, gives him a home, and makes him popular among the upper classes. Treves is the kindhearted, able-bodied buffer whose life is changed through his interactions with Merrick. One of the central conflicts of their relationship is proving to the world that Merrick is an intelligent man. Treves makes a point of working on Merrick's communication, reminiscent of Annie Sullivan and Helen Keller in *The Miracle Worker*. Funnily enough, Oscar-winner Anne Bancroft, Annie Sullivan herself, makes an appearance in this movie. She has a cameo not just because of her association with that 1962 film but also because her husband, director Mel Brooks, was a producer on this movie.

Merrick is a poor, disabled victim who is robbed, beaten, and enslaved with no real agency of his own. The truth behind the story is that the real Merrick lived a pretty peaceful, uneventful, and short life that, if he weren't so spectacularly disabled, probably wouldn't have warranted a movie at all. As we see in movies of the 1930s, or the Victorian times in which *The Elephant Man* is set, Merrick's entertainment value is that he is a disabled spectacle. This is something Cindy Lacom discusses in her 2005 article "'The Time Is Sick and Out of Joint': Physical Disability in Victorian England" while discussing the real-life Merrick with regard to Victorian labor and the economic potential of disabled bodies. As she explains, the Victorian freak show calmed able-bodied anxieties because they placed the disabled in situations where they mimicked cultural norms. We see this in the movie when Merrick reads books and performs Shakespeare opposite actress Madge Kendall (Bancroft). Drawing comparisons to the good-hearted, blind flower seller in *City Lights*, the movie has Madge Kendall and Treves's own wife act as arbiters of whether Merrick is socially acceptable. Madge goes so far as to kiss Merrick and declare, "You are not an elephant man at all." "Elephant man," in this case, refers to him as animalistic and primitive, and his performance shows him as intelligent and educated to those who are able-bodied. Madge also acts as a surrogate mother; Merrick's own is said to have abandoned him. Merrick is so grateful as to be pathetic at times. He cries at one point, saying, "I'm not used to being treated so well by a beautiful woman." Merrick says he "tries to be good" so that he can make his mother proud. In reality Merrick, whose deformities didn't start until he was five years old, enjoyed a close relationship with his mother until she died when he was eleven.

The movie forces a literal rewriting of Merrick's own history to sell his victimhood. If not for Treves's beneficence, he would be lost to history, it claims. The script used Treves's own account of John (real name Joseph) Merrick: 1923's *The Elephant Man and Other Reminiscences* as its main source material. Treves and British anthropologist Ashley Montagu crafted the narrative that "[Merrick] was a captive slave . . . in the position of a dog tied to a post, traded like an animal from one showman to another." So it makes sense that Treves is written as Merrick's savior who refuses to see himself as the man's owner but as his teacher and friend. It also ignores Treves's own writing on Merrick, whom he first describes as "the most disgusting specimen of humanity that I had ever seen . . . at no time had I met with such a degraded or perverted version of a human being."

Lynch's film makes Treves conflicted and, in some instances, unlikable. When he first discovers Merrick, he asks Merrick's owner if he can see him at the hospital. Once he gets to the Royal Hospital of London, Treves puts him on display to his medical society, stripping him naked and showing him off to his colleagues like a sideshow oddity. He refers to Merrick as an example of the "perverted or degraded conditions of the human body" and makes a point of saying that his genitals remain "entirely intact," conjuring up memories of the marketing of 1932's *Freaks* that said it answered the question "Do the Siamese Twins make love?" or "Can a full-grown woman truly love a midget?" As Leslie A. Fiedler writes in "Pity and Fear: Images of the Disabled in Literature and the Popular Arts," the real Treves was specific in how he wrote Merrick's narrative. "His [Treves's] book did not appear, in fact, until 1923, but the events he relates in it had occurred between 1894 and 1890. . . . Over that gap of forty years actual events had been recast to conform to certain Victorian archetypes of the disabled." Publishing it during the Edwardian era allowed the story to become a "Victorian fable," as Fiedler calls it, that shows people's new progressive sympathy for those with disabilities and the benefits of science and healthcare (subsidized by the rich, who were such good people). It said loathing and fear of the disabled were irrational and those who exhibited it the most were the lower classes. Even the story that Merrick's mother was frightened/attacked by an elephant and it resulted in giving Merrick the moniker of "The Elephant Man" is steeped in the nineteenth-century idea of maternal impression, the belief that any shock to the mother's system is imprinted on her child. It's something Merrick believed throughout his entire life, and Lynch plays it up as a literal thing. As Treves spends more time with Merrick, the audience sees he has changed emotionally, but he also makes good professionally by his association with Merrick. His wife says, "John Merrick is happier and more fulfilled in his life and it's all because of you [Treves]." Treves does question his inner goodness, however, because he is still showing Merrick to others and exploiting the man's deformities. This is unnecessary by the end when Merrick, always the grateful disabled, tells Treves, "I am happy every moment of the day because I know that I am loved. I could not say that if it weren't for you."

History is written by the winners, or the abled, in this case. Merrick's story has been co-opted and transformed by abled people since his death at twenty-seven. His real manager, showman Tom Norman, said Merrick didn't truly like Treves because the doctor stripped and sold him like "an animal in a cattle market." Treves believed Merrick was abandoned by his mother and had no family because, according to Norman, Merrick didn't trust Treves enough to tell him. Considering Norman was trying to position himself as Merrick's true guardian angel, his account is as dubious and steeped in ableism as is Treves's. In actuality, Merrick had far more agency than either man, or Lynch's film, give him credit for. He did what he had to do to survive by exploiting his own disabilities. After Merrick's mother died, his father got him a hawker's license to sell items door to door. He struggled to make money in the profession because of his deteriorating speech, coupled with people's fear of him. A severe beating by his father forced Merrick to turn to the workhouse, a place where the destitute did hard labor in return for food and shelter. He eventually turned to the sideshow circuit because, as Lacom writes, "Merrick's body remains other, but his earning potential is familiar." He started touring the world and made a decent living until changing mores in Europe regarding freak shows saw them close down and left Merrick destitute. It was only then that he turned to Treves.

By the end of the movie, Merrick tells Treves how grateful he is for his friendship and is taken to see Madge perform. Madge compels the audience to give Merrick a standing ovation and he receives the public adulation and validation he's been seeking, like Quasimodo in *Hunchback*. This public love is the last thing on Merrick's narrative bucket list and, upon finishing the model castle he constructed throughout the movie, removes the pillows from his bed and commits suicide by lying flat, something he is told by Treves not to do because of the weight of his head.

Merrick's death was determined to be an accident. It was the real Treves who promoted and sold Merrick's death as a suicide, saying in his book, "He [Merrick] often said to me that he wished he could lie down to sleep 'like other people' . . . he must, with some determination, have made the experiment. . . . Thus it came about that his death was due to the desire that had dominated his life—the pathetic but hopeless desire to be 'like other people.'" As Treves would have you believe, Merrick just wanted to be a normal, abled man who wanted to lie down flat like everyone else. How "pathetic but hopeless" he was to think he could ever be 100 percent like an abled man. If you don't hate the real Frederick Treves by now, it's worth pointing out that upon Merrick's death, Treves dissected him and took plaster casts of his head and limbs (which were used in Hurt's makeup for the movie), keeping samples of his skin and mounting his skeleton. That skeleton still stands in the pathology collection of the Royal London Hospital for medical students to study. Interestingly, it's not on public display anymore. Perhaps they're afraid of people asking why the body of a disabled man was cut up and saved without his consent?

The Elephant Man was nominated for eight Academy Awards and walked away with none, though John Hurt's physical transformation was hyped up in the lead-up to the Oscars, again using the real-life casts of the real Merrick's body taken after his death. Hurt's makeup took seven to eight hours to apply and two hours to remove and played on the same commitment to art as Lon Chaney Sr.'s. The "spectacular presentation of physical pain and unwanted bodily transformation," to quote Angela M. Smith, that Chaney underwent in his films lives on. Although, where Chaney did it to enhance the shock and horror, today's actors use it as evidence of artistic commitment. Sadly, Hurt went home empty-handed.

The best year to play a disabled character at the Oscars was 1990, the year I've lovingly dubbed the "Battle of the Crips." Daniel Day-Lewis and Tom Cruise squared off in the Best Actor in a Leading Role category that year for their dueling disabled characters: Cruise as über-patriot Ron Kovic in Oliver Stone's *Born on the Fourth of July* and Day-Lewis as the wildly brilliant Christy Brown in *My Left Foot*. Each has a screenplay based on memoirs written by their respective real-life counterparts, and each was nominated for Best Picture. What's interesting about the two is how they show different versions of disability as crafted by directors from two different continents. The American-born Oliver Stone looks at American patriotism and how disabled Vietnam vets were treated at the time, with Ron a symbol for American sacrifice rather than a person. Irish director Jim Sheridan crafts a proper biopic of his subject that looks at disabled struggles in a way that doesn't demean those with disabilities. (Can you tell I prefer one over the other?) Stone beat out Sheridan for the Best Director Oscar and Day-Lewis famously took home the Best Actor award, though neither movie won Best Picture in the end. That honor went to *Driving Miss Daisy*, a movie with its own host of historical problems.

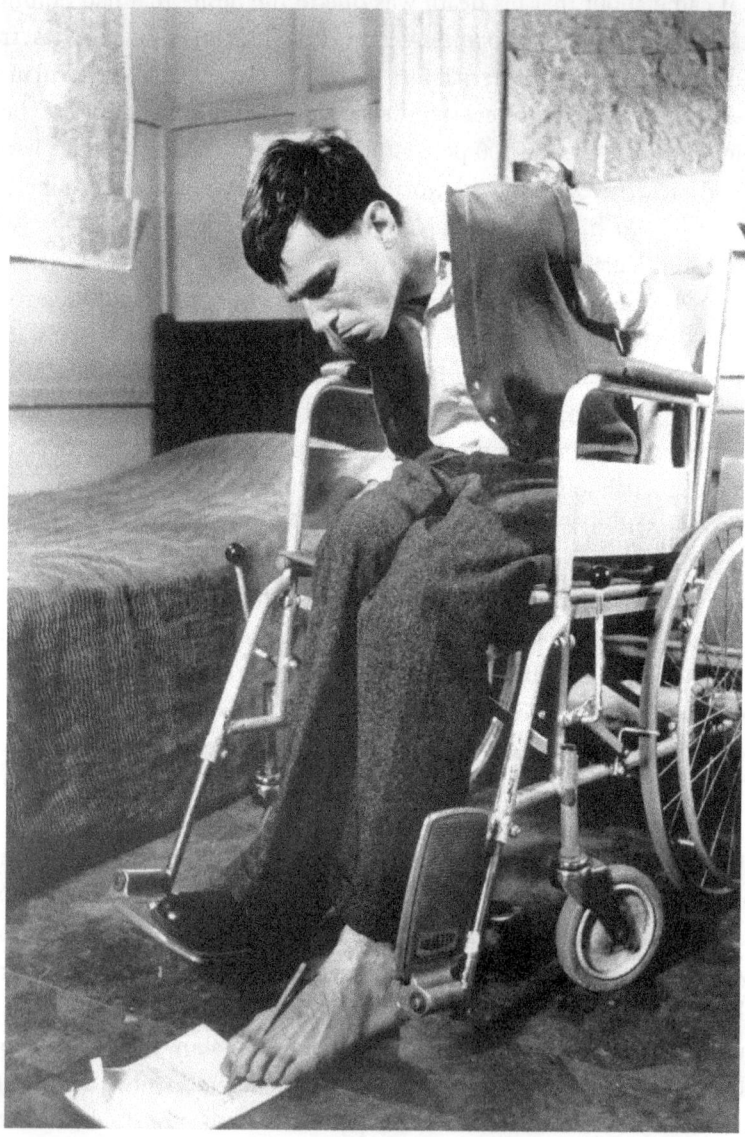

Daniel Day-Lewis won the Oscar for playing painter Christy Brown in 1990's *My Left Foot*. Miramax Films / Photofest ©Miramax Films

My Left Foot tells the story of Christy Brown (Day-Lewis), an artist and writer with cerebral palsy. The movie recounts his poor upbringing in 1932 Dublin and how he learned to paint with the help of the only limb he could control: his left foot.

I actively avoided watching *My Left Foot* prior to working on this book because of how frequently able-bodied film lovers mentioned to me what a "hard sit" it was. Other terms I heard when bringing it up were that it was "over the top" and "uncomfortable." It's apparent now that much of that stems from able audiences being uncomfortable with too much disability. But what makes *My Left Foot* unique is how it doesn't focus exclusively on Christy learning to paint. Yes, he enjoys painting, but Sheridan explores Brown's desire to craft his own life alongside his disability, and that through painting he finds an outlet for his repressed emotions. There are plenty of opportunities to root for Brown, but *My Left Foot* is really a movie about a man who lived a different life from most people and how he worked within it. There's nothing to transcend or overcome; Brown just lived.

In comparison to other movies wherein the disabled character is isolated in their experience, *My Left Foot* places Brown's family right alongside him, not in front of him. They are Brown's support system, but they don't take away from Brown as the central character. People are so comfortable with Brown's disability that even the neighborhood kids accept him during a flashback to his childhood. He's not bullied at all. He's one of the gang who gets pushed around in a wheelbarrow because his family can't afford a wheelchair. Brown goes through specific teenage rites of passage, like playing Spin the Bottle with his friends and kissing a girl, but the camera and script sensitively remind the audience that societal biases mean Brown is always at a disadvantage compared to his abled counterparts. That Spin the Bottle scene culminates with the girl he's kissed preferring Brown's brother and rejecting him. Brown's brother ends up rejecting the girl for her cruelty to Christy. Christy also has numerous friends outside the home. He plays British football like any other kid and stops a ball with his head before kicking a goal. These moments give off an air of emotional manipulation but the camera and musical score sell them as fun, not magical or miraculous like Forrest Gump breaking out of his leg braces. They're simply Christy's childhood memories.

Christy's parents each relate to him in a different way. Where *The Elephant Man* says John Merrick had a face his own mother couldn't love (which is historically untrue), *My Left Foot* is about the tenderhearted and close-knit bond between Brown and his mother, Bridget (played by an equally astounding

Brenda Fricker) and his community. Bridget is his advocate. and devoted to Christy. She tries to bring him independence by saving up to buy him a wheelchair. Kudos to Sheridan and crew for including a scene where she looks at a catalog of different wheelchair models. Finally, someone acknowledges that wheelchairs come in different looks! But while Bridget is Christy's main caregiver, she also has to provide for Brown's other siblings and that's balanced with Christy confronting issues on his own. Christy's issues with his father aren't centered around his disability at all. Both men have repressed anger they can't express about their lot in life.

Christy Brown is no saint, nor does he have a "come to Jesus" moment that causes him to learn the error of his ways. He gets angry and is rude to people, including loved ones. This is true to life, as the real Christy Brown struggled with alcoholism, which we see on-screen. The fictional Christy hides booze, complete with a straw, in his jacket. Brown is also depicted as incredibly jealous. He has a fit when he discovers the doctor he's fallen in love with is engaged to another man. It's a pretty presumptuous leap for him to have made, as there's little sexual tension between the two prior to this reveal. It's the one moment where *My Left Foot* falls into stereotype, with Christy trying to find love through the medical personnel he meets, though there is truth to this. This is coupled with the movie celebrating Brown's eventual marriage to caregiver Mary Carr.

Daniel Day-Lewis's Oscar win for playing Brown also hearkens back to the methods of Lon Chaney Sr. Where Chaney used painful devices to make him look as disabled as possible, Day-Lewis did something similar. As a Method actor, a popular acting technique wherein the performer seeks to become so bonded with a character that they act as them off-screen, the performance by Day-Lewis is considered the gold standard, and it is pretty impressive. He learned to use his foot to manipulate things and he never broke character, living in the wheelchair for the entire duration of filming, as well as having crew members lift him over obstacles and feed him. He broke two ribs on his own replicating Brown's hunched-over stance.

It's hard not to see every actor trying to one-up him since. Al Pacino drew on research from attendees of the Associated Blind Foundation to play Lt. Col. Frank Slade in 1992's *Scent of a Woman* (a performance he'd get an Oscar for). Tom Cruise spent time in a wheelchair to play Ron Kovic in *Born on the Fourth of July*. Director Oliver Stone wanted Cruise to go so far as to receive a chemical injection to make the actor temporarily paralyzed, but the idea was vetoed by the insurance company. (I would love to know if Cruise, still a daredevil at over sixty years old, entertained the idea at all.) For the 2017 film *Stronger*, Jake Gyllenhaal dragged himself across concrete pavement while acting out a traumatic flashback scene for over thirty minutes to inhabit Boston marathon bombing survivor Jeff Bauman. And Andrew Garfield never broke character playing Robin Cavendish in *Breathe*, right down to making actress Claire Foy, who played his wife, scratch any itches he'd have during breaks. These certainly sound like commitment to the bit, but Method Acting has several well-documented issues and examples of bad behavior. When actor Jared Leto played the Joker in the 2016 film *Suicide Squad*, he sent costars used condoms and brought a dead pig on set as a means of getting into character. There was nothing that extreme during the production of *My Left Foot*, though crew members on the set thought Day-Lewis's process taxed them more than anything else could.

What's funny is, despite the Method training movie marketing doesn't sell their actors as their disabled characters. Some don't even sell the movie as a disabled narrative at all. If you look at the poster for *My Left Foot* that's on Prime Video it's a glamour shot of Daniel Day-Lewis's hunky, disembodied head in the foreground with a nondescript field in the back. Are we watching a movie about a man with cerebral palsy or the story of how Daniel Day-Lewis died and went to heaven? *Stronger*'s poster has a gorgeous Jake Gyllenhaal standing and holding onto some bars at the bottom of the poster with his character's legs completely unseen. Is he disabled or learning the uneven bars? The posters for *Breathe* and *Theory of Everything* focus on the couples' romantic relationship, with each poster showing its respective actors in an ambulatory state. *Breathe* has Garfield and Foy embracing, while *Theory of Everything* has Redmayne and Jones presumably reenacting the dance scene from *Titanic*. The advertising wouldn't have you believe over half of the runtime has these men in wheelchairs or flat on their back. That's the point: Never put the male leads in positions of weakness or emasculation. These movies are about male strength and, in turn, the men's stunning and brave performances that demand response by the Academy in the form of Oscars. Fun fact: *My Left Foot* also changed the way movies were marketed. The movie had the first marketing campaign aimed at targeting disabled viewers. Home studio Miramax pulled the movie from theaters that weren't wheelchair accessible.

What usually happens in true-story biopics about the disabled is that while they may be flawed, there is always a grand redemptive arc to highlight the real-life subject's personal accomplishments against their disabled challenges. In *My Left Foot*, Christy Brown succeeds regardless of his personal demons.

The movie is about a man's attempt to get out of his own way. Christy's artistry and the publication of his book is a launchpad to tell a story about a man looking for meaning in life while creating art. Brown was a fabulous painter and writer, period, according to the movie's marketing, and it was enhanced by his disability.

The 2004 musical biopic *Ray*, about the life of blind musician Ray Charles, won two Oscars and does something similar to *My Left Foot*, though it devolves into a formulaic narrative that has less to do with being a disabled story and more about being a musical biopic. (The 2007 music spoof film *Walk Hard: The Dewey Cox Story* used *Ray* as one of many references.) There are two dueling narratives in *Ray*: One is Ray's refusal to be "turn[ed] into a cripple," a fear brought on by his mother who tells him, "Nobody's gonna have pity on you just because you're blind." The other is his personal struggles involving his womanizing and heroin addiction. Released four months after the death of the real Ray Charles, and with one of Charles's sons as a producer, the film isn't like *Breathe* in that it doesn't paint a rosy picture of Charles or his blindness. His blindness is a part of the narrative, but it's not the movie's main priority. A young Ray is taught to memorize the layout of his home. When he hits a chair and falls to the ground, he cries for his mother, who is standing a few feet away. Instead of helping Ray, she lets him lie there and get back up himself. As we discussed in chapter 6, Black disabled people remain a rarity. Ray is a blind man and a Black man, so his mother's attitude doesn't come from a lack of pity but as a reminder that the world is harsher to him because of his race and disability. *Ray* emphasizes Charles's blindness and blackness and reiterates that the two coexist.

Becoming disabled and surviving it is an accomplishment worth telling a movie about, as we've seen numerous times in this book. The disabled person stands in as a representation of the human spirit. You see this in the 2017 feature *Stronger*, a film that, in spite of being part of the dueling Boston Marathon bombing movies that debuted that year, does some fascinating things with its conflicted disabled protagonist. *Stronger* is a tale of strength in the face of terrorism that plays on America's love of patriotic stories, whether that be the Vietnam-centric *Born on the Fourth of July* or the various features that debuted post-9/11. What sets *Stronger* apart is its critique of the disability/survivor narrative, that is, "Just because someone becomes disabled, does that make them interesting?"

Jeff Bauman (Jake Gyllenhaal) is a survivor of the Boston Marathon bombing and has to acclimate to his new life as a double amputee, having lost both his legs above the knee. Gyllenhaal's Bauman is kind of a fuck-up, even before the terrorist attack. He's working the rotisserie chicken section at Costco and has recently broken up with his girlfriend Erin (Tatiana Maslany) for the third time. He's a thoroughly basic Boston boy, and it's hard not to wonder if the sole qualification for why we're watching his story is that he's played by perpetual dreamboat Gyllenhaal. Once Jeff is wounded in the bombing the movie transition into not just how Jeff deals with his disability but how people manipulate and cannibalize a person's story of survival for their own catharsis. I doubt director David Gordon Green and screenwriter John Pollano saw that secondary reading, but I'm glad to point it out for them.

We watch Jeff's discomfort at how eager people are to get a glimpse of him. When Jeff is wheeled out of the hospital to go home, he passes through a phalanx of cameras and well-wishers. Jeff doesn't know how to respond other than to awkwardly throw out a thumbs-up, a surface acknowledgment that he's okay because that's all people want to see. The script undercuts the stereotype that everyone who becomes disabled later in life is courageous and brave. When Jeff makes a public appearance at a hockey game he's introduced by the announcer as someone worth celebrating due to his "strength and perseverance in the face of adversity." No joke, that's exactly what my high school principal said about me at my high school graduation.

Jeff shows little strength and perseverance after his disability though. There's no magic switch that's flipped for him to make him—or those around him—a better person. This is what's happened and everyone, not just Jeff, must learn to live under these new circumstances. The movie isn't afraid to show the "how" behind disabled living, either, once Jeff returns home from the hospital. Disabled narratives acknowledge inaccessible housing but it's played off as a joke, when it's included at all. *Breathe* has a scene where everyone laughs at the inability to carry the wheelchair around. But *Stronger* deserves a hat tip for showcasing how the average disabled person lives without wealth in a landscape where ADA-accessible housing is a pipe dream. Jeff transfers into a car with a transfer board. Later, we see him move from the toilet in his small bathroom into an equally tiny bathtub. He later falls off that same toilet trying to reach for toilet paper on an opposite wall.

These movies say disability makes a family come together in the wake of "tragedy." When exploitation is shown, it's only in overt forms of abuse, such as physical violence, perpetrated by one bad apple. Jeff's mother Patty (Miranda Richardson) is an alcoholic who immediately volunteers Jeff for publicity appearances, including a sit-down interview with Oprah he refuses to do. Jeff's entire family is good-natured and, outside of Patty, they come off as unknowingly selfish. They see Jeff's disability as a way to benefit them. His friends urge him to do other events so they can enjoy free food and drinks. Ableist microaggressions fly under the radar, and *Stronger* does a good job of pointing them out.

Jeff's relationship with Erin could, and does, fall into caretaker cinema, but more often than not it has real moments of authenticity in showing an interabled romance. Erin isn't the gorgeously capable superwoman who bears her troubles with grace and a smile. She's a Boston woman and when she's upset with Jeff she tells him flat out. Erin wants Jeff to be a partner. She understands he needs help, but she has no intention of mothering him. The audience has already seen Jeff as selfish prior to the attack, unable to be a good boyfriend, so it's understandable when Erin tells him to "acknowledge" everyone, including her, who has helped him. She tells Jeff she's pregnant, which causes him to go on a tear about how he's unable to care for a kid because of his disability. Erin doesn't let him use that as an excuse. She agrees that he'll mess up their child, not because he doesn't have legs but because, she tells him, "You're a . . . kid still."

I love Erin, but she loses some points during a scene where she and Jeff argue. Erin, in anger, leaves Jeff in the car without his wheelchair, which leads him to an epiphany as he pulls himself across the parking lot to the door. It is an infantilizing and triggering moment that comes off crueler than intended. And for as frequently as *Stronger* sets itself as an anti-disability stereotype movie, it ends with Jeff realizing why he should embrace himself as a smiling, public figure, as the movie closes with an audience of fans telling Jeff how much seeing him inspires them to feel more American. One guy even says that seeing Jeff "made me feel a little better." *Stronger* turns Jeff into a patriotic messiah who elevates the spirit of abled people. It's hard to watch it and not recall the neighbor who stopped and thanked me for taking my dog for a walk every day and said, "I see you doing it in that wheelchair, and it makes me realize the problems in my life could be worse."

It's sad that a film like *Stronger*, which aims for something close to accurate representation of disability, failed to get any Oscar nominations. It goes to show that Oscar voters go for very specific disabled narratives.

We've spent a lot of time talking about true stories, but looking at the Oscars for best performers implies that, if you're an actor or actress seeking an award for playing a disabled person, it's best to look for either an original story or adapted material. Marlee Matlin won the Oscar for Best Actress for *Children* of a Lesser God, and Jane Wyman won for *Johnny Belinda*, both adapted from stage plays. Leonardo DiCaprio was nominated in the same category for *What's Eating Gilbert Grape*, an adaptation of a book.

But it's in original stories where there's more to mine. Hilary Swank won for *Million Dollar Baby*, and Troy Kostur won Best Supporting Actor for *CODA*. Don't forget Al Pacino's Best Actor win for *Scent of a Woman*, Dustin Hoffman in *Rain Man*, or Tom Hanks in *Forrest Gump*. Hell, as *Tropic Thunder* will forever remind us, even Sean Penn got an Oscar nomination for an original disabled narrative like *I Am Sam*. So while it seems riskier to win an Oscar working outside the true-story framework, the proof is in the pudding that there are more hits than misses with original storytelling. This is probably because true stories are bound by history and require a screenwriter to work with a predetermined narrative formula or to write up to a specific accomplishment or milestone. With an original story, there's room for creativity. Just throw in an abled person alongside the disabled one, and you have a recipe for a narrative that prioritizes abled perspectives, serious dramatic beats, and Oscar glory!

Let's look at Al Pacino's win for the 1992 drama *Scent of a Woman*, a movie that today faces social media backlash (according to my social media, "no one liked it at the time") at odds with its critical and commercial success upon release. *Scent of the Woman* asks the viewer: "You know everyone's favorite racist uncle? What if he was blind?"

Pacino's win was long overdue by 1992. He'd already walked away empty-handed after receiving nominations for *Serpico*, *Godfather 2*, *Dog Day Afternoon*, and *And Justice for All*. Yes, this is the painful reminder that he didn't win the Oscar for *Godfather 2* and wasn't even nominated for the first! The Academy clearly thought the best was still to come, because playing Michael Corleone sure wasn't the high point for them. The Oscar hopes finally bore fruit in the role of Lt. Col. Frank Slade, a blind man who spends Thanksgiving weekend with a precocious prep school boy named Charlie (Chris O'Donnell).

Frank is a disabled character you'd slap with the "quirky" or "eccentric" label to cover up the fact that he's racist, vaguely misogynist, and says "hoo-ah" enough times to induce alcohol poisoning if you sipped every time he said it. Frank also has the ability to detect a woman's mere presence in the room due to his incredible sense of smell. Gotta give it up to the Academy for thinking Al Pacino sniffing women was a better performance than as Michael Corleone. I'm not over it! Frank's goal over the weekend is to complete some items on his to-do list before he kills himself. He and Charlie drive around New York to experience life as Frank imparts words of wisdom only your favorite uncle over fifty would tell you. Frank talks about his life before becoming blind in a hand grenade accident and gives us glimpses into who he was before, though that's sold as a ruse. A family dinner scene introduces us to Frank's nephew Randy (Bradley Whitford), who tells Charlie, "He [Frank] was an asshole before" his accident. I appreciate the need to dispel the idea that Frank's blindness is what turned him into a complete cynic. Charlie wants to convince Frank to change his mind on the whole death thing and thus you have the narrative in a nutshell. Also, Frank dances the tango with a random woman the pair meet in a restaurant (played by Gabrielle Anwar one year after *Wild Hearts Can't Be Broken*, which I'd love to believe was the reason she was cast) which is pretty much the only sequence from the movie that gets brought up.

Film critic Roger Ebert called this Pacino's "best and riskiest performance." But Ebert didn't see the risk stemming from a sighted actor like Pacino playing a blind man, more that "the character is so abrasive we can hardly stand him, and only gradually do we begin to understand how he works and why he isn't as miserable as he seems." Ebert goes on to say that "the colonel's ideas are not Politically Correct. On the other hand, he is not a sexist animal, either." Set aside the capitalization of "politically correct," just starting to come into vogue in the '90s; Ebert lays out a good point we see often in disabled movies. If the disabled character is horrible and does terrible things to people, the viewer should see it as balanced out by their charm. Will Traynor is an angry, entitled man of privilege in *Me Before You*, but he's so dreamy and charming that, by the end, the audience is told to ignore everything that came before. Cliff Robertson's Charly attempts to sexually assault a woman in *Charly*, but his mental meekness at the beginning undercuts and contextualizes that it's not him enacting rape but the mind-altering chemicals he's consumed. And Joaquin Phoenix's wheelchair-using John Callahan makes crass, uncomfortable comments to women in 2018's *Don't Worry, He Won't Get Far on Foot*, but we're told it's his attempt at humor and the women find it funny! These movies say disabled men can't be rapists, can't be sexual harassers, can't be evil. It's mitigated by their ability to spit out a beautiful turn of phrase. That's a false and dangerous precedent.

Pacino was a dual nominee the year of *Scent of a Woman*. He was concurrently nominated in the Best Supporting Actor category for *Glengarry Glen Ross*, and people today see his win as more of a career Oscar than for being particularly great in *Scent*. This was also the year Denzel Washington was nominated for *Malcolm X*; do with that what you will. The dislike for *Scent of a Woman* by today's audiences plays more like post-Oscar hindsight that accompanies movies so massive at the time that they smothered any goodwill they built up during the season. Look at the collective carping about *Forrest Gump* today, which people still debate. Ebert's *Scent of a Woman* review gave the movie 3.5 stars, saying it was formulaic and similar to other prep school movies released around the same time, like *Taps* and *Dead Poets Society*. It's surprising Ebert didn't compare it to the disabled movie that immediately pops up when referencing *Scent* today: *Rain Man*. It isn't just that both movies have a main character named Charlie, or that Pacino's "hoo-ah" was imitated as often as the speech patterns of Dustin Hoffman's Raymond. The films have similar plots too. The abled man (O'Donnell's Charlie) has a financial chip on his shoulder and discovers the meaning of life through his interactions with a disabled man. Charlie in *Rain Man* has a financial chip on his shoulder and discovers the meaning of life through his interactions with his disabled brother.

Another famous entry in the "people actually loved this" Oscar discussion is the 2004 Clint Eastwood–directed boxing feature *Million Dollar Baby*. As with *Ice Castles*, *Million Dollar Baby* barely qualifies as a disabled narrative but its inclusion is imperative because of how it makes a meal out of what little disability discourse it contains. If *Scent of a Woman* gives off *Rain Man* vibes, then *Million Dollar Baby* comes off like a 2000s version of *Gilbert Grape*. *Million Dollar Baby* was nominated for seven Academy Awards and won four, including Best Picture, and acting awards for Morgan Freeman and Hilary Swank.

Eastwood plays Frankie Dunn, a boxing coach with a chip on his shoulder who seems a lot like Clint Eastwood in general. Frankie starts training neophyte boxer Maggie Fitzgerald (Swank), and the two develop a close father-daughter bond. Maggie is the definition of poor white trash; she's even called that in the narration, provided by Freeman. Her sister is a welfare queen, her father is missing, and her mother "weighs 312 pounds." (Add fatphobic to this movie's list of sins.) Maggie is a forgotten person in the world, and though Frankie initially curls his lip and refuses to train her, saying, "I don't train girls," he is worn down by her inner grit and determination.

Everything about Maggie's life is telegraphed to the audience in advance, right down to Freeman's Mr. Scrap—is it a first name or a last name?—telling a folksy story about how a neck only goes so far before it breaks. Shocker, Maggie falls onto a footstool during a fight gone bad and snaps her neck, becoming paralyzed. The movie loves reveling in Maggie's sad life and transitions into showing how disabled people's lives are the worst lives ever lived. Frankie is committed to finding a way of fixing her, literally and metaphorically, because she stands in for the relationship he can't fix with his own daughter. Frankie seeks second opinions while the camera stays focused on Maggie, looking waxy and sad, lying in a cold hospital bed.

The cinematography captures Maggie's life as icy and sterile in her most vulnerable moments. The camera watches an orderly scoop her out of bed and place her in a wheelchair with so much voyeuristic cringe it's surprising there's no Sarah McLachlan needle drop. *For less than the price of a cup of coffee you, too, can stare at this helpless disabled woman and feel better that your legs work.* Make no mistake, the intent is to show how much sadness and trauma one woman can endure. Because Maggie is set up as a forgotten woman she has no one outside of Frankie. Maggie's family shows up after having a great day at Disneyland and wants her to sign power of attorney papers so they can take her assets. Actress Margo Martindale is a national treasure and I stand by that . . . even as she, playing Maggie's mom, shoves a pen in her daughter's mouth to get her signature.

Jenni Gold's 2012 documentary *CinemAbility* looks at disabled representation in film and discusses *Million Dollar Baby*. A talking head says that, while quadriplegics and, really, anyone who becomes disabled experience a period of depression it dissipates with the benefit of time and therapy. We don't know how long Maggie is hospitalized for, but the idea of therapy is never touched on. Maggie will live and die in this hospital for the rest of her, hopefully, short life, and that's all there is to it. As if that's not enough, the audience watches Maggie bite through her tongue so she can choke herself (or bleed out, whatever comes first), and has a leg amputated due to infection. When it rains, it pours for us disabled, amiright? So when Maggie asks Frankie to end her suffering we're all about ready to shout "Just kill her already!" I mean, jeez, they're already carving her like a turkey while she's still alive. Maggie welcomes death because she can't envision a life without the acclaim and respect of being a boxer. Maggie tells Frankie, "I got all I wanted. . . . Don't let me lie here 'til I can't hear those people chantin' no more," akin to John Merrick in *The Elephant Man*. Frankie complies and gives her a fatal dose of adrenaline. Maggie dies beaming. Swank's Oscar win comes off like it's to say thank you for how much suffering the character endured.

The Disability Rights Education Fund called out *Million Dollar Baby* for its depiction of the disabled in 2005, releasing a statement saying, "Perhaps the most central stereotype fueling disability prejudice is the mistaken assumption inherent in the message of the movie that the quality of life of individuals with disabilities is unquestionably not worth living." Eastwood came out in defense of the ending, explaining that the movie is about the American Dream. "I've gone around in movies blowing people away with a .44 Magnum. But that doesn't mean I think that's a proper thing to do," he responded to the *LA Times*—the old "It's a movie and people are too precious about it" routine. Writer Wesley J. Smith argued in a 2005 article that there were plenty of ways for the script to turn Maggie's disability into a redemptive arc. "The movie could have ended with Maggie triumphing once again, perhaps having obtained an education and becoming a teacher; or, opening a business managing boxers; or perhaps, receiving a standing ovation as an inspirational speaker." These are trite suggestions, but they make more sense than using a disabled woman's death to stand in for the American Dream. The script uses disability as a quick and easy way to make the audience sad . . . for Clint's Frankie. Frankie, after all, is the one tasked with watching Maggie suffer. Frankie is the one who has to come to grips with her decision to die. Frankie is the one who puts her down like a dog. Why don't you feel bad for Frankie?! The entire movie is recounted as a letter written by Freeman's Mr. Scrap to Eastwood's estranged daughter to convince her to forgive her dad, after all. I can only imagine the opening line of that letter: "Ma'am, let me tell you the story about the time your father murdered a disabled woman. It's a beautiful story I think you'll enjoy."

We started this chapter discussing cripping up and how able actors play disability. This hasn't disappeared completely, but the debates that pop up when these movies hit theaters and the conversations abled actors have to navigate, have them look at these roles with more trepidation than in years past. In 2021, the question of whether the disability Oscar was still a thing and whether it might benefit disabled creatives popped up when *CODA* won the Oscar for Best Picture.

CODA is far from a perfect movie, and it didn't solve the entire history of disabled representation in movies, but it made hearing audiences aware of what could be and what a good, not great, example of disabled representation looks like. *CODA* stands for a Child of Deaf Adults. The movie is adapted from a 2014 French-Belgian film of the same name and follows teenager Ruby Rossi (Emilia Jones). Ruby is the hearing conduit for her Deaf parents, Jackie and Frank (Marlee Matlin and Troy Kotsur), as well as her older brother, Leo (Daniel Durant). Ruby takes an interest in the school choir which opens up an opportunity for her to attend a prestigious music school after graduation. But Ruby is torn between following her own dreams and acting as her family's communicator.

CODA is written and directed by a non-disabled director and screenwriter, and the focus of the story is a white, ambulatory family. Ruby, the hearing child, is the main protagonist and is the caretaker for her family. All these things are true, *however* . . . what makes *CODA* work is that it doesn't revel in tragedy. Ruby's story is no different than any other coming-of-age narrative. She wants to leave home against what her family wants. It shows the struggle, yes, but also the fun, the cringe, and the average, everyday moments of a family who happen to have more Deaf than hearing members in it. Having Ruby's family be Deaf and, most importantly, played by Deaf actors, make the movie accessible to hearing audiences and shows a highly specific experience that connects with disabled viewers. I'm not Deaf, but there are moments of squabbling between Ruby and her mother, or Ruby and her brother, that anyone can identify with. A common narrative tweaked to fit a disabled story illustrates the universality of life and shows disabled people have the same problems as the abled—we just require a bit more hardware.

It's interesting to watch Marlee Matlin in *CODA* and I'd like to think it's part of the same universe as the movie that secured Matlin her Oscar: *Children of a Lesser God*. Maybe Matlin's Sarah got tired of James's shit, peaced out, and settled down with Kotsur's Frank. Also, *CODA* gives us disabled sex scenes performed by Deaf actors! The movie's opening has Ruby explain to a doctor why her parents have genital irritation—it's discovered they have jock itch—only for Ruby to jokingly tell them they can't ever have sex again, a fact that horrifies both Frank and Jackie. Where *Children of a Lesser God* focuses so heavily on James making Sarah speak so she can make hearing people comfortable, the Rossis create boundaries between their world and the outside world. They know they need to adapt so people can understand them, but they also go home and communicate in a way that's totally comfortable for them, and everyone thinks that's fine! Actor and Oscar nominee Paul Raci said, in a 2020 interview about being a CODA himself, "When you go to buy a car with your parents, they're talking about the interest. I don't know what the interest is. I don't know what the hell you're talking about, and yet I'm interpreting from this adult, to my father, and I'm doing the best I can but I know that something's wrong and I'm not doing it right. It's a big responsibility." The movie deftly transitions between Ruby's relationship as daughter and interpreter to her parents, as well as between Frank and Jackie's role as her caregivers and as Deaf individuals.

We've seen poorly depicted examples of disabled parenting (*I Am Sam*), but *CODA* has such a sweet, kindhearted presentation of the range of feelings that crop up between disabled parents and their children. *CODA* may look at Deaf adults, but it does a great job emphasizing the facets of a family where disability is omnipresent. Frank realizes his complicity in relying on Ruby and how it, no doubt, affected her life. When Jackie tells him she's afraid to send her baby off to college, he replies, "She was never a baby." Jackie tells Ruby that she was worried about being a Deaf mother to a hearing daughter: "I was worried we wouldn't connect." Her family's reliance on her is never malicious; it's second nature. It's what everyone is used to. The audience watches Ruby help run her family's fishing business and negotiate fair prices for their catch. When Frank wants to start a fishing co-op, it is Ruby who speaks for him and convinces others to join. When Ruby wants to go to singing practice, Jackie demands Ruby stay and interpret for them during a TV interview. "Do you want us to fail?" she asks. That is what motivates Rossi's dependence on Ruby, the fear of failure.

There are numerous movies about disabled characters who either fear they're a burden or fear struggle. We see codependency in disabled narratives as the disabled person's downfall, or sometimes it's presented in a horror light (*Baby Jane*). *CODA* shows how the tentacles of codependency aren't always intentional, nor do they affect just Ruby. Ruby's brother Leo sees his younger sister as the golden child in his parent's eyes. He wants to speak for himself because he knows Ruby deserves her own life, and so does he. Leo is the older brother who wants to be treated like an adult. He agrees when Ruby says, "I can't always be that person," that is, the interpreter for her family. Leo tells her, "You can't stay here. They'll be looking to you to do everything . . . we're not helpless." He calls out his parents, sure, but he also calls out Ruby for coddling her family. It's hard not to lean on the kindness of the abled to make things easier. The door swings both ways. When Ruby finally auditions for the music school she wants to attend she signs her audition song, Joni Mitchell's "Both Sides Now," to her family sitting in the balcony. Before this moment Frank, Jackie, and Leo don't have a connection to Ruby's singing because they can't hear. When she signs the lyrics they may not know the melody but they feel unified as a family and as part of a community. You have to have a heart of stone not to tear up.

CODA won three Oscars (Best Picture, Best Adapted Screenplay, and Best Supporting Actor for Kotsur), yet it hasn't ushered in a wave of disabled storytelling. As of this writing, none of the major studios has disabled narratives, starring disabled actors, on their slates. There's no momentum to make more movies like *CODA*, certainly not ones starring or being directed/written by disabled talent. Troy Kotsur hasn't starred in another feature film as of this writing, nor has Matlin (though a documentary on her life was released in 2025) or Daniel Durant. What do studios want from their disability narratives? Cripping up continues to win the day.

EPILOGUE

ARE WE THERE YET?

We've made it to the end, or more like we've made it to the present. We started in the silent era, traced a path through the eugenic discourse of the 1930s, talked about disabled characters played by (predominantly) abled actors, war vets, characters of color, disabled women, sex, caretakers, and the Oscars. No doubt you're exhausted and maybe a tinge demoralized. And why not? The myth of disability in these movies perpetuates false promises and lies about the disabled experience—lies that disability makes one unlovable, unsexy, and fixable. But from what and whose standards? Able-bodied screenwriters and directors are the ones making the call, alongside studio executives, but it's also up to the viewer. As I mentioned at the beginning of this book, my goal isn't to make you feel bad for watching these movies and enjoying them. I love several of the movies included here, from *Forrest Gump* to *The Hand That Rocks the Cradle*. The hope is that, after reading this, you'll look at disabled characters on-screen a little closer, ask some questions, and demand Hollywood do better. (I also hope you've laughed at a few of my jokes too.) If someone were to ask me if I see my disabled experience on-screen, I would still say no, but I'm happy to have so many friends who are now able to point out why a hospital wheelchair isn't right or who use the term "able-bodied buffer" in conversation.

Movies about disability today still don't reflect the one in four people in the US who live as disabled. We remain woefully underrepresented when it comes to directors, screenwriters, and below-the-line talent. The 2024 Annenberg Inclusion Initiative study showed that of the most popular movies released over the last sixteen years, 2.4 percent had a character with a disability, a 0.5 percent increase since their previous study. More importantly, viewers are more aware and desirous of content created by, starring, and about disabled people. A 2024 poll conducted by the Inevitable Foundation showed that 66 percent of audiences were displeased with the current representation of the disabled community in entertainment. Over 25 percent felt the majority of what they saw on-screen was inauthentic to the disabled experience. And with disability being a trillion (again, with a T) dollar industry, the poll shows Hollywood leaves a lot of money on the table by not investing in disabled buying power. According to Inevitable, 35 percent of disabled people watch twenty or more hours of TV per week compared to 25 percent of non-disabled people, and 40 percent of those polled said they'd recommend a film or TV show that had authentic representation.

Casting is easy, as I said. Casting, in theory, is the quickest way to create a pipeline for new talent and tell more disabled stories. But if casting is such a tough nut to crack, then how can the disabled community expect Hollywood to boost the numbers of disabled directors and screenwriters? The few disabled actors allowed into the industry are tasked with representing every disabled person, which is a tough cross to bear. Even once a disabled person is let into Hollywood, they still have to grapple with how inaccessible the industry remains. Harold Russell spent so much of his time in Hollywood selling himself as a disabled man for the *Best Years of Our Lives* press tour that when he fought to be seen as more than his disability, it took him forty years to get another role. Marlee Matlin continues to advocate for better representation on-screen and better access for disabled performers already in the industry. She was a vocal proponent for making Academy Awards screeners contain subtitles so that hard-of-hearing voters could actually enjoy them.

There's never been more awareness of the need for disabled characters to fill the frame, which has yielded directors and screenwriters to make some, shall we say, unique attempts at accomplishing that. There's a trend in Hollywood movies these days wherein a movie includes a disabled person somewhere in the frame to acknowledge their existence in the world without actually giving them a character, lines, or anything to do other than act as set dressing or world building. Creatives acknowledge they can't get away with a world they've created having zero disabled people in it, especially if it's set in a large city or another locale where disabled people are bound to be, but that's where the buck stops. Greta Gerwig's 2023 feature *Barbie* brought the 1950s fashion doll into the modern day while celebrating women of all makes and models. It also did its best to include disabled women in a world where every woman is Barbie, and Barbie is every woman. There are two scenes where the audience's attention is drawn to unnamed disabled Barbies. One has a limb difference and is silently talking to another character in a background scene with Issa Rae's President Barbie. Another unnamed Barbie is in a wheelchair in the front of a dance sequence during a party. Neither character has a name, nor are they an active part of the narrative but, hey, they're there. In the case of the unnamed wheelchair-using Barbie it's particularly galling considering there *is* a wheelchair-using Barbie named Becky, not to mention an entire line of disabled Barbies Mattel released in 2023. And while social media picked apart Mattel employee Gloria's (America Ferrera) now-iconic speech about how it's "impossible to be a woman," little was written about how it ignores disability.

Other movies that do this: 2018's *Mamma Mia! Here We Go Again* also has a disabled dancing wheelchair user in an ensemble scene, as well as 2024's *Wicked*, which after making the Munchkins nonlittle people, decides to place a little person actor just walking through Oz . . . that's it. Instead of acknowledging the fraught history of the Munchkins, there's a hope that viewers have forgotten that part of the 1939 movie and an indication that little people simply live in Oz. Thankfully, the addition of Marissa Bode as the wheelchair-using Nessarose, marking the first time a wheelchair user has played the character in an adaptation of the Broadway show, is great! Disney's recent live-action remake of *Snow White* divorces the seven dwarfs from the little people community by calling them "magical creatures" who can sniff out diamonds in the mine they work in. The movie goes the extra mile of including an actual character who is a little person, as well as several little people in a crowd scene, but that came after months of outcry about the movie's outdated depiction of disability.

Other movies, fearful of any criticism of their film's disabled representation, erase disability completely. These moments reduce internet discourse and awkward interviews, but also remove any potential contributions disabled actors and creatives have made in the medium's history, and they limit opportunities for disabled writers to champion the films. Actor Herve Villechaize's role as Tattoo is one of the most identifiable parts of the 1970s–1980s TV show *Fantasy Island,* yet the 2020 feature film adaptation erased the character and turned him into a punchline (the joke is one of the characters has a tattoo of the word "Tattoo").

Sean Durkin's 2023 film *The Iron Claw,* a biopic about the Von Erich wrestling family, is a prime example of how the continued lack of education about disability representation in movies put directors in a position where they fall into a trap and don't even know it. The main narrative of *The Iron Claw* is how the four Von Erich brothers cope with the weight of their domineering father's desire for them to be superstars in wrestling. There were five Von Erich sons though only four are given stories on-screen. Chris Von Erich, who had brittle bone disease, was nixed from the movie entirely. It was said to have nothing to do with his disability but only, as Durkin explained in a 2023 interview, for narrative purposes. "One of the hardest decisions possible was cutting Chris," he said. "And the reason why [is] Chris was in the script for a lot of years and I loved him and loved the character. But ultimately as a writer and filmmaker, I had to separate the real humans from the characters on the page at some point." Since so much of *The Iron Claw*'s narrative surrounds the deaths of the Von Erichs, Durkin didn't want to get repetitive. As Durkin laid out, and as we've seen happen with true stories, the family gave their blessing to excise the character.

The Iron Claw has two of the brothers dealing with disability issues. Kerry (Jeremy Allen White) loses a foot in a motorcycle accident, and Mike (Stanley Simons) suffers brain damage after a coma. These moments come toward the movie's back half as the brothers try to maintain their wrestling status and hold onto their father's love. As their real-life counterparts did, Kerry and Mike eventually commit suicide. But after their deaths, *The Iron Claw* ends with a troubling coda that returns us back to the Victorians yet again. The finale shows Kerry, immediately after his death, going outside to an idyllic version of his childhood home. It's clear he's in his version of the afterlife, where he discovers his missing foot has returned to him. He reunites with his other dead brothers, including Mike, who is now cognitively normal. This is perceived to be a happy ending, where everyone is reunited in a place where they experienced so much happiness. But it returns us to the idea that in order to find happiness, one must be abled, and the surest way to be a whole person is exclusively through death. The afterlife becomes the great washer away of all disabled sins. It's doubtful Durkin knew this was how disabled audiences would interpret the film, but this is what a lack of disabled awareness in the movies does. You don't know what you don't know. Who recognizes a good or bad example of representation if no one knows what to look for, or if they don't know the history of what's come before?

Back in chapter 8, I mentioned my concerns for the next generation of disabled girls, and that statement should be expanded out to the next generation of disabled kids, period. Getting comfortable with disability should start early, and Disney is one of the only studios making an active push toward increasing disabled representation on-screen—though they don't always stick the landing. The studio that Walt built has, by far, the most disabled characters (either coded as or explicitly stated), and it is these depictions that are a helpful tool to teach children about disability and combat ableism by exploring difference and using that to open up a conversation around disability. Take the 2003 animated movie, *Finding Nemo*, the story of a clownfish who goes out into the ocean to find his kidnapped son, Nemo. Nemo is a bright, adventurous little boy whose asymmetrical "lucky" fin, coupled with losing his mother and siblings in an attack, causes him to be endlessly coddled and watched by his father, Marlin (voiced by Albert Brooks). Marlin is the central caretaking protagonist, but his search for Nemo forces him to control his parental smothering and the way he undermines his son's ability to do things out of fear Nemo will fail. Nemo is his own character with his own plot. Trapped in a fish tank with other fish, including the disabled-coded Gill (voiced by Willem Dafoe), Nemo is forced to learn how to rely on himself and live without his dad taking care of him. Marlin and Nemo eventually find common ground and have a more loving father-son relationship that isn't contingent on Marlin controlling and limiting his son.

But not even Disney is immune to being unaware of disabled stereotypes, and film history leaves some movies exhibiting unintentional ableism. Such is the case with *Finding Nemo*'s 2016 sequel, *Finding Dory*. In this one, Marlin's friend and companion Dory (voiced by Ellen DeGeneres) tries to find her parents from whom she became separated as a child and, due to her short-term memory loss, can't remember. There is a level of sympathy for Dory and her parents who, in the opening scene, look at their daughter with fear in their eyes when she can't recall information recently imparted to her. But Marlin forgets the lessons he previously learned in *Finding Nemo* and uses Dory's disability against her when he and Nemo are in danger. "Go wait over there and forget, it's what you do best," he says.

Finding Dory garnered controversy upon release by disabled activists and journalists for how it appeared to poke fun at characters coded as neurodivergent. New characters are introduced in the film, including the sea lion Gerald and a bird named Becky. Both characters are animated as having offbeat characteristics. Gerald has a thick unibrow and Becky has rumpled feathers and bulging eyes. Compared to the other classically animated characters, the implication that they are different is apparent. Each is mocked and made fun of. In Becky's case, it is Marlin who makes comments about her; and with Gerald, it's two fellow sea lions, Rudder and Fluke, who bully him. As disabled author and activist Alice Wong wrote in 2016, the fact that Gerald seemed coded as disabled resonated with her. "I relate to Gerald intensely, his wanting to be accepted and taken advantage of by faux friends/allies," Wong writes. "I was angry for Gerald but was delighted to see him in a scene after the credits where he manages to nestle himself on the rock behind Rudder and Fluke and gives a bit of a snicker. He does have agency and is tenacious at getting his place in the sun." The criticism caused codirector Andrew Stanton to make a statement and say Gerald wasn't disabled but was written to be a nerd in a tribute to the crew who worked behind the scenes on the film.

A Disney character I saw as coded disabled, and I absolutely love, is talking doll Gabby Gabby (voiced by Christina Hendricks) in the 2019 film *Toy Story 4*. This fourth installment to the long-running *Toy Story* franchise sees cowboy doll Woody (voiced by Tom Hanks) and the gang trying to reunite with their current owner, Bonnie, and finding themselves in a small town with a traveling carnival. While visiting a local antique store, Woody meets Gabby Gabby, a doll from the 1950s who has lived in the antique shop in the hopes that the store owner's granddaughter, Harmony, will notice her and take her home. But Gabby doesn't believe Harmony will love her because Gabby has been defective since her creation. Her broken voice box makes her unable to throw out quippy catchphrases like the other toys. Gabby wants to take Woody's voice box, by force if necessary, to restore her to working condition. Gabby Gabby believes in a magic cure, that fixing her voice box will—the equivalent of erasing her disability—make her worthy of Harmony's love, and that the little girl will reciprocate. But her isolation is self-imposed, and Harmony's disinterest isn't because of Gabby's nonworking voice box. When Woody willingly parts with the box, Gabby waits for Harmony, who remains disinterested in her. Gabby makes her disability her sole problem in life, so when Harmony still rejects her, Gabby has to reconcile finding a new identity. Her plotline is resolved when she meets a new little girl who immediately falls in love with her.

What's interesting is Gabby is contrasted with another disabled character, that of Bo Peep (voiced by Annie Potts). Bo Peep has lost an arm. Where Gabby is isolated and angry, Bo Peep lives on her own among a community of friends. She saves Woody and his friends in spite of her missing arm and just lives her best life. The fact that both characters exist in one film illustrates the varied nature of disability and how it goes hand in hand with a person's sense of identity and self-worth. But Disney still has a ways to go. Its 2023 film, *Wish*, features a character named Dahlia, the best friend of the film's hero Asha (voiced by Ariana DeBose). Dahlia uses a crutch and is a disabled bestie/cheerleader integrated into Asha's group of friends and not valued just for her own character. Dahlia is voiced by wheelchair user Jennifer Kumiyama whom you might remember from when we talked about *The Sessions* back in chapter 9.

Disabled activists and writers like M. F. Norden have pointed out the studio's use of the "sweet innocent," in movies like *The Hunchback of Notre Dame*, a stereotype wherein disabled characters are sweet, innocent, and willing to help the abled. Or they're "supercripples," where the character's disability gives them a power that is of use to abled characters. From a production standpoint, Disney has yet to work with disabled directors or screenwriters.

And though we talked about *Snow White* earlier, it's worth coming back to in order to show how new technologies are limiting disabled roles. In 2022, actor Peter Dinklage appeared on a podcast and discussed that he was "taken aback" by Disney resurrecting the Seven Dwarfs. Dinklage said at the time, "Take a step back and look at what you're doing there. It makes no sense to me. You're progressive in one way, but you're still making that fucking backward story about seven dwarfs living in a cave together. Have I done nothing to advance the cause from my soapbox? I guess I'm not loud enough."

Little Women: LA star and producer Terra Jolé said in 2022, "Because of equality, and voices stating that they weren't okay with things like elf roles, or dwarf roles, or leprechaun roles, they've been eliminated. And not only are you not seeing a lot of little people in the acting industry anymore, but you're not seeing productions being created to give little people an actual role, either." This same backlash accompanied the 2023 release of *Wonka*, a prequel that looks at the early life of fictional chocolatier Willy Wonka (played by Timothée Chalamet). If you watched the 1971 version, *Willy Wonka and the Chocolate Factory*, you saw another foundational look at disability in the Oompa Loompas, Wonka's potentially indentured servants who were played by little people. Even the 2005 remake directed by Tim Burton had the Oompa Loompas remain little people, albeit just one actor (Deep Roy) plays them all. And now technology allows for abled actors to be shrunk down to Oompa Loompa size. *Wonka* went this route to cast abled/non-LP actor Hugh Grant as an Oompa Loompa, while the *Snow White and the Huntsman* series did the same for the dwarfs.

Disney said they wanted to "avoid reinforcing stereotypes from the original animated film" so were "taking a different approach with these seven characters and have been consulting with members of the dwarfism community." The finished product has the characters look like CGI versions of their 1937 counterparts, with the exception of Dopey, who looks like he took Ozempic. In 2012, director Tarsem Singh directed *Mirror Mirror*, another adaptation of the *Snow White* fairy tale that cast its dwarf characters with authenticity in mind. The script gives all seven characters individual personalities and plotlines.

It's not 100 percent terrible, thankfully. There are creatives, both disabled and non, doing their part to improve disabled representation in film, and movies being made that are telling unique disabled stories. In 2021, directors Nicole Newnham and wheelchair-user Jim LeBrecht were nominated for the Best Original Documentary Oscar for their film *Crip Camp*, exploring the campers at Camp Jened, a Catskills-based summer camp for disabled kids. LeBrecht attended Camp Jened in the 1970s and uses the doc to show how it was a place for disabled teens to be independent and engage in all manner of summer hijinks, including sex. LeBrecht and Newnham don't limit the scope of their doc to the camp's impact as a revolutionary place for disabled teens; they also look at how its campers became integral activists in the disability rights movement that swept the US in the '70s and led to the passage of the ADA. *Crip Camp* showed real, explicitly disabled people who went on to found a movement that generations of disabled people have benefited from. It's unfortunate the Academy voters decided a movie about a guy's interest in an octopus, *My Octopus Teacher*, was more worthy of the award. It's hard not to wonder if the overtly disabled faces, coupled with the frank discussions of the campers getting crabs and having sex, turned off a voting body still committed to outdated disabled stereotypes. That octopus and I will never be friends! A year later *CODA* won the Oscar for Best Picture, which has its fair share of critiques, as we've already looked at. Either way, these movies are crowd-pleasers and awards darlings that people do want to watch.

The 2019 feature *Sound of Metal*, nominated for six Academy Awards and winning two, is another great example of a movie with a nuanced conversation about disability that dispels a multitude of myths with the purpose of telling a great story. (Funny how simple that sounds.) What I love the most is how it smashes the idea that disability aids are quick fixes. Riz Ahmed plays Ruben, a drummer in a hard rock band who is losing his hearing. As his deafness intensifies, Ruben thinks getting a cochlear implant will automatically solve the problem. He reluctantly joins a support group for Deaf addicts run by Joe (Paul Raci), who hopes to show Ruben that a hearing device won't fix his own ableist insecurities. You should watch this alongside *Scent of a Woman* because everything *Scent* does with its "blind, flawed yet lovable" narrative, director Darius Marder does with more nuance and detail in *Sound of Metal*'s portrayal of deafness and addiction. There's a moment where Joe says his wife and kids left him "not because I was Deaf" but for being an alcoholic, reminiscent of the dinner scene in *Scent of a Woman*. As he tells his story, having Joe explain the lines drawn between his personality, his disability, and his addiction is a tiny script tweak that gives more authenticity.

The script, credited to Marder and his brother Abraham, looks at the nature of ableism and how those with disabilities feel the greatest ableism and insecurity within themselves. We meet Ruben while he experiences ringing in his ears. What starts as a small, tinny sound explodes into muffled voices and his inability to make out coherent words. (The use of sound here is so exceptional, it's unsurprising it won the Oscar for it.) A pharmacist tells him to see a doctor. Ruben tries to hide it, but the terror on his face is subtle yet palpable. When Ruben sees a doctor he's told, "The hearing that you have lost is never coming back." Within the first few minutes we know there is no miraculous turnaround or cure coming. All he can do is preserve what hearing he has and adapt. But Ruben has no doubt watched a lot of movies and has no background with Deaf people, so when he hears about cochlear implants, he thinks that is what he needs. Right now. He tells his girlfriend Lou (Olivia Cooke) that his hearing will "come back" after his surgery.

The lack of understanding regarding those with deafness and disability contributes to misguided beliefs that wheelchairs, hearing aids, prosthetics, and other adaptive equipment give you perks. Use a wheelchair and get to the front of the line at Disney! Wear a hearing aid and you get supersonic hearing! This sounds silly to read but if you don't know any disabled people, what else do you think? At the bare minimum a hearing or abled person thinks these things replicate the experience of being abled. *Sound of Metal* shows these devices for what they are: methods to help Deaf and disabled people function at a different capacity than an abled person. Once disability is introduced the playing field is never level again. Joe verbalizes this to Ruben upon his entering the rehab program: "We're looking for a solution to this [points to head] and not this [points to ears]." The goal is to make Ruben okay with his deafness. Okay that his life has changed. Not to cure him.

Raci, as previously mentioned, is a CODA; his mother lost her hearing at age five, and his father was born Deaf. Raci grew up around deafness every day and was frank about how the media has laid out the Deaf experience in a 2020 interview. "I was born in 1948 [and] that was the year that *Johnny Belinda* came out, starring Jane Wyman. She won the Academy Award for playing a Deaf mute who gets raped and can't even scream. . . . Six or seven years later, that movie came to television and my mother was very excited," he said. "She made me sit down and watch it because she was excited that a Deaf person was being portrayed. I just watched it again, cringing all the way. Jane Wyman is a hearing person. When you look at her, you can tell that she's not a native [ASL] signer." Raci shows the realities of deafness that movies like *Johnny Belinda* were too afraid, or unaware of, to illustrate. "Deaf people have addictions. Guess what? There are Deaf rapists. There are bad Deaf people," he says. *Sound of Metal* would not be what it is without him, and the fact he didn't win the Oscar for Best Supporting Actor hurts a little bit. "Deaf people will tell you themselves they're sick of this pristine portrayal of them," he said. Showing a group of Deaf addicts removes any connection between their disabilities and their addictions, between the medical and the personal.

Ruben is the outsider surrounded by people who speak via American Sign Language, a flip from previous movies where the disabled person is usually outnumbered by the abled. Where the disabled person is the one to feel the shame of being different, it is Ruben, a formerly hearing person, embarrassed at not being part of the status quo. Imagine if Sarah in *Children of a Lesser God* was in this group and didn't have to rely on speaking as a way to feel integrated into hearing society. At dinner, Ruben is unable to speak to anyone because he refuses to learn ASL. "I'm sorry, I don't get sign language," he says. He thinks he won't need it after the cochlear implant is inserted. It's funny to watch Ruben continue talking to people verbally, hoping someone will magically understand him. It hearkens back to scenes like in *Johnny Belinda* where the doctor character thinks if he yells loudly enough at the deaf Belinda or speaks super slow, she'll understand. Ruben falls into this trap, slowing down his speech because he thinks everyone reads lips.

Joe challenges Ruben to spend some time sitting in silence, since that is much of what Ruben's future will consist of. Joe tells Ruben, "Everybody here [in the rehab] shares in the belief that being Deaf is not a handicap. That it's not something to fix." But as with Ruben's stubbornness to get the implant he is resistant to appreciate the quiet. When he finally gets the surgery, which the movie watches in all its gory glory to see what is involved in the process, he's upset that everything he hears comes with an undercurrent of static. Everything sounds fake, loud, and scratchy. The sound mix mimics this, making everything Ruben hears robotic, with little personal connection or inflection. Ruben is reminded, "This is not sound like you remember." Ruben wants things as they were, even his relationship with Lou, which changes and eventually ends during his time at the rehab. When Ruben disconnects the implant in the film's final moments and finally sits in the silence it's in acknowledgment that his relationship to hearing, to music, to people, to the world is irrevocably altered. Not something to mourn, but just something that is.

Sound of Metal truly looks at disability issues from a disabled perspective in spite of its casting. Ruben goes through the stages of grief during the film and comes out the other side. Raci himself discussed this in that same 2020 interview: "My mother was always—I hate to say this—tortured a little bit because she did have [hearing] till she was five years old," he said. "So she was tortured by not being able to hear Elvis. I went to see the Beatles. I came back and I told her what it was all about, and she had tears in her eyes because she had seen Frank Sinatra in Chicago as a young girl and loved the excitement so much." Ruben, much like Raci's mother, understands a piece of him is forever lost. As the movie's ambiguous ending says, he has to be willing to change and make peace with the loss of connection to things he once knew. *Sound of Metal* makes a point of showing that deafness and disability aren't death sentences. They are an opportunity for rebirth.

Horror remains a genre still hospitable to disabled stories. In 2024, director Aaron Schimberg's *A Different Man* hit theaters. If one were to ask me what a great movie about disability looks like, I point straight to this one. The movie tells the story of Edward (Sebastian Stan), a man with a disfigured face due to the effects of neurofibromatosis. He lives alone and deals with the bevy of stares and rude comments people say to those with disabilities, let alone to someone with such a severe facial deformity as his. Things change when an experimental drug offers the ability to heal Edward's face and turn him into a conventionally attractive man. Edward jumps at it, and the treatment quickly works. Determined to start a whole new life, Edward reinvents himself as Guy, a successful real estate agent. But the arrival of Oswald (Adam Pearson), a man with Edward's same past facial deformity who appears to have a better life than him, causes Edward to lose his newfound sense of identity as he tries to figure out the secret to Oswald's success.

What makes *A Different Man*, well, different is how it takes the established disabled tropes we've discussed in this book and plays with them. Schimberg, who also wrote the script, uses them to deconstruct what a disability narrative is and how an audience's sympathy changes when those expectations are played with. Edward's neighbor Ingrid (Renate Reinsve) gasps upon seeing Edward for the first time. But when people aren't staring at him, he's invisible. There are several small bits of business the movie includes that resonate with disabled viewers. Someone comes up to Edward and says they think they know him. "I get this a lot," Edward says, because people are quick to assume disabled people, particularly with the same disabilities, all look alike. A random passerby stops outside the diner Edward is eating at and waves at him. "Sometimes these things happen to me," he tells Ingrid. As someone who gets a lot of random waves by people, I, too, feel so seen.

Medical equipment permeates the movie's opening credits, a landscape common to the disabled experience. Edward's doctor says, "Words like 'heal' and 'cure' are anathema in my profession," but when a cure pops up he's quick to recommend it to Edward. But there's less magic found in the cure only more trauma and pain. Once Edward takes the serum, the body horror starts. Edward, understandably freaked out, tells his doctor, "My face is falling off in clumps." But Edward's doctor tells him, "Perhaps the risk is worth the reward." His doc mimics what the average person who sees Edward would say: *Anything is better than living with the face he has.*

Instead of telling a "be careful what you wish for story," *A Different Man* looks at the intertwining of disability with ableism and identity and how so often the combination fuels a self-fulfilling prophecy. Edward thinks every problem he has—his loneliness, his singleness, and his failed acting career—can be fixed with the removal of his disfigurement. And, for a bit, it is. Now looking like Sebastian Stan, the new Edward rebrands himself, sells his apartment, and tells the doctor who gave him the serum, in true Taylor Swift mode, that Edward is dead. Edward starts hooking up with girls and gets everything that society has told him beautiful, non-disabled people get. But Edward can't resist the pull back to Ingrid, the one woman who knew him when he was his old self and who is now peddling an off-Broadway show called *Edward*.

Ingrid is a prime example if you ever need an example of ableist microaggressions. It's not just the blunt way she asks Edward, "What happened to you?" when she first meets him or that she's surprised that Edward's facial deformities started later in his life and he looks aesthetically normal in childhood photos. It's Ingrid commenting on how oily Edward's skin is or presuming that she has ownership and experience in Edward's life purely because she knew him. The movie deftly looks at the ethics permeating disabled representation on-screen and questions its very existence. "Is it wrong to cast someone because of their disfigurement?" Ingrid asks. "Will people come to gawk?" What are the ethical boundaries of abled directors and screenwriters to tell disabled stories? How do narrative tropes play into an audience's expectation of disability? These are questions that don't have easy answers. The fact the movie even considers this at all is amazing. In a 2024 interview, Sebastian Stan, who garnered a Golden Globe nomination for his performance as Edward, expressed hope that audiences would look at the movie and challenge the stereotypes they've come to expect from these movies. "Those stereotypes, they've always been around, and that's all people know," he said. "Largely because there hasn't been enough exposure for people to see things differently."

When Edward discovers Ingrid's play is about him, he has no problem auditioning for it even though he is no longer disfigured. Edward feels he deserves to play the character, and he's right: The character is based on him. But playing the character with his new face forces the audience to confront disabled appropriation and whether Edward *should* play the role. Edward goes up against several other disabled performers, including a few of color, also auditioning. No doubt white privilege plays a heavy role in whoever gets the part. The audience's sympathy turns because Edward can't have it both ways. When Oswald arrives, having the same facial disfigurement as Edward, he is a breath of fresh air. "By the end of this film, Sebastian Stan is going to be looking at Adam Pearson and feel envy and jealousy, and that's something that I don't think audiences have ever seen before, and they're going to understand why he's jealous," Schimberg said in that same 2024 interview. Where Edward is awkward (even post-transformation), Oswald is accomplished. Oswald plays the saxophone, has a large group of friends, an ex-wife, and a child. Oswald flirts with being a disabled overachiever, a character who is so highly accomplished in order to show that their disability doesn't slow them down. It's obvious Edward's disability wasn't just the limiting factor in his life; it was also his perception that the limitation existed. Edward lets Oswald push his buttons because, in Edward's mind, if Oswald can do something, then why can't Edward? What makes Oswald so special?

"In order to challenge stereotypes they first need to establish they exist," said Pearson in that same 2024 interview. *A Different Man* confronts the audience with every one of them to show how disabled people feel having these stereotypes heaped on their shoulders. How much does Edward's self-esteem equate to his opportunities or lack thereof? How much of our perception of the outside world plays into our conceptions of ourselves? Oswald is doing everything Edward wants to do, and does it as a disabled man, therefore Edward thinks he needs to go back to being disabled. He's not willing to accept his own decisions. He wishes to recover what he gave up. As a neighbor says to Edward at the beginning of the movie, "All unhappiness in life comes from not accepting what is." Edward is unable to accept himself first as a disabled man and then as a non-disabled man. He's unwilling to accept his life, period. For Edward, his disability is his identity, and to remove it is to remove his sense of self. But allowing it to be his only defining characteristic in life also forces him to limit himself.

Only time will tell whether *A Different Man* makes an impact on Hollywood at large. Its distributor, premiere boutique label A24, opened the movie up to audiences who might never have seen it otherwise. It also received numerous critics' awards, won the Gotham Award for both Best Feature Film and Best Performance for Pearson, and garnered Sebastian Stan a Golden Globe. During his speech, Stan used his time to demand more disabled stories. "Our ignorance and discomfort around disability and disfigurement has to end now," he said. "We have to normalize it and continue to expose ourselves [and our children] to it. Encourage acceptance. One way we can do that is by continuing to champion stories that are inclusive." Fingers crossed it marks some sort of turning point, if only to let Aaron Schimberg continue to make more movies.

How do I feel about disability in the movies after talking about the good, the bad, and *The Other Side of the Mountain*? I can't say I'm enthusiastic, but I'm not utterly defeated either. There's a helluva long way to go in making representation in Hollywood close to equal. Sets are still inaccessible, and people are still content to celebrate just letting us in the room but without letting us get behind a camera. We still need disabled executives in power at all the studios, ones who can greenlight projects and compel people to hire disabled people. Those things take time and continued activism, but if the movies have told us anything, we're nothing if not persistent. We can find Swedish death chalets after all! What about me? Have I learned something about myself after talking about the movies I've watched? Yes. I grew up watching and loving the movies, even when the movies taught me not to love myself. I'm still unlearning a lot about what the movies have taught me about disability, but I know what I'm looking for now when I talk about good and bad representation. So when you're watching a movie with a disabled character, make sure to ask some questions, or at least point out the hospital wheelchair and tell someone why it's inaccurate.

WORKS CITED

#RepresentationMatters: Content as a Mirror to Culture. National Research Group, 2021.
Adams, Guy. "Film About Stephen Hawking's Life Has Split His Family." *Mail Online*, December 12, 2014.
Balun, Chas. "Long Live Leatherface!" *Fangoria* 70, no. 1 (January 1988): 49–51.
Bergan, Ronald. "Obituary: Harold Russell." *The Guardian*, February 6, 2002. https://www.theguardian.com/news/2002/feb/06/guardianobituaries.
Bergman, Anne. "Film Clips: A True Veteran Actor; Sure, It's Typecasting—but He's Used to It." *Los Angeles Times Calendar*, September 8, 1996.
The Best Years of Our Lives. Directed by William Wyler. The Samuel Goldwyn Company, 1946.
Born on the Fourth of July. Directed by Oliver Stone. Universal Pictures, 1989.
Borowsky, Larry. "Herbert Marshall: The 1st Amputee Movie Star." *Amplitude*, March 8, 2023. https://livingwithamplitude.com/herbert-marshall-amputee-actor.
Breathe. Directed by Andy Serkis. Bleecker Street Media, 2017.
Calvario, Liz. "Why Was One Von Erich Brother Left Out of 'The Iron Claw'?" *Yahoo Entertainment*, June 6, 2024. https://www.yahoo.com/entertainment/iron-claw-leaves-one-von-022101492.html.
Brest, Martin. "Production Notes." *Scent of a Woman* (DVD). 2006.
Carter-Long, Lawrence. "The Evolution of Disability in Film: After the Accolades, the Work Continues | PBS." *Independent Lens*, July 16, 2020. https://www.pbs.org/independentlens/blog/the-evolution-of-disability-in-film-after-the-accolades-the-work-continues.
Case, Ariana, et al. *Inequality in 1,600 Popular Films*. 2023. https://assets.uscannenberg.org/docs/aii-inequality-in-1600-popular-films-20230811.pdf.
CDC. "Disability Impacts All of Us Infographic | CDC." Centers for Disease Control and Prevention, January 5, 2023.
Champions. Directed by Bobby Farrelly. Focus Features, 2023.
Charles, John. "Susan Peters." Turner Classic Movies, www.tcm.com/tcmdb/person/151081%7C143413/Susan-Peters/#overview. Accessed March 16, 2024.
Charly. Directed by Ralph Nelson. Fox Video, 1968.

Child, Beckie, et al. "Understanding the Experience of Crime Victims with Disabilities and Deaf Victims." *Journal of Policy Practice* 10, no. 4 (2011): 247–67. https://doi.org/10.1080/15588742.2011.605829.

Children of a Lesser God. Directed by Randa Haines. Paramount Pictures, 1986.

CinemAbility. Directed by Jenni Gold. Leomark Studios, 2012.

City Lights. Directed by Charlie Chaplin. Criterion Collection, 1931.

Coming Home. Directed by Hal Ashby. United Artists, 1978.

Crivello, Kirk. *Fallen Angels: The Lives and Untimely Deaths of Fourteen Hollywood Beauties*. Sphere, 1988.

Cult of Chucky. Directed by Don Mancini. Universal Studios, 2017.

Curse of Chucky. Directed by Don Mancini. Universal Studios, 2013.

D'Agostino Lloyd, Annette. "August 24, 1919 . . . Witzel Photographers." Harold Lloyd Dot US, December 22, 2011. https://haroldlloyd.us/the-life/august-24-1919-witzel-photographers. Accessed March 31, 2024.

Davis, Joy. "The Radical Lives of Helen Keller." *Disability Studies Quarterly* 25, no. 1 (December 2005).

Davis, Leigh Ann. *People with Intellectual Disabilities in the Criminal Justice Systems: Victims & Suspects*. The Arc, August 2009.

Dean, Michelle. "The Theory of Everything Does Jane Hawking a Disservice." *The Guardian*, November 14, 2014.

DeVault, Nancy. "Why Interabled Relationships Are the New Normal." *Latest National Disability News*, February 9, 2022.

"Disability Groups Protest 'Tropic Thunder.'" TODAY.com, August 12, 2008. https://www.today.com/popculture/disability-groups-protest-tropic-thunder-1C9412425.

"Discrimination and Language: The Word 'Boy.'" *The Takeaway*, WNYC Studios, September 10, 2010. https://www.wnycstudios.org/podcasts/takeaway/segments/93569-when-word-boy-and-isnt-discriminatory.

Ebert, Roger. "Scent of a Woman Movie Review." RogerEbert.com, December 23, 1992. https://www.rogerebert.com/reviews/scent-of-a-woman-1992.

Edward Scissorhands. Directed by Tim Burton. Twentieth Century Fox, 1991.

The Elephant Man. Directed by David Lynch. Paramount Pictures, 1980.

Elsbury, William. "Racial, Ethnic, and Religious Minorities in the Vietnam War: A Resource Guide." Library of Congress, September 12, 2022. https://guides.loc.gov/racial-ethnic-and-religious-minorities-in-the-vietnam-war.

The Enchanted Cottage. Directed by John Cromwell. RKO Radio Pictures, 1945.

Erickson, Hal. *Encyclopedia of Television Law Shows*. McFarland, 2009.

"Executions by Race and Race of Victim." Death Penalty Information Center, 2019.

Ferrero, Lee. "Actress Susan Peters, Paralyzed 7 Years, Dies." *Milwaukee Sentinel*, October 25, 1952, 3.

Fiedler, Leslie A. "Pity and Fear: Images of the Disabled in Literature and the Popular Arts." *Salmagundi* 57 (Summer 1982): 57–69.

Finding Dory. Directed by Andrew Stanton and Angus MacLane. Walt Disney Company, 2016.

Finding Nemo. Directed by Andrew Stanton. Walt Disney Animation, 2003.

Forrest Gump. Directed by Robert Zemeckis. Paramount Pictures, 1994.
Frankenstein. Directed by James Whale. Universal Pictures, 1931.
Freaks. Directed by Tod Browning. MGM, 1932.
Freeman, Mark. "A Guide to the Study of Vietnam War Films." Mark Freeman Films, February 3, 2020. https://markfreemanfilms.sdsu.edu/film_resources/guide-to-the-study-of-vietnam-war-films.
Friday the 13th: Part 2. Directed by Steve Miner. Paramount Pictures, 1981.
George, Diana, and Diane Shoos. "Deflecting the Political in the Visual Images of Execution and the Death Penalty Debate." *College English* 67, no. 6 (2005): 587–609.
Glantz, Michael J., et al. "Gender Disparity in the Rate of Partner Abandonment in Patients with Serious Medical Illness." *Cancer* 115, no. 22, November (2009): 5237–42. https://doi.org/10.1002/cncr.24577.
Glenn, Cerise L., and Landra J. Cunningham. "The Power of Black Magic: The Magical Negro and White Salvation in Film." *Journal of Black Studies* 40, no. 2 (2009): 135–52.
Graham, Peter W., and Fritz Oehlschlaeger. *Articulating the Elephant Man: Joseph Merrick and His Interpreters*. Johns Hopkins University Press, 1992.
Graham, Regina F. "I'm a Black, Disabled Actor. This Is How I'm Making My Place in Hollywood." Refinery29, September 16, 2020. https://www.refinery29.com/en-us/2020/09/9903981/lauren-ridloff-danielle-perez-disabled-actress-women-of-color.
The Green Mile. Directed by Frank Darabont. Warner Bros., 1999.
The Hand That Rocks the Cradle. Directed by Curtis Hanson. Buena Vista Pictures, 1992.
Hansen, Gunnar. *Chain Saw Confidential*. Chronicle Books, 2013.
Harrell, Erika. "Crime Against Persons with Disabilities, 2009–2019." Bureau of Justice Statistics, November 2021.
Harris, Leslie. "Disabled Sex and the Movies." *Disability Studies Quarterly*. 22, no. 4 (2002): 144–62.
Heisel, William. "Time for Hollywood to Make Disabilities More than Just Oscar Material." USC Anneberg Center for Health Journalism, February 7, 2020.
"Helen Keller in College—Blind, Dumb and Deaf Girl Now Studying at Radcliffe." *Chicago Tribune*, October 13, 1900, 16.
Hereditary. Directed by Ari Aster. A24, 2018.
Herzogenrath, Bernd. *The Films of Tod Browning*. Black Dog Publishing, 2006.
Holcomb, Jeanne, and Kenzie Latham-Mintus. "Disney and Disability: Media Representations of Disability in Disney and Pixar Animated Films." *Disability Studies Quarterly* 42, no. 1 (2022).
Home of the Brave. Directed by Irwin Winkler. Metro-Goldwyn-Mayer, 2006.
Howell, Michael, and Peter Ford. *The True History of the Elephant Man: The Definitive Account of the Tragic and Extraordinary Life of Joseph Carey Merrick*. Skyhorse Publishing, 2010.
"How Many People Are in the US Military?" USAFacts, February 21, 2024. https://usafacts.org/articles/how-many-people-are-in-the-us-military-a-demographic-overview.

The Hunchback of Notre Dame. Directed by Wallace Worsley. Universal Pictures, 1923.
Hush. Directed by Mike Flanagan. Netflix, 2016.
I Am Sam. Directed by Jessie Nelson. New Line Cinema, 2001.
Ice Castles. Directed by Donald Wyre. Columbia Pictures, 1978.
The Iron Claw. Directed by Sean Durkin. A24, 2023.
Jay and Silent Bob Reboot. Directed by Kevin Smith. Saban Films, 2019.
Johnny Belinda. Directed by Jean Negulesco. Warner Bros., 1948.
Karger, Dave. *50 Oscar Nights*. Running Press, 2024.
Karraker, Amelia, and Kenzie Latham. "In Sickness and in Health? Physical Illness as a Risk Factor for Marital Dissolution in Later Life." *Journal of Health and Social Behavior* 56, no. 3 (2015): 420–35. https://doi.org/10.1177/0022146515596354.
Kincheloe, Pamela. "The New 'A Quiet Place: Day One' Trailer Is Here—but Will the Sequel Do Enough for Deaf Representation?" *BBC*, February 12, 2024.
Lacom, Cindy. "'The Time Is Sick and Out of Joint': Physical Disability in Victorian England." *PMLA* 120, no. 2 (2005): 547–52. http://www.jstor.org/stable/25486182.
Leatherface: Texas Chainsaw Massacre III. Directed by Jeff Burr. New Line Cinema, 1990.
Lee, Chris. "'Baby' Plot Twist Angers Activists." *Los Angeles Times*, January 27, 2005. https://www.latimes.com/archives/la-xpm-2005-jan-27-wk-mdb27-story.html.
"The Links Between Disability & Domestic Violence." Sanctuary for Families, July 28, 2022. https://sanctuaryforfamilies.org/disability-domestic-violence.
Llewellyn, Gwynnyth, and Gabrielle Hindmarsh. "Parents with Intellectual Disability in a Population Context." *Current Developmental Disorders Reports* 2, no. 2 February (2015): 119–26.
Lombardo, Cristiana. "5 Facts about Horror Icon Lon Chaney, Sr." *American Masters*, PBS, October 24, 2022. https://www.pbs.org/wnet/americanmasters/5-facts-about-horror-icon-lon-chaney-sr/23549.
Lopez, Kristen. "A24's 'A Different Man,' Starring Sebastian Stan, Shatters Tropes around Disfigurement and Ableism." *Salon*, September 21, 2024. https://www.salon.com/2024/09/21/a-different-man-sebastian-stan-adam-pearson-and-director-schimberg-shatter-ableism-tropes.
———. "Christopher Reeve and 1998's 'Rear Window.'" *Kristomania!*, November 25, 2022. kristenlopez.substack.com/p/christopher-reeve-and-1998s-rear. Accessed April 2, 2024.
———. "Don't Look to the Movies to Learn About Disability." *Pacific Standard*, July 8, 2016. https://psmag.com/news/dont-look-to-the-movies-to-learn-about-disability.
———. "Film Under the Influence, A: Gender, Homage and 'Midsommar.'" *Forbes*, July 1, 2019.
———. "'Get Out' and the Overlap of Disability and Racism." Silent Saints and Tragic Monsters, March 13, 2017. https://crookedmarquee.com/get-out-and-the-overlap-of-disability-and-racism.
———. "How 'Christopher Robin' Erases Part of Winnie the Pooh History." *Hollywood Reporter*, August 3, 2018.

———. "How Deafness in Horror Evolved Beyond Damsels in Distress." IndieWire, October 20, 2020.
———. "How 'Shape of Water' Breaks Down Barriers About Sex and Disability." *Hollywood Reporter*, December 24, 2017. https://www.hollywoodreporter.com/movies/movie-news/shape-water-sex-scenes-break-down-barriers-sex-disability-1069815.
———. "Interview with Don Mancini." Heard Tell, May 2, 2018.
———. "Kevin Smith & His Cast Talk Disability, Reboots, and 25 Years of View Askew." *Forbes*, October 14, 2019. https://www.forbes.com/sites/kristenlopez/2019/10/14/kevin-smith--his-cast-talk-disability-reboots-and-25-years-of-view-askew.
———. "Let's Talk About 'Shazam's' Freddy Freeman and Disabled Superheroes." *Forbes*, April 8, 2019. https://www.forbes.com/sites/kristenlopez/2019/04/08/shazams-freddy-freeman-disabled-superheroes.
———. "*NCIS: New Orleans* Star Daryl Mitchell Says Race Similar to Disability." IndieWire, February 12, 2021. https://www.indiewire.com/features/general/ncis-new-orleans-fear-the-walking-dead-daryl-mitchell-disability-1234615898.
———. "On the Representation of Disabled Women in Cinema." RogerEbert.com, March 30, 2018. https://www.rogerebert.com/chazs-blog/on-the-representation-of-disabled-women-in-cinema.
———. "Peter Dinklage Said the Seven Dwarfs Are an Insult, but the Reality Is More Complex." IndieWire, February 5, 2022. https://www.indiewire.com/features/general/peter-dinklage-snow-white-and-the-seven-dwarfs-backlash-little-people-1234695983.
———. "'Pet Sematary': Zelda and Women in Horror." IndieWire, October 12, 2022. https://www.indiewire.com/features/general/pet-sematary-zelda-women-horror-1234771017.
———. "Popcorn Disability: Does Anyone Even Like 'Scent of a Woman' (1992)?" Film Maven, July 26, 2024. https://thefilmmaven.substack.com/p/scent-of-a-woman-al-pacino.
———. "*Sound of Metal* Star Paul Raci Challenges Hollywood: Deaf People Are Sick of Saintly Portrayals." IndieWire, December 8, 2020. https://www.indiewire.com/features/general/sound-of-metal-paul-raci-1234598013.
———. "Ten Years of Missing the Point of 'Tropic Thunder's' Thoughts on Mental Disability." Forbes, November 2, 2018. https://www.forbes.com/sites/kristenlopez/2018/11/02/ten-years-of-missing-the-point-of-tropic-thunders-thoughts-on-mental-disability/?sh=338836ed34bd.
———. "We Weren't Wrong About 'I Am Sam' but We Are About Mental Disabilities in Movies." Film Maven, May 6, 2024. https://thefilmmaven.substack.com/p/we-werent-wrong-about-i-am-sam-but.
———. "'Unbreakable' Through the Eyes of Someone with Osteogenesis Imperfecta." Crooked Marquee, February 21, 2017. https://crookedmarquee.com/unbreakable-through-the-eyes-of-someone-with-osteogenesis-imperfecta.
———. "Women and Disability Panel: The 30th Anniversary of the ADA Only Shows How Much Work Remains." IndieWire, July 24, 2020.

Macor, Alison. *Making* The Best Years of Our Lives. University of Texas Press, 2022.

Magnificent Obsession. Directed by Douglas Sirk. Universal, 1954.

Mansky, Jackie. "P. T. Barnum Isn't the Hero the 'Greatest Showman' Wants You to Think." *Smithsonian*, December 22, 2017.

The Man Who Laughs. Directed by Paul Leni. Universal Pictures, 1928.

Margaritoff, Marco. "Bryan Cranston Says He 'Got Sh*t' for His Role in 'The Upside,' Announces Sequel." *HuffPost*, January 27, 2023.

McCarthy, Jay. "'Rain Man' at 30: Damaging Stereotype or 'The Best Thing That Happened to Autism'?" *The Guardian*, December 13, 2018.

McTaggart, Ninochka, et al. "Representations of Black Women in Hollywood." Geena Davis Institute, 2021.

Me Before You. Directed by Thea Sharrock. Warner Bros., 2016.

MGM: When the Lion Roars. Directed by Frank Martin. Warner Bros. Home Entertainment, 1992.

Midsommar. Directed by Ari Aster. A24, 2019.

Million Dollar Baby. Directed by Clint Eastwood. Warner Bros., 2004.

"Million Dollar Baby Built on Prejudice About People with Disabilities." Disability Rights Education & Defense Fund, February 13, 2005. https://dredf.org/2005/02/13/million-dollar-baby-built-on-prejudice-about-people-with-disabilities.

The Miracle Worker. Directed by Arthur Penn. United Artists, 1962.

"Miramax—My Left Foot." EIN SOF Communications, 2024. https://www.einsofcommunications.com/success-stories/miramax-left-foot.

Moore, James. "Disabled Children Are Not Scary so Please Stop Using Able-Bodied Actors to Portray Them in Horror Films." *The Independent*, July 13, 2019.

Morton, Andrew. *Tom Cruise: An Unauthorized Biography*. St. Martin's Press, 2008.

My Left Foot. Directed by Jim Sheridan. Miramax, 1989.

Nightmare on Elm Street 3: Dream Warriors, A. Directed by Chuck Russell. New Line Cinema, 1987.

O'Dell, Cary. "Discovering TV's 'Miss Susan.'" *Library of Congress* (blog), February 8, 2023. https://blogs.loc.gov/now-see-hear/2023/02/discovering-tvs-miss-susan. Accessed March 16, 2024.

The Other Side of the Mountain. Directed by Larry Peerce. Universal Pictures, 1975.

The Other Sister. Directed by Garry Marshall. Buena Vista Pictures Distribution, 1999.

Otterbourg, Ken, et al. *Race and Wrongful Convictions in the United States 2022*. National Registry of Exonerations, 2022.

"Our First Interview with Christopher Reeve." *Ability Magazine*, February 1998. https://abilitymagazine.com/christopher-reeve-the-man-behind-the-cape Accessed April 2, 2024.

A Patch of Blue. Directed by Guy Green. MGM, 1965.

Parish, James Robert. *The MGM Stock Company: The Golden Era*. Arlington House, 1973.

The Penalty. Directed by Wallace Worsley. Kino Video, 1920.

Pet Sematary. Directed by Mary Lambert. Paramount Pictures, 1989.

The Phantom of the Opera. Directed by Rupert Julian. Universal Pictures, 1925.

Powell, Robyn. "Parents with Disabilities Face an Uphill Battle to Keep Their Children." *Pacific Standard*, January 3, 2018. https://psmag.com/social-justice/parents-with-disabilities-face-an-uphill-battle-to-keep-their-children.

Pride of the Marines. Directed by Delmer Daves. Warner Bros., 1945.

The Princess and the Scrivener. "The Shape of Ableism: How We Restrict Disabled and Disfigured Stories." YouTube, July 21, 2018. https://www.youtube.com/watch?v=HK1KLVPipmY.

Prochnow, Alexandria. "An Analysis of Autism Through Media Representation." *ETC: A Review of General Semantics* 71, no. 2 (2014): 133–49.

A Quiet Place. Directed by John Krasinski. Paramount Pictures, 2018.

Radio. Directed by Michael Tollin. Sony Pictures Releasing, 2003.

Rain Man. Directed by Barry Levinson. Warner Bros., 1988.

Rear Window. Directed by Jeff Bleckner. ABC, 1998.

Reeve, Christopher. *Still Me*. Random House, 1998.

Reilly, Philip J. *The Phantom of the Opera*. Magicimage Filmbooks, 1996.

Rich, Frank. "How Dirty Harry Turned Commie." *New York Times*, February 13, 2005. https://www.nytimes.com/2005/02/13/arts/how-dirty-harry-turned-commie.html.

The Ringer. Directed by Barry W. Blaustein. Fox Searchlight Pictures, 2005.

Robbins, Tod. *Freaks; or Spurs (Fantasy and Horror Classics)*. Read Books Ltd, April 2013.

Robinson, David. "Charlie Chaplin: Filming City Lights." Charlie Chaplin, 2004. https://www.charliechaplin.com/en/films/5-City-Lights/articles/4-Filming-City-Lights.

Rodas, Julia Miele. "Tiny Tim, Blind Bertha, and the Resistance of Miss Mowcher: Charles Dickens and the Uses of Disability." *Dickens Studies Annual* 34 (2004): 51–97. http://www.jstor.org/stable/44372091.

Roppolo, Michael. "16,000 People with Disabilities Are in State-Operated Institutions." *CBS News*, April 30, 2024. https://www.cbsnews.com/news/16000-people-disabilities-institutions-no-place-like-home-cbs-reports.

Ryerson, Jade. "Disability and the World War II Home Front." National Park Service. https://www.nps.gov/articles/000/disability-and-the-world-war-ii-home-front-introduction.htm.

Saad, Nardine. "Hugh Grant Faces Backlash as an Oompa Loompa in 'Wonka.'" *Los Angeles Times*, July 28, 2023. https://www.latimes.com/entertainment-arts/movies/story/2023-07-28/hugh-grant-oompa-loompa-dwarfism-actor.

Safran, Stephen P. "Movie Images of Disability and War: Framing History and Political Ideology." *Remedial and Special Education* 22, no. 4 (2001): 223–32. https://doi.org/10.1177/074193250102200406. Accessed March 31, 2024.

Sankar-Gorton, Eliza. "The One Glaring Problem with 'Finding Dory.'" *HuffPost*, June 22, 2016. https://www.huffpost.com/entry/the-one-glaring-problem-with-finding-dory_b_10616630.

Scent of a Woman. Directed by Martin Brest. Universal Pictures, 1992.

Schemering, Christopher. *The Soap Opera Encyclopedia*. Ballantine Books, 1988.

"The Screen; His Grim Grin." *New York Times*, April 28, 1928. https://www.nytimes.com/1928/04/28/archives/the-screen-his-grim-grin.html.

Seal, Karen H., et al. "Trends and Risk Factors for Mental Health Diagnoses Among Iraq and Afghanistan Veterans Using Department of Veterans Affairs Health Care, 2002–2008." *American Journal of Public Health* 99, no. 9 (2009): 1651–58. https://doi.org/10.2105/ajph.2008.150284.

The Sessions. Directed by Ben Lewin. Fox Searchlight Pictures, 2012.

Severo, Richard. "Harold Russell Dies at 88; Veteran and Oscar Winner." *New York Times*, February 1, 2002. https://www.nytimes.com/2002/02/01/arts/harold-russell-dies-at-88-veteran-and-oscar-winner.html.

"Sexual Abuse." Disability Justice, 2023. https://disabilityjustice.org/sexual-abuse.

Shamsian, Jacob. "The 'Finding Dory' Director Says Gerald Is Not Disabled." *Business Insider*, November 15, 2016. https://www.businessinsider.com/finding-dory-gerald-2016-11.

The Shape of Water. Directed by Guillermo del Toro. Fox Searchlight, 2017.

Shapiro, Joseph P. *No Pity: People with Disabilities Forging a New Civil Rights Movement*. Times Books, 1994.

Short, Kelly. "Elder Abuse Statistics for 2024." Senior Living, April 1, 2024. https://www.seniorliving.org/research/elder-abuse-statistics.

Siebers, Tobin. "Disability in Theory: From Social Constructionism to the New Realism of the Body." *American Literary History* 13, no. 4 (December 2001): 737–54. https://doi.org/10.1093/alh/13.4.737.

The Sign of the Ram. Directed by John Sturges. Columbia Pictures, 1948.

Skal, David J., and Elias Savada. *Dark Carnival : The Secret World of Tod Browning, Hollywood's Master of the Macabre*. Anchor Books, 1995.

Sling Blade. Directed by Billy Bob Thornton. Miramax, 1996.

Smith, Angela M. *Hideous Progeny: Disability, Eugenics, and Classic Horror Cinema*. Columbia University Press, 2012.

Smith, Wesley J. "A Million Dollar Miss." *CBS News*, March 2, 2005. https://www.cbsnews.com/news/a-million-dollar-miss.

Sound of Metal. Directed by Darius Marder. Amazon Studios, 2019.

"SSI Federal Payment Amounts for 2024." Social Security. https://www.ssa.gov/OACT/COLA/SSI.html.

Stronger. Directed by David Gordon Green. Lionsgate Films, 2017.

Super/Man: The Christopher Reeve Story. Directed by Ian Bonhôte. Fathom Events, 2024.

"Susan Peters Takes Stage in Wheelchair." *Toledo Blade*, June 27, 1949.

Taylor, Drew. "Disney Assures Peter Dinklage on 'Snow White' Reboot: 'We Are Taking a Different Approach' on Dwarf Characters." TheWrap, January 25, 2022. https://www.thewrap.com/snow-white-peter-dinklage-disney-response.

The Texas Chain Saw Massacre. Directed by Tobe Hooper. Criterion, 1974.

The Theory of Everything. Directed by James Marsh. Focus Features, 2014.

There's Something About Mary. Directed by Bobby Farrelly and Peter Farrelly. 20th Century Fox, 1998.

Thomas, Matthew. "Why Daniel Day-Lewis Once Made Crew Members Feed Him by Hand Daily." TheThings, October 15, 2021.

Thompson, Vilissa. "Understanding the Policing of Black, Disabled Bodies." Center for American Progress, February 10, 2021.

Tikkanen, Amy. "Anne Sullivan." *Britannica*, December 23, 2023. https://www.britannica.com/biography/Anne-Sullivan.

"Tod Browning—Biography." IMDb. https://www.imdb.com/name/nm0115218/bio/?ref_=nm_ql_1. Accessed February 19, 2024.

Tofi, Alice. "On-Screen Representation Changes How People Feel About Themselves and Others." Paramount Insights, December 7, 2021.

Trepany, Charles. "Ben Stiller Says He Makes 'No Apologies' for Controversial 'Tropic Thunder': 'Proud of It.'" *USA TODAY*, February 24, 2023.

Treves, Frederick. *The Elephant Man and Other Reminiscences*. Cassell and Co., 1923.

Tropic Thunder. Directed by Ben Stiller. Paramount Pictures, 2008.

Turner, Adam. "A History of Neglect." Nursing Clio, July 8, 2014, https://nursingclio.org/2014/07/08/a-history-of-neglect/#note5_footnote.

Unbreakable. Directed by M. Night Shyamalan. Touchstone Pictures, 2000.

The Unknown. Directed by Tod Browning. Metro-Goldwyn-Mayer, 1927.

The Upside. Directed by Neil Burger. STX Entertainment, 2017.

Vigor-Mungovin, Joanne. *Joseph: The Life, Times and Places of the Elephant Man*. MANGO Books, 2017.

Wait Until Dark. Directed by Terence Young. Warner Bros., 1967.

Warner, Kara. "*Me Before You*: Real Story Behind Jojo Moyes' Best-Seller and New Movie." *PEOPLE*, June 3, 2016. https://people.com/books/me-before-you-real-story-behind-jojo-moyes-best-seller-and-new-movie.

Waxman, Olivia. "The Helen Keller You Didn't Learn About in School." *Time*, December 15, 2020. https://time.com/5918660/helen-keller-disability-history.

Welk, Brian. "Bryan Cranston Calls Playing Disabled Character in 'The Upside' a 'Case of Catch-22.'" TheWrap, January 12, 2019. https://www.thewrap.com/bryan-cranston-calls-playing-disabled-character-in-the-upside-a-case-of-catch-22.

What Ever Happened to Baby Jane? Directed by Robert Aldrich. Warner Bros., 1962.

What's Eating Gilbert Grape. Directed by Lasse Hallström. Paramount Pictures, 1993.

"Why 'Million Dollar Baby' Infuriates the Disabled." *Chicago Tribune*, February 2, 2005. https://www.chicagotribune.com/2005/02/02/why-million-dollar-baby-infuriates-the-disabled.

Wild Hearts Can't Be Broken. Directed by Steve Miner. Walt Disney Pictures, 1991.

The Wizard of Oz. Directed by Victor Fleming and King Vidor. Warner Bros., 1939.

Wolf, Naomi. *The Beauty Myth: How Images of Beauty Are Used Against Women*. Vintage Classic, 1991.

Wong, Alice. "Finding Dory, Disability Culture, and Collective Access." Disability Visibility Project, June 27, 2016. https://disabilityvisibilityproject.com/2016/06/27/finding-dory-disability-culture-and-collective-access.

Wood, Bret. "The Witch, the Devil, and the Code: A HORROR STORY OF HOLLYWOOD IN THE GOLDEN AGE." *Film Comment* 28, no. 6 (1992): 52–56. http://www.jstor.org/stable/43453945.

Yin, Michelle, et al. *A Hidden Market: The Purchasing Power of Working-Age Adults with Disabilities.* American Institutes for Research, 2018. https://www.air.org/resource/report/hidden-market-purchasing-power-working-age-adults-disabilities.

INDEX

2024 Annenberg Inclusion Initiative study   195

able bodied buffer   6, 12, 32, 79, 80, 87, 90, 91, 101, 105, 143, 155, 170, 176, 195
An Affair to Remember (1957)   134
Ahmed, Riz   202
All That Heaven Allows (1955)   143
American Civil Liberties Union   160
American Foundation for the Blind   160
American Institutes of Research   6
American Sign Language (ASL)   13, 54, 56, 107, 123, 146, 204
Americans with Disabilities Act (ADA)   1, 69, 71, 74, 76, 113, 202
Amurri, Eva   136
Andrews, Dana   43
animosity   61
Anwar, Gabrielle   153, 188
The Arc   84
Arkin, Alan   117, 118
Ark of the Covenant   124
Arrested Development   82
Ashby, Hal   68, 69, 71
Aster, Ari   124
autism   7, 80, 81
Ayres, Lew   146, 149

Babylon (2022)   26
Baby-Sitters Club   132
Baclanova, Olga   23, 24, 30, 33, 35
Baker, Kathy   128
Bancroft, Anne   157, 175, 176
Barbie (2023)   6, 7, 196
Barnum, P. T.   31, 41, 175

The Barretts of Wimpole Street (1934)   52
Barrymore, Lionel   40
Barty, Billy   26
Bay, Michael   66
A Beautiful Mind (2001)   54, 83, 169
The Beauty Myth (Wolf)   133, 145
Benson, Robby   152
Bergman, Ingrid   132
The Best Years of Our Lives (1946)   42–8, 51, 52, 62–5, 70, 74, 75, 135, 174, 175, 196
Bickford, Charles   49
Biel, Jessica   70, 74, 75
The Birth of a Nation (1915)   96
Bisutti, Danielle   120
bitter cripples   61, 66, 67, 71
Black, Lucas   86
Bloom, Claire   84
Blunt, Emily   124
Bogdan, Robert   26
Bogdanovich, Peter   142
Born on the Fourth of July (1989)   66, 69–71, 112, 169, 179, 182, 184
"Both Sides Now" (song)   193
Bottoms, Timothy   169
"Boy Wonder." *See* Thalberg, Irving
Breathe (2017)   169–72, 183–5
Breen, Joseph   45
Bride of Frankenstein (1935)   19, 139
Bridges, Beau   151, 159
brittle bone disorder   1
Brody, Adrien   149
Brooke, Hillary   64, 136
Brooks, Albert   199
Brooks, Mel   139, 176
Brown, W. Earl   89

Browning, Tod 8, 16, 17, 29–33, 36–8, 47, 68
Bureau of Justice 84
Burns, Marilyn 111
Burr, Jeff 111
Burton, Tim 127, 201
Butler, Gerard 20, 135, 136

Campbell, Neve 121
caregiver cinema 81
caretaker cinema 142, 155, 160, 162, 165, 172, 186
Carter, Jimmy 69
Cartman, Eric 87
casting 196
Chained for Life (1952) 37
Chalamet, Timothée 201
Champions (2023) 90
Chaney, Lon 8, 12–20, 23–5, 27, 30, 31, 37, 51, 134, 135, 179, 182
Chaplin, Charlie 21, 22, 25, 132
Charles, Ray 184
Charles Sherwood Stratton. *See* General Tom Thumb
Charly (1968) 83, 188
Chazelle, Damien 26
Cher 142, 143
Cherrill, Virginia 21, 22, 132
Cheu, Johnson 17
child of Deaf adults (CODA) 13
Children of a Lesser God (1986) 53, 54, 56, 57, 107, 124, 131, 132, 159, 174, 185–6, 192, 204
Childs, Charles 69
A Christmas Carol (Dickens) 11
Christopher Robin (2018) 174, 175
A Cinderella Story 40
CinemAbility (2012) 2, 190
City Lights (1931) 21, 22, 55, 123, 132, 144, 145, 176
Claflin, Sam 164
Clark, Dane 63
Clarke, Emilia 164
Cleland, Max 69
CODA 174, 187, 191–4, 202
Cohen, Jeff 82
Coming Home (1978) 66–71, 82, 112, 141, 168, 169

Cook, Meira 32
Cooke, Olivia 132, 203
Corleone, Michael 187
Cox, Alaqua 108
Cox, Charlie 171
Cranston, Bryan 160, 173, 174
Crawford, Joan 16, 118, 132, 156
Crip Camp (2020) 6, 202
Cromwell, John 136
Crosby, Denise 126
Crothers, Scatman 99
Crowe, Russell 54, 83
Crowther, Bosley 62
Cruise, Tom 80, 91, 112, 179, 182
Culkin, Macauley 136
Cult of Chucky (2017) 119, 121, 122
Cunningham, Landra J. 99, 101, 102, 104
Curse of Chucky (2013) 119, 121, 122
Curtis, Jamie Lee 121
Cyrano de Bergerac 139

Dafoe, Willem 199
Daredevil 107
Davis, Bette 118, 156
Davis, Geena 2
Davis, Joy 160
Day-Lewis, Daniel 15, 179–83
Dean, Michelle 170
DeBose, Ariana 200
DeGeneres, Ellen 199
de Havilland, Olivia 48, 82
del Toro, Guillermo 148
Depp, Johnny 82, 85, 127
Dern, Bruce 68
Dern, Laura 142
Diary of a Sergeant (1946) 42
Diaz, Cameron 17, 88
DiCaprio, Leonardo 82, 85, 86, 187
Dickens, Charles 11, 12, 19, 79
A Different Man (2024) 45, 155, 205–7
Dinklage, Peter 201
Disability Justice 145, 148
disability narratives 2, 8, 11, 101, 205
disability politics 98, 153
Disability Rights Education Fund 190
disabled actors 35, 37, 39, 57, 59, 60, 173
disabled audiences 5, 27, 95, 198

disabled characters   2, 5, 6, 8, 11–14, 20, 27, 30, 32, 33, 35, 37, 39, 50, 51, 54, 63, 67, 68, 75, 85, 109, 113, 122, 124, 158, 160, 193, 196, 201, 208
disabled movies   2, 8, 27, 123, 162, 188, 189
disabled viewers   3, 56, 183, 192, 205
Dixon, Ivan   141
Donner, Richard   47
Don't Worry, He Won't Get Far on Foot (2018)   188
Dourif, Fiona   120
Downey, Robert   77, 78
Dracula (1931)   30
Driving Miss Daisy (1989)   180
Duff, Hilary   40
Duke, Patty   156-7, 159, 175
Duncan, Michael Clarke   99
Dungeons and Dragons (game)   113
Dunn, Frankie   189
Durant, Daniel   191, 194
Durkin, Sean   197, 198

Earles, Harry   30, 36
Ebert, Roger   188, 189
Eck, Johnny   32, 38
Edmond, Treshelle   106, 107
Edward   206
Edward Scissorhands (1991)   8, 127, 134
The Elephant Man (1980)   175, 176, 179, 181, 190
The Elephant Man and Other Reminiscences (Treves)   177
The Enchanted Cottage (1945)   64, 136, 138
Englund, Robert   113
Entertainment Tonight (TV show)   77
The Eternals (2021)   107
eugenics   12, 19, 25, 33, 45, 109, 125
Evans, Lee   88

The False Cripple (1900)   11
Fanning, Dakota   90
Fantasy Island (TV show)   197
Farnum, Joseph   17
Farrelly, Bobby   90
Fear the Walking Dead   44, 108
Ferguson, Margaret   49, 51

Ferrera, America   7, 197
Fiedler, Leslie A.   177
50 Oscar Nights (Karger)   57
Finding Dory (2016)   199
Finding Nemo (2023)   199
Finger, Bob   23
Fitzgerald, F. Scott   35
Flanagan, Mike   122, 123
Fletcher, Louise   56
Flowers for Algernon (Keyes)   83
Fonda, Jane   67, 168
Ford, Gerald   69
Ford, Wallace   32, 140
Forrest Gump (1994)   2, 8, 41, 55, 61, 64, 69–73, 78, 82, 86, 98, 166, 187, 189
Foy, Claire   171, 183
Frankenstein (1935)   139
Freaks (1932)   8, 16, 29–38, 45, 47, 63, 79, 128, 139, 153, 177
Freeman, Morgan   189
French, Phyllis   54
Fricker, Brenda   182
Friday the 13th   110, 111, 119, 120
Friday the 13th: Part 2 (1981)   110, 113, 115, 119
Friday the 13th: Part 3 (1982)   110

Gallagher, John   122
Garfield, Andrew   171, 183
Garfield, John   62, 64, 65
General Tom Thumb   31
George, Diana   102
Gerwig, Greta   6, 196
Get Out (2017)   16, 82, 97
Gibson, William   156
The Glass Menagerie (Williams)   52
Glee (TV show)   93
Glengarry Glen Ross (1992)   188
Glenn, Cerise L.   99, 101, 102, 104
Godfather 2 (1974)   187
Gold, Jenni   190
Goldbeck, Wallis   31
Gold Diggers of 1933 (1933)   26
Goldwyn, Samuel   42, 46, 47
Gooding, Cuba   82, 102-4
The Goonies (1985)   82
Gottsagen, Zack   93

Granger, Farley   42
Grant, Cary   134
Grazer, Jack Dylan   114
The Greatest Showman (2017)   175
The Greatest Show on Earth (1952)   37
Green, David Gordon   185
The Green Berets (1968)   66
The Green Mile (1999)   99, 101, 102
Griffith, D. W.   96
The Guardian   81, 170
Guess Who's Coming to Dinner (1967)   139
Gyllenhaal, Jake   183–5

Halloween   110, 121
Hamilton, George   132
Hands Across the Table (1935)   138
The Hand That Rocks the Cradle (1992)   96, 97
Hanks, Tom   55, 78, 79, 91, 99–100, 187, 200
Harris, Ed   102
Hart, Kevin   160
Hartman, Elizabeth   139
Hassett, Marilyn   150, 169
Hawkes, John   166, 167
Hawking, Jane   170–2
Hawking, Stephen   170
Hawkins, Sally   148
Hedges, Peter   85
Heiden, Ira   113
Heidi   79, 136
Hellman, Jerome   69
Hendricks, Christina   200
Henkel, Kim   111, 112
Hepburn, Audrey   116–18, 122, 172
Hereditary (2018)   124
Herrod, Julie   117
Hideous Progeny (Smith)   6, 12, 17, 32, 79
Hitchcock, Alfred   59
Hoberman, J.   35
Hoffman, Dustin   78–82, 104, 187, 189
Hollywood Production Code   27, 35, 45, 141
Home of the Brave (2006)   70, 74, 75, 169
hooks, bell   95
Hooper, Tobe   111, 112
Hopkins, Anthony   176

Howard, Bryce Dallas   149
Howard, Ron   169
Hubatsek, Andrew   126
Hudson, Ernie   96
Hudson, Rock   143
Hugo, Victor   17, 23
The Hunchback of Notre Dame (1923)   8, 15, 17, 18, 20, 23
The Hunchback of Notre Dame (1939)   20
The Hunchback of Notre Dame (1996)   20, 135, 178
Hunt, Helen   166
Hurst, Brandon   20
Hurt, John   176, 179
Hurt, William   54, 57, 132
Hush (2016)   122, 123, 149
The Hustler   132
Hyams, Leila   32

I Am Sam (2001)   78, 84, 90, 91, 96, 187, 193
Ice Castles (1978)   152–4, 189
I'll Scream Later (Matlin)   54
in-home healthcare aide   160
Inside Moves (1980)   47
International Center for Deafness and the Arts   53
The Intouchables (2011)   160
The Iron Claw (2023)   197, 198

Jackman, Hugh   175
Jackson, Samuel L.   4, 74
Jay and Silent Bob Reboot (2019)   106
Jensen, Dean   37
Jerome, Jharrel   105
Jimenez, Neal   136, 169
Johnny Belinda (1948)   132, 146, 149, 187, 203, 204
Johnson, Dakota   93
Johnson, Lynn-Holly   152
Jolé, Terra   201
Jones, Doug   148
Jones, Emilia   191
Jones, Felicity   170
Jones, Freddie   176
Jones, O-Lan   128
Jory, Victor   157

222   INDEX

Kaluuya, Daniel 97
Kane, Bob 23
Kantor, MacKinley 42
Karger, Dave 57
Karloff, Boris 19, 27
Keaton, Diane 92
Keep Your Powder Dry (1945) 48
Kempley, Rita 96
Kendrick, Anna 174
Kerr, Deborah 134
Kerry, Norman 16
Kidman, Nicole 98, 162
Killing Rage (hooks) 95
King, Stephen 99–101, 126
Kirk, Norman T. 41, 43, 175
Knox, Alexander 50
Knoxville, Johnny 89
Kotsur, Troy 174, 187, 191, 192, 194
Kramer vs. Kramer (1979) 81
Krasinski, John 124
Kumiyama, Jennifer 167, 200

LaBeouf, Shia 93
Lacom, Cindy 13, 34, 176, 178
Lanchester, Elsa 20
LA Times 191
Laughton, Charles 20
Laurie, Piper 56, 132, 134
Leatherface: The Texas Chainsaw Massacre III (1990) 111
LeBrecht, Jim 202
Legally Blonde 3
Leni, Paul 23
Leroux, Gaston 20
Leto, Jared 183
Levinson, Barry 80
Lewis, Juliette 92, 93
Light in the Piazza (1962) 82, 132
The Little Foxes (1941) 40
The Little Mermaid (1989) 3
Little Women: LA 201
The Lives and Loves of Daisy and Violet Hilton (Jensen) 37
Lloyd, Harold 40
Lloyd Webber, Andrew 135
Lombard, Carole 138
Lopez, Jennifer 105
Los Angeles Daily News 46
Los Angeles Times 35
The Lost Weekend (1945) 84
Love, Actually (2003) 156
Love Story (1970) 150–2
Lynch, David 175, 177, 178

McBride, Tom 115
McCarten, Anthony 170
McGonegal, Charles 41
MacGraw, Ali 150
McGregor, Ewan 174
McGuire, Dorothy 137
MacMurray, Fred 138
McNally, Stephen 146
Macor, Alison 41, 44
magic cure 17, 58, 122
Magnificent Obsession (1954) 132, 143, 146
Making the Best Years of Our Lives (Macor) 41, 44
Malcolm X (1992) 188
Mamma Mia! Here We Go Again (2018) 197
Mancini, Don 119, 120, 122
"Man of a Thousand Faces." *See* Chaney, Lon
The Man Who Laughs (1928) 23, 30, 33, 55, 110, 117, 123, 125, 128, 145
March, Fredric 43
Marder, Darius 202, 203
Maren, Jerry 27
Margulies, Julianna 64, 163
Marks, Annika 167
Marshall, Garry 92
Marshall, Herbert 40, 41, 138
Martin, Ann M. 132
Martindale, Margo 190
Martinsville, U.S.A. 52
Marx, Samuel 35
Mask (1985) 142, 156, 163, 166
Maslany, Tatiana 185
Matlin, Marlee 53–7, 131, 174, 186, 191, 192, 194, 196
Matuszak, John 82
Me Before You (Moyes) 164, 167, 169, 170, 172, 188
medical cure 17
"medicalizing" disability 18
medical marvels 18

Meet McGonegal (1944) 41
Memphis Belle 43
Menounos, Maria 77
Meredith, Burgess 80
Method Acting 13, 183
#MeToo movement 145
Mewes, Jason 106
Midkiff, Dale 126
Midsommar (2019) 124
Miller, Patsy Ruth 17
Million Dollar Baby (2004) 187, 189, 190
Milne, A. A. 174
Mimieux, Yvette 82, 132
The Miracle Man (1919) 14
The Miracle Worker (1962) 157–9, 175, 176
The Miracle Worker (Gibson) 156
Mirror Mirror (2012) 201
Miss Susan 52, 53
Mitchell, Daryl 44, 108
Mitchell, Joni 193
Montagu, Ashley 177
Montgomery, Belinda 151
Moore, James 125
Mornay, Rebecca de 96
Morris, William 47
Morrow, Barry 81
Motion Picture 40
Moyes, Jojo 164, 165
My Fair Lady 140
My Left Foot (1989) 15, 71, 179, 181–4
My Octopus Teacher (2020) 202

Nash, John 54, 83
Natural Born Killers (1994) 93
Network 175
neurodivergence 80, 84
Newman, Paul 134
Newnham, Nicole 202
Nielsen, Kim 160
Nightmare on Elm Street 3: Dream Warriors (1987) 113, 114, 122
non-disabled body 17
Norden, M. F. 200
Norman, Tom 178

O'Brien, Mark 166, 167
O'Dell, Cary 52
O'Donnell, Cathy 44, 46, 64, 135
O'Donnell, Chris 187
Of Mice and Men (Steinbeck) 79, 83, 86, 87, 101
The Other Side of the Mountain (1975) 150, 152, 156, 169, 208
The Other Side of the Mountain: Part II (1978) 169
The Other Sister (1999) 84, 91–3
Out of Africa 171
The Outward Room 48

Pacific Standard 26
Pacino, Al 2, 71, 182, 187–9
Parker, Eleanor 63
A Patch of Blue (1965) 139–41, 146
The Peanut Butter Falcon (2019) 93
Pearl Harbor (2001) 66
Pearson, Adam 205, 207
Peele, Jordan 16, 97, 98
The Penalty (1920) 14–18, 20, 27
Penn, Sean 78, 90, 91, 104, 156, 187
Pertain, Paul A. 111
Peters, Susan 48–53, 131, 133
Pet Sematary (1989) 126, 131
Pet Sematary (2019) 126, 131
Pet Sematary (King) 126
Pfeiffer, Michelle 90
Phantom of the Opera (2004) 20
The Phantom of the Opera (1925) 15, 17, 23, 24, 134
Philbin, Mary 17, 23
Phoenix, Joaquin 149, 188
Picturing Disability (Bogdan) 26
Pinedo, Isabel Cristina 109
Platoon (1986) 66
Playboy 54
Poitier, Sidney 139, 140
Pollano, John 185
Potts, Annie 200
President's Committee on the Employment of People with Disabilities 1948 47
pretty disabilities 21, 64, 116, 131, 132, 136, 150
Pride of the Marines (1945) 62–5, 67, 71, 72, 144

Prine, Andrew   158
Prochnow, Alexandria   80
Puczkó-Smith, Levente   124

A Quiet Place (2018)   123
Quine, Richard   48, 52

Raci, Paul   192, 202, 203, 205
Radio (2003)   82, 99, 102, 103
Rain Man (1988)   71, 78, 80, 81, 84–6, 90, 92, 156, 187, 189
Randian, Prince   32
Random Harvest (1942)   48
Ray (2004)   184
Ready Player One (2018)   132
Rear Window (1954)   59
Rear Window (1998)   59, 165
Recreational Terror: Women and the Pleasures of Horror Film Viewing (Pinedo)   109
Redmayne, Eddie   170, 183
Reeve, Christopher   57–9, 114, 165
Rehabilitation Act of 1975   47
Reinsve, Renate   205
The Return of the Texas Chainsaw Massacre: The Documentary   111
Ribisi, Giovanni   92
Richardson, Miranda   185
Ridloff, Lauren   107
The Ringer (2005)   89, 90
Ringwald, Molly   2
Ritter, John   87
Robbins, Tod   31, 36
Robertson, Cliff   83, 188
Robinson, Jerry   23
Rockwell, Sam   101
Rodas, Julia Miele   11, 12, 18, 31
Rogue One (2016)   107
Roosevelt, Franklin Delano   66
Root, Stephen   97
Rossum, Emmy   135
Roy, Deep   201
Rusk, Howard A.   45
Russell, Harold   41–8, 52, 53, 62, 75, 174, 175, 196
Ryder, Winona   127, 134

Sackter, Bill   81
Safran, Stephen P.   62, 66
Savage, John   47
Saved! (2004)   136
Scary Movie (2000)   88
Scent of a Woman (1992)   2, 71, 182, 187–9, 202
Schimberg, Aaron   37, 45, 205, 207, 208
Schoeffling, Michael   153
Schumacher, Joel   20, 135
Scorsese, Martin   26
Scream   110, 121
Scrooge, Ebenezer   12, 22, 41
The Secret Garden   136
The Sessions (2012)   166, 200
Shannon, Michael   148
The Shape of Water (2017)   148, 149, 163
Shapiro, Milly   124
Shazam! (2019)   83, 114, 138
Shelley, Mary   19, 139
Sheridan, Dave   88
Sheridan, Jim   179–82
The Shining (1980)   99
Shoos, Diana   102
Short, Don   15
Shyamalan, M. Night   4, 149
Siebers, Tobin   6
Siegel, Kate   122, 123
The Sign of the Ram (Ferguson)   49, 51, 52, 54, 55, 120, 131, 133
Simmons, Millicent   123
Simons, Stanley   198
Simple Jack   77
Singh, Tarsem   201
Sinise, Gary   80, 101
Sirk, Douglas   143
Sixteen Candles (1984)   3, 153
The Sixth Sense (1999)   4
Slade, Frank   182, 187
Sling Blade (1996)   84, 86, 87, 90
Smith, Angela M.   6, 12, 13, 15, 17, 32, 79, 106, 179
Smith, Harley Quinn   106, 107
Smith, Wesley J.   191
The Snake Pit (1948)   84
Snow White and the Huntsman   201
Snow White and the Seven Dwarfs   8, 197, 201

social parasites 18
Social Security Disability Insurance (SSDI) system 70
Sound of Metal (2019) 42, 202–5
Spacey, Kevin 88
Spears, Britney 81
Spurs (Robbins) 36
"Spurs" (1920) 31
Stan, Sebastian 45, 155, 205–8
The Stand 101
Stanton, Andrew 200
Steel, Amy 110
Steinbeck, John 79, 86, 101
Stewart, Jimmy 59
Stewart, Patrick 4
Stiller, Ben 77, 78
Still Me (Reeve) 58
Stohl, Ellen 54
Stoker, Bram 30
Stoltz, Eric 136, 142
Stone, Oliver 66, 69, 71, 72, 179, 182
Stronger (2017) 183–6
Sturges, John 49
Suicide Squad (2016) 183
Super/Man (2024) 58
Supplemental Security Income (SSI) 70
Swank, Hilary 187, 189, 190
Swenson, Inga 157
Swift, Taylor 163, 206

Taylor, Lauren-Marie 115
The Texas Chain Saw Massacre (1974) 110–13
Thackeray, William Makepeace 11
Thalberg, Irving 30, 31
Thaxter, Phyllis 49
The Theory of Everything (2014) 169–71, 183
There's Something About Mary (1998) 17, 88–9
"This Is Me" (song) 175
Thomson, John 32
Thornton, Billy Bob 86, 87, 91
Time (magazine) 42
Tofi, Alice 40
Toles, G. 64
Toy Story 4 (2019) 200
A Trip to the Moon (1902) 11

Tropic Thunder (2008) 77–9, 83, 86, 90, 91, 93, 104, 173, 174, 187
Trouble in Paradise (1932) 40

Unbreakable (2000) 4, 5
The Unholy Three (1925) 37
The Unknown (1927) 16, 17, 20, 30
Unstoppable (2024) 105, 106
The Upside (2017) 64, 160–4, 173
USC Annenberg 6, 39, 95
USC Annenberg Center for Health Journalism 174
The Usual Suspects (1995) 87

Variety 35, 38
Veidt, Conrad 23
The Village (2004) 4, 149
Villechaize, Herve 197
Voight, Jon 66–8, 168

Wait Until Dark (1967) 116–18, 122, 123
Walk Hard: The Dewey Cox Story (2007) 184
Walter Reed Army Medical Center 70
Washington, Denzel 188
The Waterdance (1992) 135, 169
Wayne, John 66
Weigert, Robin 167
Wen, Alice 106
Wexler, Haskell 68
Whale, James 19
What Ever Happened to Baby Jane? (1962) 118, 156
What's Eating Gilbert Grape (1993) 82, 85, 156, 158, 187, 189
When the Lion Roars (1992) 27
White, Jeremy Allen 198
Whitford, Bradley 188
Wicked (2024) 197
Wiest, Dianne 128
Wild Hearts Can't Be Broken (1991) 153, 154, 188
Williams, Tennessee 52
Williamson, Mykelti 98
Willis, Bruce 4
Willy Wonka and the Chocolate Factory (1971) 201

Winger, Debra   104
Winkler, Henry   53
Winnie the Pooh (Milne)   174
Winters, Shelley   139
Wish (2023)   200
The Wizard of Oz (1939)   8, 25, 26, 37
Wolf, Naomi   133, 139, 145
The Wolf of Wall Street (2013)   26
A Woman's Face (1941)   132
Wonka (2023)   201
Wood, Robin   110
Woodard, Alfre   103, 104
Worsley, Wallace   14
Wright, Robin   73

Wright, Teresa   135
Wyler, William   42–4, 46
Wyman, Jane   132, 143, 146, 187, 203

Yen, Donnie   107
Yoakam, Dwight   87
Young, Robert   136
Young, Terence   117
Young, Waldemar   17
Young Frankenstein (1974)   139

Zayid, Maysoon   30
Zeno Mountain Farms   93
Zimbalist, Efrem   117